INDIA AND THE ASIAN POPULATION PERSPECTIVE

INDIA AND THE ASIAN POPULATION PERSPECTIVE

By
Ashish Bose

1993

B.R. Publishing Corporation

[A Division of D.K. Publishers Distirbutors (P) Ltd.]
Delhi-110007

Sales Office:
D.K. Publishers Distributors (P) Ltd.
1, Ansari Road, Darya Ganj,
New Delhi-110002.
Phone: 3261465, 3278368
Fax : 091-011-3264368

ISBN 81-7018-765-6

Published by:
B.R. Publishing Corporation
[Division of D.K. Publishers Distributors (P) Ltd.] at
Regd. Office 29/9, Nangia Park, Shakti Nagar,
Delhi-110007. Phone: 7120113

Typeset by:
ABC *for* **DTP**
Delhi-34, Ph.: 7183087

Printed at:
D.K. Fine Art Press
Delhi. Ph.: 7116929

PRINTED IN INDIA

*In
memory of my
mother*

Preface

Most national and international seminars and conferences on Population invariably recommend that the media should be effectively mobilised in making people population-conscious. As far as India is concerned, there is very little evidence that our national and regional newspapers in English and in vernacular languages have shown a sustained interest in population issues. The radio and TV programmes on population and family planning are more of a routine nature and, in my opinion, have not shown enough innovation in communicating with illiterate Indian masses.

Demographers, who have the expertise to tackle massive population data, particularly from the Census are not good at communicating their research findings to planners, policy-makers and the readers of newspapers and magazines. It is unfortunate that many of our social scientists downgrade newspaper articles just because they are of a popular variety. Books and journals, both Indian and foreign, have become extremely costly and students in particular find it very difficult to buy books or subscribe to journals. This is true even of libraries in our universities and research institutions. Therefore, there is a great danger of a big knowledge gap between the tremendous flow of new research material all over the world and the availability of such material to our scholars, administrators, planners and policy-makers. The newspapers and in particular, the national newspapers, have an important role in bridging this gap. I must, therefore, congratulate *Financial Express* and, in particular, Professor A.M. Khurso, the Editor of this important national newspaper for introducing a fortnightly column titled 'Population Scan'. Ever since April 1992, I have been writing this column.

It is often complained that Indian newspapers do not carry much material on Asian countries, while there is a lot of coverage of USA and Europe. At least in population matters, this complaint seems to be valid.

I had the fortune of participating at the First, Second, Third and Fourth United Nations Asian Population Conferences held at New Delhi (1963), Tokyo (1972), Colombo (1982) and Bali (1992) respectively. I had also the opportunity of discussing population issues with members of the government delegations from Asian countries to these Conferences. On the basis of the material which I received as a United Nations ESCAP Resource Person at the Bali Conference, I wrote a series of articles for *Financial Express* on China, Japan, Korea and Indonesia (which are reproduced in this book). These articles do not give an in-depth analysis of the demographic situation in these countries but they do give a glimpse of the demographic scene. It should be clear to the reader that the World Population problem is now zeroing in on South Asia (India, Pakistan and Bangladesh). Several major countries in Asia where the population problem was acute are now on the road to demographic transition; for example, China, Korea, Indonesia and Thailand, apart from Singapore and Hong Kong. Unfortunately, the demographic scene in India, Pakistan and Bangladesh is far from encouraging, in spite of the massive expenditure on family planning and all the foreign aid that has poured in. In my view, much of this aid is not backed by a proper conceptualisation of the population problem in India and shows ignorance of grassroot reality.

I have ventured to put issues somewhat dramatically by describing the present international approach to the family planning programme in India (which has failed to deliver the goods) by coining an acronym: COMIEC, where CO stands for contraceptive technology, M for monetary incentives and IEC for information, education and communication. I have pleaded for an alternative strategy which I call BLISS, where B stands for basic needs, LI for literacy (100 per cent both for boys and *girls*), S for schooling and the next S for skill formation (See chapter 2). In my view, skill formation rather than extension of education beyond secondary level should have the highest priority. In that spirit, I have put forward a new scheme to be administered by TARA (Technology-oriented Adolescent Resource Development Agency) which should specially focus on adolescent girls in the age group 14-18 years. I have given a brief outline of my scheme in this book (Chapter 21).

For the use of the average reader, I have given a statistical appendix which presents the latest data from Census and other sources for Asian countries. I have also included the latest statistical material separately for China and India. In order to update this material, I have also included a set of supplementary tables for India based on the latest Census Paper published by the Registrar General. For those who are not statistics-minded, I have presented a series of graphs and charts which are self-explanatory.

New Delhi,   **Ashish Bose**
9 June, 1993

Acknowledgements

I am grateful to Professor A.M. Khusro, Editor, *Financial Express*, at whose initiative I started writing a regular fortnightly column titled 'Population Scan'. I acknowledge with thanks the permission given by him to reproduce the articles which I wrote for *Financial Express* (from 7 April, 1992 to 8 June, 1993).

I am deeply indebted to Mr. A.R. Nanda, Registrar General, India and Census Commissioner for his continued help in giving me quick access to 1991 census data.

I am grateful to Mr. T.N. Chaturvedi, M.P., Editor of the *Indian Journal of Public Administration* for inviting me to contribute a paper to the Special Number of this journal on 'India's Population Policy and Its Implementation: The Emerging Scenario' (July-Sept. 1992, Vol. XXXVIII, No. 3), which is reproduced in Chapter 21. The material in this paper is based on my research on a project financed by the Family Planning Foundation (FPF). I am grateful to Mr. J.R.D. Tata, Chairman, and Mr. Harish Khanna, Executive Director of FPF for their help and cooperation which enabled me to complete my project on family planning.

I am thankful to Mrs. Alaka Basu of the Institute of Economic Growth, and Professor Roger Jeffery of the Department of Sociology, University of Edinburgh, for inviting me to present a paper at their Workshop on 'Female Education, Women's Autonomy and Fertility Change in South Asia' (New Delhi, April, 1993). My paper for this important workshop is reproduced in Chapter 2.

I am grateful to Dr. C. Gopalan, Chairman, Nutrition Foundation of India for giving me his research papers. I had the benefit of several rounds of personal discussion with him on population issues. His insight has been valuable for my research.

I acknowledge my gratitude to the United Nations Population Division, New York, and the United Nations ESCAP at Bangkok, for regularly sending me valuable material on Population and allied topics. I have reproduced in the Statistical Appendix, data from the *1992 ESCAP Population Data Sheet* circulated at the Fourth Asian and Pacific Population Conference at Bali, Indonesia (August, 1992).

I am deeply indebted to China Population Information and Research Centre, Beijing for sending me regularly their Bulletin on *China Population Today, China Population*

Data Sheet and other material on China. This has enabled me to have access to the latest Chinese statistics on Population.

I have also used the material from *INDIA 1991: Population Data Sheet* issued by the Registrar General, India, in the Statistical Appendix. While preparing the Supplementary Tables for India, I have drawn heavily from Census of India 1991 Paper Z of 1992: *Final Population Totals: Brief Analysis of Primary Census Abstract*.

While preparing my articles, I have used the *Country Statements* issued by each country participating at the United Nations ESCAP Fourth Asian and Pacific Population Conference (Bali, 1992). I am grateful to the UN ESCAP for enabling me to participate at this Conference, as a Resource Person.

I am grateful to Dr. Shanti R. Conly and Dr. Sharon L. Camp of the Population Crisis Committee, Washington for sending me in advance their two recent publications: *China's Family Planning Program: Challenging Myths* (Washington, 1992), and *India's Family Planning Challenge: From Rhetoric to Action* (Washington, 1992). I had also the benefit of personal discussion with them. I am happy to note that recently the Population Crisis Committee has been renamed as Population Action International.

My sincere thanks go to Mr. R.P. Tyagi from the Population Research Centre, Institute of Economic Growth for his able editorial help. I wish to record my appreciation of the excellent research backup of Miss Prachi Dwivedi. I received competent assistance from other members of my research staff: Mr. M.S. Bist, Mrs. Anita Haldar and Miss Ipsita Banerji. My secretarial work was very efficiently handled by Mr. H.L. Mehta.

Ashish Bose

Contents

SECTION V: VULNERABLE POPULATION

SECTION VI: URBANIZATION

SECTION VII: STATISTICAL APPENDIX: BASIC DEMOGRAPHIC DATA FOR ASIAN COUNTRIES, CHINA AND INDIA

SECTION VIII: GRAPHICS: INDIA 1951-91

List of Text Tables

List of Appendix Tables

SECTION I

ASIAN PERSPECTIVE

1

Asian Population Perspective

"If countries are given time to speak in accordance with the size of their population, my country will not get any chance", observed the lone delegate from the Pacific island of Kiribati, at the recent United Nations ESCAP Asian and Pacific Population Conference (Bali, Indonesia, 19-27 August 1992). The population of Kiribati is only 73 thousand. There are even smaller countries in the Pacific. Niue has a total population of only 2 thousand, Nauru has 10 thousand people, Tuvalu 11 thousand, Republic of Palau 16 thousand and Cook Islands 17 thousand. The largest island country in this region is Papua New Guinea which claims a population of a little over 4 million.

In the UN system, countries are listed in alphabetical order and not according to population size. So the delegate from Kiribati got the same time as China with a population nearing 1.2 billion. China fielded a big delegation with 30 members, including delegates, alternates and advisers. The Indian delegation had only 3 members.

The main theme of the Bali Conference was 'Population and sustainable development: goals and strategies into the 21st century'. This comprehensive and somewhat elusive theme was sub-divided into eleven sub-themes as follows: (1) demographic situation and outlook, (2) population, environment and development, (3) metropolitan growth and urbanization, and their implications, (4) developing more effective family planning/ family health and welfare programmes, (5) policies and programmes for fully involving women in the development process, (6) human resources development and poverty alleviation issues: (a) population and human resource development, (b) population and poverty alleviation, (7) internal and international migration and its implications for socio-economic development policies, (8) mortality and fertility transitions in Asia and the Pacific and their consequences, (9) population ageing and its economic and social implications, (10) population data and information issues, and (11) policy formulation and implementation issues.

Appeared in *Financial Express*, 15 September, 1992

On each of these sub-themes, UN ESCAP Secretariat had produced a background paper, in addition to a working paper prepared by a consultant (designated as a Resource Person and Discussion Leader). The documents included a country paper for each country which gave the official position in regard to population issues listed above. The Conference began with the participation of Senior Officials from all the Asian and Pacific countries and ended with the somewhat nominal participation of Ministers (mostly of Health or Family Welfare) during the closing days and the unanimous adoption of the Bali Declaration.

The Senior Officials Meeting was inaugurated by Prof. Emil Salim, Minister of state for Population and Environment in Indonesia, while Prof. Alwi Dahlan, Assistant Minister of State for Population was elected the Chairman. The Ministers Conference was inaugurated by President Soeharto of Indonesia. The Indonesian presence was marked by a high degree of competence, matchless grace and oriental hospitality. The arrangements for the conference were perfect.

As a United Nations Resource person, I sat with the UN ESCAP staff and could objectively observe the performance of different delegations. The Chinese delegation was ably led by Mme. Peng Peiyun, Minister in charge of State Family Planning Commission. I had met her in New Delhi and Beijing and I was delighted to meet her in Bali. She conducts herself with great tact and gentle diplomacy. I heard her say at the Bali Conference: "It is incorrect to say that China has a one-child population policy." What she implied was that people are themselves realising that one child was enough, given the excessive population of China. The country report for China states that "The voluntary participation in family planning by more people especially in rural areas in the western part of China will be the crucial factor determining the future fertility trends in the country."

The leader of the Japanese delegation. Mr Hiroyuki Sonoda, Parliamentary vice-Minister in the Ministry of Foreign Affairs made a spirited speech and talked of the Asian Forum of Parliamentarians on Population and Development. Prof Shigemi Kono of Japan was elected as a Vice-Chairman of the Conference conducted the deliberations with great competence. He is a technical demographer and had worked for years with the United Nations Population Division in New York.

Pakistan's alternate delegate, Mr Mahbub Ahmad, Additional Secretary in charge of the Ministry of Population Welfare was also elected as Vice-Chairman of the Conference and he impressed everybody with his dynamism. He was also chairman of the Drafting Committee.

Having attended all the four Asian Population Conferences (New Delhi, Tokyo, Colombo and Bali), I cannot help observing that the lead which India had in population matters in 1963 was totally lost at the Bali Conference, perhaps because of the short-sighted view of the Finance Ministry. On all previous occasions, the Registrar General and Census Commissioner was a member of the Indian delegation and had played a key role in the deliberations of the Conference. Considering the fact that India has successfully conducted the second largest census in the world in 1991, it was all the more necessary that the 1991 Census Commissioner was included in the Indian delegation. His absence was noticed by all friends of India. It may be noted in passing that Pakistan did not succeed in conducting the Census of 1991 (they are hoping to do so in the near future).

I see no reason why India kept such a low profile at the Bali Conference. The three member delegation did their best. Mr K.K.Mathur was a persuasive speaker but he was transferred from the Department of Family Welfare to that of Chemicals just before the Bali Conference. Professor Sudesh Nangia, the non official member of the Indian delegation (she is the General Secretary of the Indian Association for the Study of Population) was one of the few delegates who had the technical competence to speak on environment in relation to population. The leader of the Indian delegation, Mrs Tharadevi Siddartha conducted herself gracefully and during the closing session, she moved a resolution adopting the Bali Declaration.

To sum up, the major areas of concern reflected in the Bali Declaration are: (a) the urgent need "to bring into balance population dynamics, socio-economic development, use of natural resources and environmental quality"; (b) "recognise that urbanization is inevitable" and therefore "be concerned with the environment and sustainable development and improvements in the quality of life in cities and the country-side, particularly slums and other disadvantaged areas"; (c) realise that "the success of family planning and MCH programmes is closely associated with the improved role and status of women, lower infant, child and maternal mortality rates, better birth-spacing and breast-feeding practices, and the delivery of services by trained personnel"; (d) recognise that "demographic factors are strategically important in human resources development because of their inter-relationships with employment, education, skill and capability development; health and nutrition, and the status and role of women"; and (e) strengthen "the family support system by providing economic incentives such as tax exemptions and special privileges to families taking care of their elderly members."

The Bali Declaration was almost silent on the issues concerning international migration, legal as well as illegal. This would have perhaps raked up a lot of political controversy. Most delegates to this Conference observed that there was no controversy of any kind at the Bali Conference. Perhaps, the physical environment of the beautiful island of Bali and the grace and charm of the people around made everything so harmonious. The next such Conference is likely to be held in Korea after ten years.

2

Fertility Transition in South Asia Comiec Versus Bliss Strategy

It has become internationally fashionable to talk of sustainable development. It is our contention that we should also think in terms of sustainable family planning strategies. This paper pleads for the rejection of the current family planning strategies followed in countries like India, Pakistan, Bangladesh and Nepal (largely inspired by foreign ideas and funding agencies). Our plea is that, given the level of poverty in south Asia, the family planning programme would have no credibility unless the basic needs of the people are fulfilled.

Primary health is a basic need. Family Planning is a part of reproductive health and therefore should automatically be covered by primary health care. Jawaharlal Nehru was responsible for the incorporation of family planning under the rubric of health in the very first five year plan of India (1951-56). But under misguided foreign advice, family planning was put in a separate basket in 1966 and the practice continues till today. Again, under misguided foreign advice, monetary incentives were introduced in the family, planning programme. This has lead to widespread corruption and commercialisation of the programme. It was thought that in a poor country, the best way to motivate people was to give them monetary incentives. In this process, another shortcut was applied, namely. over -emphasis on sterilisation, which is a terminal method of family planning. Looking back at the experience of India and on the basis of the extensive fieldwork which we have done for the last 30 years, it appears to us that the illiterate masses in India have outwitted our bureaucracy and the foreign experts. They have accepted cash incentives and sterilisation but only after completing thieir family building which means at least two living sons or a family size of 5 or 6 children, Obviously, this has not brought about a significant dent on the birth-rate. This has been at last realised by the Government of India and the international donor agencies. But strangely enough, the solution offered is to put more money on the so called IEC (Information, Education, communication) programme. We believe that under conditions of mass illiteracy, IEC programmes have limited value.

Paper presented at a Workshop on Female Education, Autonomy and Fertility Change in South Asia, New Delhi, 10-11 April, 1993

Now there is a shift in Government policy: from sterilisation to spacing methods. This is also not likely to produce the desired results because under conditions of mass illiteracy, any programme based on spacing methods cannot be sustained, because such methods require sustained motivation. Given the level of illiteracy, the average age of marriage cannot also be increased. Our plea, therefore, is that governments is South Asia and the donor agencies must back an effective basic needs programme, coupled with a massive programme for stamping out illiteracy in the shortest possible time. In our view, this is the best family planning input.

Reassessing Intervention Strategies

The Fourth Asian and Pacific Population conference (United Nations, 19-12 August 1992, Bali, Indonesia) provided an excellent opportunity for planners and policymakers to take stock of the demographic situation in Asian countries. From the individual country statements and also background papers prepared by ESCAP it was evident that South Asia is lagging behind East Asia and South-East Asia on the road to demographic stabilisation. Considering the absolute size of the population, the comparatively high level of fertility and the low levels of income, South Asia may be regarded as the world's most vulnerable demographic region. In fact, the world population problem is zeroing in on India, Pakistan and Bangladesh. It was also evident from the deliberations of the Bali Conference that in spite of ever-expanding family planning programmmes in South Asian Countries, their success in reducing the birth rate was somewhat limited. While analyzing the reasons for the slow progress in containing population growth in these countries (except in Sri Lanka), it may be worthwhile to have a good look at the current intervention strategies in order to reorient some of these strategies.

India has the longest experience of state-sponsored intervention strategies to contain the population growth rate and other countries can benefit from the Indian experience and avoid the pitfalls. It is not suggested that the Indian expcience should guide population policies of other countries in this region. South Asia is not a homogeneous region. Nevertheless, one must recognize that the similarities in the demographic, economic and social characteristics of the countries in South Asia are perhaps much greater that dissimilarities.

The Bali Declaration on Population and Development rightly asserts that "the emerging population issues in the region will become more diverse and complex during the 1990s, requiring flexible and innovative approaches to sustain the achievement made in the last three decades." In regard to family planning, the Bali Declaration does recognize the need to undertake "comprehensive and critical reviews of existing policies and programme strategies" (Recommendation 17) but it is only is the context of urbanization that the Bali Declaration recommends that "Governments should reassess policies relating to urbanization and seek to implement policies that recognise that urbanisation is inevitable." (Recommendation 5). This paper makes a plea for reassessing intervention strategies in regard to family planning in South Asian countries. It is also our plea that governments in this regions should recognize that there can be no sustainable family planning programme unless the literacy level (both for males and females) is raised to near one hundred per cent. Pumping more and more money into current programmes is unlikely to deliver the goods.

For the sake of brevity, we shall describe the present intervention strategies (supported by international and bilateral donor agencies) by an acronym--COMIEC where CO stands for contraceptive technology, M for monetary incentives and IEC for information, education and communication. The implicit assumption behind this strategy is that modern technology (and in this context, the latest contraceptive technology, say, norplant) can come to the rescue of masses of poor and illiterate people, if only they are given some monetary incentives and a good dose of IEC to generate demand for family planning. In our view, this strategy has not succeeded in India nor is it likely to suceeed, The same may be true of Bangladesh, Nepal and Pakistan.

In spite of policy pronouncements that India's family planning programme follows a cafeteria approach, sterilisation is the mainstay of the family planning programme (this is true of Nepal also), The reason why sterilisation is favoured by the family planning administrators is that it is a once for all, terminal method and therefore cost-effective. Other methods require sustained motivation and in most cases sustained medical attention. It is recognized that the basic issue is how to generate motivation. Given the poverty of the people, perhaps the best method bringing them into the family planning fold is incentives in cash and kind. In India, historically speaking, in the earlier stages of the family planning programme, there was only "compensation" money for loss of wages (initally for acceptors of vasectomy and later extended to tubectomy which became more prevalent) but over the years, compensation yielded place to monetary incentives, supplemented in several states by incentives in kind. In several states the monetary incentives given by the Central Government were also supplemented by enhanced monetary payments on behalf of the State concerned. In the case of several organised industries also the monetary incentives were substantially higher than those given by the government. Interestingly, the monetary incentive for IUD insertions is a very negligible amount and in the case of condoms (called "conventional contraceptives" in Indian family planning jargon), there is no incentive except that there is free distribution of condoms through Primary Health Centers and other outlets. This is true of oral pills also. Though the age at marriage is recognized as an important factor in bringing down the birth rate, there is no incentive for raising the age at marriage (some posters and publicity material as well as radio and TV programmes talk of the benefits of raising the age at marriage of girls).

It is not often recognized that inherent in this system of differential compensation and monetary incentives is a marked bias in favour of sterilisation. In the name of monitoring the programme, a rigid system of target-setting was introduced in the Central Ministry of Health and Family Planning and detailed targets are set out for each method of family planning. The Central Government also makes it obligatory for all State Governments to submit monthly and quarterly reports on family planning performance, setting out the achievements against the targets. The States in turn demand from each district, monthly and quarterly figures on similar lines and the district medical Officer of each PHC in turn demands performance figures from each Sub-Centre, catering to a population of 3000 to 5000 persons. So what is aimed at is command performance, with the Central Ministry of Health and Family planning financing, directing, controlling and monitoring a huge monolithic programme.

Unfortunately, in most States in India (and particularly in the large states of Bihar, Madhya Pradesh, Rajasthan and Uttar Pradesh which account for 40 percent of India's population--our acronym is BIMARU) this command performance is weak both on the technical front and the social front, laparoscopy as a method of female sterilization in the modern world cannot be opposed but in the absence of adequte chech-up and in particular, follow-up after the operation, this method which was initially welcomed by female acceptors fell out of grace. Doctors were vying with each other in maximising the number of laparoscopic operations per day, in violation of all medical ethics. But much more than the logistics and technical aspects of the method, what really went wrong was the social environment created by the over-advocacy of this method. In the eyes of the people, family planning got identified with sterilisation and that too, female sterilisation. All other methods were edged out, but the pertinent question is: Did this terminal method which is so very effective really succeed in bringing down the birth rate significantly? Unfortunately the answer is in the negative.

Numerous studies show that most of the acceptors of this terminal method are women beyond 30 years, with more than 4 or 5 children, Thus in spite of the growing number of sterilisation cases, the dent on the birth rate could be only marginal, It took a long time for the Government to realise this. The international donor agencies and bilateral donor agencies also realised this rather late. The Government of India, on Rajiv Gandhi's personal initiative, invited suggestions for restructuring and redesigning the family planning programme in 1985 but he could not complete this task. With the blessing of international agencies, there is now a sudden upsuge of interest in IEC (Information, Education, Communication) strategy as an important mechanism for strengthening the family planning programme through emphasising non-terminal methods, raising the age at marriage, improving female literacy rates and supporting other "beyond family planning measures". Large sums are being invested on the IEC programme. But there is no evidence that things have improved. Our field work in different parts of India, and in particular , in the BIMARU states convinces us that under conditions of mass illiteracy, the impact of IEC would be marginal. In any case, there is no IEC strategy which can effectively counteract the widely accepted and widely prevalent notion among the masses that family planning means sterilisation. The masses cannot be blamed for this state of affairs. The fault lies with what we call the COMIEC strategy. What should we do then?

Focus on women

The 72nd and 73rd Amendments to the Constitution of India passed by Parliament recently make it mandatory for all local government bodies and Panchayats to have 33 per cent of the seats reserved for women. This will give tremendous power to women. In fact, the subject of women and child development has been brought under the purview of the panchayats and to that extent, the Department of Women and Child Development of the Central Government would have to shed much of its powers.

This is indeed a happy development and the Government and Parliament deserve congratulations on passing these amendments for ushering in Panchayat Raj. But what disturbs one is the shocking state of female literacy revealed by the 1991 Census of India. Can Panchayat Raj be effective with this level of illiteracy? There are only two states in

India namely, Kerala and Mizoram where more than 75 per cent of the females are literate but these are small states, On the other hand, in the large states of Uttar Pradesh, Bihar, Madhya Pradesh and Rajasthan, the female literacy rate is extremely low.

It is universally accepted that the level of literacy has direct bearing on the infant mortality rate and the birth rate, as also practice of family planning. Kerala which has the highest literacy rate has also the lowest infant mortality rate and the lowest birth rate (barring Goa which is a tiny state). Most developed countries have an infant mortality rate (IMR) of well below 30 per thousand (the lowest IMR is in Japan, namely, only four per thousand). In fact, an IMR of more than 60 is considered very bad and an IMR of over 100 is considered unacceptable in the modern world. In India in the State of Orissa the IMR is as high as 126 while in Madhya Pradesh it is 122. Only in Kerala, it is as low as 17 per thousand.

In India, for many years, the Parliament, Planning Commission and the Ministry of Health and Family Welfare have adhered to birth rate target of 21 per thousand for the country as a whole by the year 2000. The actual birth rate in Kerala in 1990 was 18.1 per thousand and in Tamil Nadu it was 20.7. Kerala and Tamil Nadu are the flagships. Sadly enough, the birth rate is higher than 30 per thousand in the large states of Uttar Pradesh, Bihar, Madhya Pradesh and Rajasthan. It is most unlikely that by the year 2000, the birth rate in these states would be 21 per thousand.

The inescapable conclusion is that whether we want effective Panchyat Raj, lower infant mortality rates and lower birth rates, the liquidation of illiteracy among women is absolutely essential. High on the agenda for women's development must be the attainment of one hundred per cent literacy rate in the shortest possible time.

Table 1 gives the female literacy rate for different states and union territories of India on the basis of the 1991 Census data

Table 2-1
Female Literacy Rates, 1991
(per cent of total females)

India 39.3%

A.   75% and above

Kerala (86.1), Mizoram (78.6)

B.   50-75%

Lakshadweep (72.9), Chandigarh (72.3), Goa (67.1), Delhi (67.0), Pondicherry (65.6), Andaman & Nicobar Islands (65.5) Daman & Diu (59.4), Nagaland (54.8), Maharashtra (52.3), Himachal Pradesh (52.1), Tamil Nadu (51.3). Punjab (50.4)

C.   25-50%

Tripura (49.7), Gujarat (48.6), Manipur (47.6), Sikkim (46.7), West Bengal (46.6), Meghalaya (44.9), Karnataka (44.3), Assam (43.0), Haryana (40.5), Orissa (34.7),

Andhra Pradesh (32.7), Arunachal Pradesh (29.7) Madhya Pradesh (28.9), Dadra & Nagar Haveli (27.0), Uttar Pradesh (25.3)

D. Below 25%

Bihar (22.9), Rajasthan (20.4)

Basic Needs Approach

The preamble of the Bali Declaration recognizes that "the alleviation of poverty is fundamental to the achievement of sustainable development". The first step in this regard in our view is the satisfaction of the basic needs of the people. Long back, India's Fifth Five Year Plan (1974-79) emphasised the importance of the Minimum Needs Programme. This is not a new demand. In the context of family planning it implies that people demanding bread must be given bread and contraceptives and not merely contraceptives. In short, the success of the family planning programme would depend largely on the success of the programme to fulfil the basic needs of the people. Literacy is a part of these basic needs but has to be spelt out separately, Time and again, reference is made to the Kerala and Sri Lanka model of fertility transition where literacy and, in particular, female literacy has played a key role. Literacy is something desirable in itself, regardless of what it does to fertility. In any case, at the fag end of the 20th century it should be more than obvious that development without near 100 per cent literacy level is not sustainable, If this is obvious, it should also be obvious to our planners and policymakers and the international donor agencies that in countries like Nepal or India, instead of spending money on IEC in the context of family planning, there should be a TOTAL mobilisation of resources and efforts to wipe out illiteracy in the shortest possible time. What worthwhile information can one give to the illiterate people? Granted that we have to popularise spacing methods like oral pills, can the rural women and women in the proliferating slums of the cities read a set of simple instruction about the pill? And what exactly in the "education" component in IEC when the pre-condition of literacy is not fulfilled? And do we really know how to communicate with the illiterate masses?

Coming back to the question of fertility decline, there are numerous studies all over the world which indicate threshold level of education of the husband and wife which bring about a decline in fertility. Mere literacy is not enough. This threshold level is generally the secondary level of schooling. Taking a broader view of population control in the context of human resource development, one can argue that even this threshold level of education is not enough unless there is an element of skill formation which leads of higher levels of productivity and therefore, higher levels of economic growth and income generation. The Bali Declaration does realise the value of human resource development and recommends that "Government should improve human resources development programmes, especially vocational and occupational training in both rural and urban areas, to open up wide range of employment option for people living in areas characterised by a surplus labour." (Recommendation 32)

For the sake of brevity, we shall give an acronym to the type of intervention strategy we are advocating to contain population growth. We shall call this strategy BLISS, where B stands for basic needs, LI for literacy (aiming at 100 per cent literacy both for males and females), S for schooling (upto secondary level, both for boys and girls) and the next S for skill formation (both for men and women).

There is nothing new about this approach. In fact, every plan of every country would provide for the fulfilment of basic needs, literacy, schooling and skill formation. These would form a part of the overall strategy of development. But what we are suggesting is that this should form a part of the family planning strategy. As things are, such a suggestion would be unacceptable to the Ministry of Health and Family Planning who would regard these issues to be outside the purview of their Ministry. For example, they would argue that literacy and schooling should be handled by the Ministry of Education, skill formation by the Ministry of Labour and Basic needs by the Planning Comn.ission through intergrated five year plans. In short, as thing are, the concerned Ministry, namely, Ministry of Health and Family Planning would concede to the logic of this approach but for operational reasons would reject such a strategy. The same holds true of international donor agencies. The solution to this dilemma, which as advocated from time to time, is to appoint a National Population Commission with the Prime Minister as the chairman to co-ordinate the activities of different Ministries. In our view this is not a worthwhile solution. It is not question of inter-sectoral cordination but of thrust areas, given to poverty and illiteracy of the masses.

In India, even the Government concedes that there is need for decentralising the family planning programme. The international donor agencies of late are the greatest champions of NGOs by siphoning off funds to them is unlikely to deliver primary health care. Health as defined by Jawaharlal Nehru, the first Prime Minister of India and the Chairman of the first Planning Commission, includes family planning. But under misguided foreign advice, in 1966, family planning was put in a separate basket in India and this has done great harm to the credibility of the health and family planning programme. Of late, it has become fashionable to talk of reproductive health. Unfortunately, the strategy of paying monetary incentives for family planning has sought to put a premium on family planning work (which in effect means, more often that not, somehow fulfilling the sterilisation targets fixed by the Ministry, regardless of the age and parity of the acceptors of sterlisation). As D. Banerji (1991), a leading critic of the family planning programme has observed, "Health has been hijacked by family planning". The credibility of the family planning programme is not high anywhere in India. There is no doubt that in Kerala, the small family norm has crystallised and even if the family planning programme is withdrawn, the people will not abandon the small family norm. The Government programme alone is not responsible for this encouraging demographic scenario. There are numerous historical, geographical, social and economic factors which have been mentioned by several scholars who have commented on Kerala.

In our view, Nehru's strategy of sponsoring family planning under the rubric of health was sound but over the years, the programme has suffered because of the separation of health and family planning growing commercialisation of the family planning programme by giving monetary incentives to indiiduals and cash award to States and the poor implementation of the family planning programme at the grassroot level, apart from the damage done to the programme during the Emergency in India (1975-77). We believe that no matter how much money is spent on IEC, the credibility of the family planning programme cannot be restored. We would, however, not reject the IEC approach altogether but plead for a fundamental reorientation of the programme by linking family planning to environment and sustainable development.

Development as understood today is by definition sustainable development. Inherent in the concept of sustainable development is concern for the future and concern for judicious use of our resources. In recent years, there has been considerable awareness of the threat to the quality of life by growing environmental degradation and the increasing strain on the ecosystem though it cannot be maintained that all our environmental problems are caused by population growth. Nonetheless, there is a greater awareness today of the need for considering population issues in the context of environment.

The nexus between population and environment is more difficult to understand than the nexus between health and family plannning. It is necessary to understand population issues not only in the limited context of fertility control but also in relation to the distribution of population, and in particular, consider the role of internal and international migration. We are heading towards an urban world in the 21st century. Urbanization is very much a demographic phenomenon. In this sense, population planning is a more appropriate term which should include intervention strategies to influence the level of fertility, mortality and migration and in so far as migration is linked to employment generation, the issue of manpower planning or human resources development becomes important.

Adolescent Girls

Like development, which should be sustainable, family planning strategy should also be sustainable. The strategy being followed at present in India (or for that matter in Nepal) is based on motivating people to practise family planning (more specifically sterilisation) by paying incentive money. Once this money is withdrawn, the programme may collapse, in other words, is not based on sustained motivation to adopt the small family norm. In our sheme of things, attainment of 100 per cent literacy, particularly among females, is a solid first step for building such motivation, in a sustained manner. Secondary schooling is the second step. Skill formation and income generation is the third step. Historically speaking, this is how demographic transition was achieved in large parts of the world. But today we are increasingly relying on modern contraceptive technology, money power and IEC. But this strategy has not delivered the goods in countries like India, Pakistan and Bangladesh. The levels of female literacy are extremely low in these countries. The secondary school enrolment rates are shocking low (and the drop out rate is high). There is widespread child labour. The age at marriage is low and teenage pregnancy common. Fertility control apart, in such a situation, the talk of raising the status of women is meaningless unless women are made literate. But in the spirit of sustainable development, we would argue that adult literacy programmes are not enough. The only way to sustain a high level of literacy and schooling is to ensure that the new generation is fully literate and has the threshold level of schooling. This changes the focus at once from the age group 15-35 years to the age group 6-14. In the context of family planning this calls for a paradigm shift from women in the age groups of 30+ (at present the prime target group for sterilisation) to those in the age group 6-14 years, and even more importantly, those in the age group 14-18 comprising adolescent girls.

In operational terms, we would plead for the extension of the Intergrated Child Development Scheme (ICDS) to include the age group 6-18 years as follows:

Age Group	Focus	Intervention Strategy
0-3	Care of the Mother and Child	Nutrition, immunisation, antenatal and postnatal care
3-9	Present ICDS Programme plus formal education	More intensive efforts for 100% school enrolment, especially of girls.
9-18	Adolescent girls	female education, skill formation, income generating activity, marriage beyond 18 years.

In short, the present ICDS programme may be modified as follows:

ICDS I   :   0-3 age group
ICDS II   :   3-9 age group
ICDS III :   9-18 age group (renamed as IADS-Intergrated Adolescent) Development Scheme)

What we are pleading for is a paradigm shift from women in the reproductive age group to adolescents who will enter the reproductive age group. Given the financial constraints, we would concentrate on girls in the age group 14-18 years. This is good economics, good sociology and good demography.

Our women must go beyond the papad and achar syndrome, They must learn modern skills, be self-reliant, marry late, produce fewer and healthier children and contribute to human resource development.

Time and again, suggestions are made that a substantial sum should be paid as incentive money to acceptors of sterilisation, say Rs. 5,000 or Rs. 10,000 per sterilisation. This is supposed to be cost-effective in the overall national context. Such cost benefit analysis is very often unreal and misguided. We would plead for diverting such money to skill formation for girls in the age group 14 to 18 years, We are aware of numerous short-term training programmes and orientation courses for women. Our plea, however, is for a sustained programme for five years (if the girl getting training is married or gets married before 18 years, she should be disqualified from joining this scheme). The new organisation we have suggested is named TARA Technology-oriented Adolescent Resource-Development Agency. This should be an independent, autonomous body and any government department, public sector industry, voluntary organisation, private sector industry or even an individual can sponsor a TARA Centre, initally for five years by paying Rs. one million per year or Rs. five million for five years (out of which Rs. 2.5

million would be spent on non-recurring expenduture). Each TARA Centre would recruit as trainees 40 to 50 girls every year. Things will change dramatically if we can start some 500 TARA Centres in the BIMARU states.

The Economic Survey for 1992-93 presented to the Parliament by Dr. Manmohan Singh, who is currently the Finance Minister of India, recognizes the unsatisfactory state of India's family planning programme in four large states of India. To quote from this report (1993:201)

> In spite of massive efforts, budgetary support and infrastructure development, the performance of the family welfare programme has lagged behind in the northern states of Bihar, Madhya Pradesh, Rajasthan and Uttar Pradesh, which continue to be characterised by high birth and total fertility rates. Effort for containment of population growth have to be intensified. This calls for an interated approach and concerted efforts through both Government and non Government organisations besides social and political commitment to make it national movement.

We believe that the COMIEC strategy of intervention will have a limited impact on the family planning programme in these four large States. We would advocate the BLISS intervention strategy as described by us. It is also important to realise that unless the question of physical accessibility is tackled, the fulfilment of basic needs will be problematic. Unfortunately, the energy crisis and the steep rise in petroleum prices make mobility an expensive proposition. This calls for very careful planning of health and family planning services at the grassroot level.

Conclusion

South Asia may be regarded as the world's most vulnerable demographic region, considering the absolute size and growth rate of population and also the low level of income. India, Pakistan, Bangladesh and Nepal are lagging behind East Asia and South East Asia on the road to population stabilization. Indeed, the world population problem is zeroing in on South Asia. This highlights the urgency of focusing attention on this region.

India has the longest experience of State sponsored family planning programme extending over eight five year plans. Yet the experience of India in reducing the birth rate is far from encouraging. Judging by the contraceptive prevalence rate, the situation is even worse in Pakistan, Bangladesh and Nepal. This calls for serious rethinking on the current intervention strategies designed to bring down the birth rate. This paper makes a plea for reassessing and reorienting such policies.

In our view, the present family planning strategy is not conceptually sound in the South Asian context. It relies heavily on contraceptive technology, monetary incentives and IEC (information, education, communication). We believe that in spite of increasing funds for the family planning programme allocated by national governments and international and bilateral donor agencies, it is unlikely that in the near future, the birth rate will go down sharply. Under conditions of mass illiteracy, motivation is sought to be generated by monetary incentives. This tends to artificially prop up the family planning programme and there is every danger of the programme collapsing if the monetary incentives are withdrawn. Like sustainable development, we must also have sustainable family planning programmes.

It is our firm conviction that the only way to sustain such a programme is to generate motivation for the small family norm on a lasting basis or in other words, bring about a fundamental change in the reproductive behaviour. This is possible only when the basic needs of the people are fulfilled, the literacy level (both for men and women) is raised to near 100 per cent, there is compulsory secondary school level education for the new generation, along with adequate skill-formation which alone can trigger off the process of higher levels of productivity, economic growth and modernisation of society and economy.

The efforts to short-circuit the lengthy demographic transtion by relying on modern contraceptive technology without creating the necessary social environment have not succeded. Increasing money power has lead to corruption and the IEC programme has been largely ineffective.

India did recognise the urgency of population control in the very first five year plan launched in 1951, but after four decades of planning, the prospect of population stabilisation remains a far cry. There is nothing wrong *per se* in advocating modern contraceptive technology. But unfortunately this approach has degenerated into target setting, primarily aimed at sterilisation and that too, female sterilisation, without any regard for the age of the acceptor or the number of children they have. No wonder the dent on the birth rate is not substantial.

We, therefore, advocate what we call BLISS strategy, based on fulfilment of basic needs, one hundred percent literacy level, socondary level schooling and skill formation. Primary Health care is of course a part of the basic needs. And we would put family planning as an integral part of primary helth care. In this sense, family planning becomes a basic need and should be recognised as such, We would also urge all donor agencies to divert the IEC money to massive literacy campaigns (Kerala offers a good example of total mobilisation with the effort of the people: it is not a question of Government versus NGOs). Wiping out illiteracy in the shortest possible time should be high on the agenda of family planning. The dividend from such an approach would indeed be high. It would enable women to fight injustice against them like dowry, unwanted and repeated pregnancies, child marriages, alcoholism of husbands, etc, and will go a long way in raising the status of women. In the context of reservation of seats for women in the *panchayats* (village councils). It is essential to empower women through literacy and education. But we must caution that our focus is not on the adult females but on the new generation and we would plead for special programmes for adolescent girls in the age group 14-18 years.

It is also our contention that the question of physical accessibility has not been adequately considered by planners and policy makers. In the context of the energy crisis, this issue becomes even more complex. The provision of basic services including health and family planning suffers in the absence of optimum physical accessibility of primary health centres and Sub-Centres. Several alternative models should be tried to improve the state of affairs.

Finally, we would plead for linking population to environment and for redesigning IEC strategies to educate the people about the need for ecological balance and environmental protection in the context of sustainable development.

REFERENCES

Banerji.D.(1990). *A Socio-Cultural, Political and administrative analysis of health policies and programmes in India*. New Delhi:Lok Paksh.

Bose Ashish (1988). *From Population of People* (in 2 volumes) Delhi: B.R. Publishing Corporation.

Bose Ashish (1992). *Family Planning--Alternative Strategies*. Report for Family Planning Foundation.

India. Ministry of Finance (1993). *Economic Survery* 1992-93. New Delhi.

United Nations (1992). *Bali Declaration on Population and Sustainable Development*.

□ **3**

Population Planning in China

The global market stems from the global population. China and India, the two demographic giants, with a combined population of 2,000 million, account for about 38 per cent of the world population.

Round the world, whenever population matters are discussed, questions like the following invariably crop up: Has the Chinese family planning programme really succeeded? Will India overtake China's population? Can India follow the Chinese model? Will it be politically counterproductive?

These are difficult questions to answer and much would depend on our demographic judgement which has a large subjective element.

Soon after the abortive student revolt in Beijing, I was in China in December 1989, attending a series of national seminars on population, rural transformation, urbanisation and aging, at the invitation of the Chinese Academy of Social Sciences. The one child policy was discussed mainly in the context of aging population and the need for social security. During coffee break, several social scientists belonging to the younger generation told me: "We cannot press our population control programme any further without inviting political trouble. We know what happened to the Indira Gandhi Government in India".

The question of a more effective family planning programme in India was invariably mentioned in my discussions with Prime Minister Rajiv Gandhi and his advisers during 1985-89. I had told Mr. Gandhi that it was a mistake to have put family planning in a separate basket, under misguided foreign advice. Pandit Nehru was right when he visualised family planning as an integral part of the health programme. In my notes to the Prime Minister, I had clearly stated: "What happened in 1977 can happen again. People in the northern states have not forgiven the Government for emergency excesses in getting sterilisation cases". I was asked : "Now that the elections are coming, what should

Appeared in *Financial Express*, 7 and 8 April, 1992

we do?" My suggestion was: "Harp on health, on the immunisation programme." Much more than my advice, the powerful UNICEF advocacy of child survival strategies influenced Mr. Gandhi to take personal interest in the immunisation programme. Unfortunately, he never got a chance to redesign India's family planning programme, which he wanted to do ever since he assumed office.

The 1990 Census of China and the 1991 Census of India have given a jolt to the Prime Ministers of both China and India. In their utterances in recent months, there is a renewed concern for a more effective family planning programme. There is also a sense of urgency brought about by the results of the census. Both in China and India, the growth rate of population revealed by the census is higher than expected. In China, there is a trend towards a slight increase in the birth rate. This is mainly due to the entry of a large number of young couples in the reproductive age group, a consequence of the baby boom in the 1960s. The somewhat "relaxed" population policy followed by China in recent years must have also contributed to the slight rise in the birth rate.

The census of 1990 in China shows that there is an excess population of 30 million in China compared to the goal set by the Seventh Five Year Plan (1985-90). In India, the Planning Commission was hoping that the annual growth rate of population during the last decade would be around 1.9 per cent or at least below two per cent per annum. The 1991 census of India shows that the growth rate during 1981-91 was 2.1 per cent per year.

Thus, both in China and India, there is a setback to the deadline for population stabilisation which remains an elusive target and a distant dream. According to the most recent United Nations projections, the population of China in the year 2000 would be around 1,300 million while in India it would be around 1,041 million (medium variant projection).

China and India accounted for 21.5 per cent and 16.1 per cent, respectively, of the world population in 1990 (or a total of 37.6 per cent). By 2025 China's share is expected to come down to 17.8 per cent while India's share will increase to 17 per cent. If we go a couple of decades beyond 2025, we can visualise India's population exceeding China's population, a situation far from flattering to India.

China took many somersaults in its population policy but there is no doubt that China has succeeded in drastically cutting down the birth rate in the last decade and a half. The birth rate which was 23 per thousand in 1975 came down to 17.5 in 1985 and since then it has risen slowly and according to the latest data, the birth rate of China was 21.1 in 1990.

In contrast, in India, the birth rate which was 35.2 in 1975 came down to 32.9 in 1985; in fact, the birth rate has stalled around 33 per thousand ever since 1977. There is a trend towards a slight decrease in the birth rate in recent years. According to the latest data the birth rate of India in 1990 was 29.9 per thousand.

It is worth noting that in Kerala, the birth rate is 19, compared to China's 21 per thousand. In Nagaland, the birth rate is 16.2 and in Goa, it is 15.5. But these are islands of demographic modernisation in an ocean of demographic inertia marked by continued high fertility. According to the latest data, the birth rate in Uttar Pradesh is 35.7, in Bihar

32.9, in Madhya Pradesh 36.9 and in Rajasthan 33.1. These politically powerful but demographically week states account for roughly 40 per cent of India's population. Statistically, speaking, Goa, Nagaland and Kerala can hardly influence the overall birth rate of India because the combined population of these three modern states is only a little over 31 million compared to the combined population of over 335 million in Bihar, Madhya Pradesh, Rajasthan and Uttar Pradesh (which I call demographically Bimaru states).

While explaining the growth rate of population, it is not enough to harp on the birth rate only. It is often forgotten that China has an impressive record of rapid decline in mortality and in particular, infant mortality. According to the latest data, China's death rate was 6.3 per thousand compared to India's 9.6. What is more striking is that even in 1971, the death rate of China was lower than India's death rate in 1990.

It is worth noting that in Kerala the death rate is only 5.9 per thousand. It is also 5.9 in Manipur and 4.1 in Nagaland and 6.8 in Goa. In contrast, the death rate in U.P. is 12.0, in Madhya Pradesh 12.5, in Bihar 10.6 and in Rajasthan 9.4.

It is recognised all over the world that the infant mortality rate (IMR = number of deaths below one year per 1000 live births) has a strong impact on the family planning programme. Is it possible to attain the Chinese level of infant mortality? In India the IMR is shockingly high. According to latest data, the IMR is 80 in India as a whole but in Uttar Pradesh it is 98, in Madhya Pradesh 111, in Rajasthan 83 and in Bihar 75. In contrast, it is only 17 in Kerala. In China it is around 32.

It will be seen that the Kerala model is a more impressive model than China's when one considers the birth, death and infant mortality rates. Could we learn more from Kerala than China?

The road to population stabilisation is long, ardous, elusive and full of political pitfalls. China's dream of population stabilisation at around 1.2 billion cannot be realised as the 1990 Census figures indicate. India's goal of Net Reproduction Rate of Unity, the first step to population stabilisation, had a target date of the year 2000. The Planning Commission pushes this date farther every time a new five year plan is formulated. India's population planning has been a frustrating experience during the last four decades, in spite of the parrot-like repetition by our planners and policymakers that India was the first country in the world to have put forward a Government policy for population control as a part of its development process.

In the last few years, the Prime Ministers have changed, the Health and Family Welfare Ministers have changed, the Planning Commission has been reconstituted several times and Family Welfare Secretaries have come and gone. Nobody knows what is happening on the family planning front.

Of late, we are coming out of this state of confusion. Both the President and the Prime Minister of India in their important pronouncements have highlighted the urgency of the population problem facing India. The 79th session of the Indian Science Congress (Baroda, January, 1991) chose "Science, Population and Development" as its central theme.

The National Development Council (NDC) under the Chairmanship of the Prime Minister met in December 1991 and appointed a Committee of Chief Ministers to urgently look into the family planning programme.

The Health Ministry has put forward a ten-point action plan for revamping the family welfare programme. International funding agencies have not given up lobbying for a population commission. This time it is not China but Indonesia which is their model. Our experts and administrators are making a beeline to visit Indonesia.

The Directional Paper for the Eighth Five Year Plan (1992-97) says: "The country will cross 1,000 million mark by the year 2000. If this trend is not halted, it will never be possible to render social and economic justice to millions of our masses". There is an element of helplessness when the Planning Commission says: "...... a national population policy needs to be enunciated and adopted by Parliament." One wonders why we are so good in enunciating POLICIES and so poor in implementing them.

Meanwhile, the Finance Minister has substantially stepped up the allocation (Rs. 1,000 crores in 1992-93) for family welfare in the latest budget. One cannot help observing that if this is meant for more of the same thing, much of the money will be wasted. May be the foreign sponsored Population Commission, as and when it is appointed, would look into the phenomenon of increasing funds and a largely non-responsive birth rate which tends to remain high. The unfortunate fact is that the PEOPLE are nowhere in picture, except in the rhetoric of making "family planning a people's movement." We are still whistling in the dark.

Let us have a look at China where, in spite of the rigorous population control programme, there is a growing concern for the sensitivities of the people, and the possible political repercussions of stretching the programme too far.

In March 1991, the National People's Congress of China adopted a report prepared by Premier Li Peng on an Ten Year Programme to "resolutely implement the basic State policies of family planning and environmental protection." In May 1991, the Central Committee of the Communist Party of China and the State Council took several DECISIONS on "strengthening the family planning programme for strict control of population growth."

The four major decisions taken at this meeting are as follows: (1) "We should have a strong sense of historical responsibility and the urgency of the time... The No. 1 leaders of party committees and governments at all levels must take charge of family planning work in person and should be responsible for the overall implementation of the family planning programme."

(2)   Resolutely carry out the current family planning policy of the late marriage and one child for each couple, and "manage the family planning programme according to laws." The "Small Hole" approach of giving permission to only-daughter families to have a second birth, which "opened up arbitrarily" and "reckless approval of birth quotas should be prohibited resolutely... third and higher parity births must be stopped."

(3)   "Take a firm hold of the rural areas as a key link and implement the family planning programme in a down-to-earth way". The emphasis should be on the "three stresses, which are explained as follows:

Publicity and education rather than economic disincentives; contraception rather than induced abortions; and constant family planning management rather than irregular campaigns.

The need for a more humane approach to the population control programme will be evident from the following exhortation:

"We should care for the people and do concrete things for them in order to win their understanding and support so that family planning can become their voluntary practice not only to achieve effective control of population growth, but also to improve the relationship between functionaries and masses, thus maintaining a situation of stability and unity."

(4)   All departments concerned must be mobilised to take charge of family planning work to ensure its smooth development. The need for implementing the policy governing the households enjoying "five guarantees" is emphasised. These guarantees refer to childless and infirm old persons who are guaranteed "food, clothing, medical care, housing and burial expenses by the villages where they live."

It should be noted that China is now emphasising the role of publicity and education rather than economic disincentives. A striking difference between China and India is in regard to the literacy rates as revealed by the 1990 Census of China and the 1991 Census of India.

The Chinese census groups illiterates and semi-literates together while the Indian Census presents data for the number of literates and the percentage of literates. In 1990, the illiteracy rate of China (inclusive of semi-literates) was 15.88 per cent or 16 per cent. That is to say 84 per cent of the population of China is literate.

In contrast, in India only 52 per cent of the population is literate according to the 1991 Census. If one examines the State-wise variations in the literacy rates, one observes that the literacy rate in Kerala is 91 per cent while it is 39 per cent in Bihar and Rajasthan, 42 per cent in Uttar Pradesh and 43 per cent in Madhya Pradesh.

A study of the differences in the literacy rates in the different regions of China show that the highest literacy rate was in Beijing region where it is 91 per cent while the lowest literacy rate is in Xi Zang where it is 56 per cent.

It may be recalled that as a result of the recent literacy campaign in Kerala, the literacy rate is almost 100 per cent whereas in other parts of India, only a few selected districts claim to have attained near 100 per cent literacy rates.

Can India attain the level of China's or Kerala's birth rate without attaining their level of death rate?

Can India attain China's or Kerala's birth rate and death rate without attaining the literacy level of China or Kerala? India's family planning programme has for a long time centred round the sterilisation programme and basically it has been sterilisation of the illiterate rural masses. We are now getting diminishing returns from this "bring cases" approach based on monetary incentives.

A frontal attack on literacy should be a high priority item on the family planning agenda.

$\boxed{4}$

The Aging Population
of Japan

We have got used to the term "population explosion", signifying a high rate of population growth caused by high fertility and declining mortality. Hence the solution of the population problem lies in effective family planning programmes. This perception is still valid in several countries of Asia, Africa and Latin America. But what this perception lacks is an adequate realisation of a serious population problem facing the developed countries, caused by an increase in the proportion of the elderly population. Family planning is certainly not the solution of this type of population problem. In fact, this problem is caused by the very success of family planning. When there is a rapid reduction in birth and death rates, there is a reduction in the proportion of the youthful population and an increase in the proportion of the adults and the elderly population. After a time lag, depending on the age structure of the population, the proportion of the elderly increases rapidly.

Take for example the case of Japan, a highly developed country with very low rates of fertility and mortality and the highest level of expectation of life at birth. Has this demographic transition (the Japanese population growth rate is below replacement level) really improved the quality of life in Japan?

Let me answer this question by quoting at length Shigemi Keno, Director General of the Institute of Population Problems in Tokyo who says in a recent study on Aging in Japan (1992):

"The term 'population aging' has become a household word to average citizens in Japan. Hardly a day passes by without referring to the issues of population aging in Japanese newspaper and weekly magazines. Population aging is viewed almost unanimously here in Japan as a process causing young labour shortages, sluggish economic growth and higher tax burdens to support social services for the elderly. The tone of argument is thus mostly pessimistic. Sometimes it is conceived that a black hole

Appeared in *Financial Express,* 16 December, 1992

named 'population aging' is approaching Japan and eventually entire Japan will be swallowed up into this ominous dark aperture".

Let me give a few facts about the Japanese demographic scene. In 1950, the proportion of population in the age group 0-14 was 35.4 per cent while that for the age group 65+ was only 4.9 per cent. In 1990, the comparable figures were 18.2 per cent and 12.1 per cent. According to population projections in 2000, the proportion of the elderly would be 16.9 per cent while the proportion of children would be 15.2 per cent. Thus, for the first time in the demographic history of Japan, the elderly will outnumber the children. By 2050, if the projections prove correct, the elderly would constitute 27.4 per cent of the population of Japan while the children would account for only 16.1 per cent.

According to the latest figures, in Japan the expectation of life at birth for males is 76 years and for females 82 years.

It must be noted that what has happened in Japan is by no means unique--the story is the same in all the developed countries where there has been a sharp reduction in birth and death rates.

In the developing countries, the proportion of the elderly is still low but in absolute terms, the number of elderly is high in counties like China and India. So, there is no escape from the explosion of the elderly even in these countries which are still youthful. In short, while in the developed countries in the West and also in Japan, the proportion of the elderly is high, in developing countries the absolute number of the elderly is high.

According to United Nations estimates, in 1950, almost 50 per cent of the world population aged 65 and over was in "more developed regions" and another 50 per cent in the "less developed regions". By the year 2025, 69 per cent of the world's population of the elderly would reside in the less developed regions (and 31 per cent in the more developed regions).

It must also be noted that in 1990, Asia had the largest share of the elderly (65+) in the world, namely 48 per cent.

China with its one child family norm has also to gear up to face the problem of aging population. It was in 1987 that Peking University and the University of Cambridge organised an international symposium on changing family structure and population aging in China. In his Introduction to the volume containing the papers for this symposium (published in 1990). Zeng Yi, a leading Chinese demographer observes:

"Rapid population aging implies serious potential socio-economic problems... If the aging process cannot be properly brought under control through proper policy making and implementation, there will be problems with labour force shortages and a great burden on each individual family as well as society, which will harm the realisation of the national goal of moderanisation."

There are serious economic, social, psychological and even political implications of aging population which have not received adequate attention from planners and policy-makers. In the West where there are fairly good social security systems, the elderly face the problem of emotional insecurity because of the erosion of the institution of marriage and family. In the developing countries, the problem of economic insecurity is paramount and with the gradual break-up of the institution of extended family under the impact of increasing urbanisation, the problem of emotional insecurity too has to be reckoned with.

It is heartening to note that in spite of the remarkable moderanisation of Japan, the family still counts. In fact, one of the most striking differences between Japanese and the Western countries is in regard to living arrangements for the elderly.

Another interesting feature of the elderly in Japan is that a fairly substantial source of income of the elderly is in the form of financial support from their children (Table 2). The situation in the Western countries, in sharp contrast, reflects weak family solidarity.

In traditional China, the elderly had a high status in the family. Even with the advent of communism in China, the Chinese mode of supporting the elderly mainly by the family was respected. The Marriage Law of 1950 stipulates that parents have the duty to rear their children and the adult children have the duty to support their parents. The Chinese Constitution also stipulates that "parents have the duty to rear and educate their minor children, and children who have come of age have the duty to support and assist their parents". The 1980 Penal Code specifies punishment (imprisonment upto 5 years) of adult children who refuse to support parents.

In India, there is no evidence that our planners and policy-makers have adequately anticipated the problems of aging population. Giving a paltry sum to destitute every month is not enough. We need a comprehensive Plan of Action for the elderly.

Table 4.1: Living arrangement for the elderly (60+)

per cent

Living arrangement	USA	Denmark	Italy	Japan
Spouse	49.0	51.0	56.9	69.5
Married son	0.7	0.8	11.1	40.4
Married daughter	2.0	1.0	11.0	10.2
Grand child	2.3	0.8	16.7	38.0
Live alone	39.6	44.0	18.8	6.7

Note: These are multiple answers. So the figures do not add up to 100.
Source: Japan Aging Research Center. **Aging in Japan**. Tokyo, 1992.

Table 4.2: Source of living expenses for the elderly

Per cent

Source	USA	Denmark	Italy	Japan
Earning from work	24.0	14.0	12.1	34.3
Public pension	84.7	76.5	82.5	77.0
Private pension	29.7	13.2	10.6	5.4
Savings	24.0	11.4	24.5	16.6
Yield from property	49.4	20.0	7.4	14.5
Support from children	2.2	0.2	10.8	21.8

Note: These are multiple answers and the figures do not add up to 100.
Source : Japan Aging Research Centre. **Aging in Japan** Tokyo, 1992.

5

Korea's Rapid
Demographic Transition

The spectacular economic growth in the Republic of Korea (South Korea) in recent years is known all over the world. But what is not so well known is the demographic transition in Korea. Korea today is more than competing with Japan. Her aggressive export-oriented economy should be a lesson for Indian industrialists. Likewise, the spectacular fall in the birth and the death rates in Korea should be a eye-opener to our planners and policymakers.

Let me give a few facts about the demographic situation in Korea. The population of South Korea was 25 million in 1960. It increased to 43 million in 1990. It is worth nothing that in 1960, the birth rate was as high as 42 per thousand. In other words, the rate of natural increase was 30 per thousand or 3 per cent per year. In contrast, in 1990, the birth rate was only 15.6 while the death rate was 5.8, thus yielding a growth rate of 9.8 per thousand or 0.98 per cent (roughly 1 percent) per year.

India is struggling with a population growth rate of over 2 per cent per year for the last three decades, in spite of our ever-expanding family planning programme. In Korea, during the last three decades, the population growth rate has come down from 3 per cent per year to less that 1 per cent per year.

While discussing the demographic situation, it is not enough to look at the birth rate and death rate only. Let us look at the urban population. The spectacular growth in the economy of Korea is reflected in the proportion of urban population which was only 28 per cent in 1960 and was as high as 74.4 per cent in 1990. In spite of the ravages of the Korean war, since the early 1960s, South Korea which was a rural agricultural country has quickly transformed itself into a modern industrial urban economy. Korea's rapid industrialization and socio-economic development has occurred along with her rapid demographic transition.

Appeared in *Financial Express*, 2 December, 1992

Korea offers a tremendous opportunity for not only students of demography but more importantly to our planners and policy-makers and in particular, the Ministry of Health and Family Welfare, to understand the factors which led to the rapid demographic transition in Korea. A key factor in this transition was the important role of education, especially secondary education. In 1960, the average number of years of schooling was 4.8 years for males. It increased to 10 years in 1990 . Likewise, in 1960, the figure for females was only 2.9 years and it increased to 8.2 years in 1990. During these years, there has been a steady increase in the enrolment rates beyond the level of primary school. In 1990, there was 100 per cent enrolment of boys and girls in primary schools. But what is more noteworthy is that 97 per cent of the boys and girls were enrolled in the middle schools. Primary education is compulsory in Korea but not secondary education. Look at the pathetic Indian scene. We are still struggling with literacy. In 1991, the female literacy rate in India was less than 40 per cent. In the rural areas it was 25 per cent and in Rajasthan the female literacy rate in rural areas was near zero; it was only 9 per cent : And we want family planning to succeed in Rajasthan.

The impact of secondary education on the age at marriage, total fertility rate and the practice of family planning in Korea will be obvious from the following figures: the mean age at first marriage in Korea in 1990 was 27.8 years for males and 24.8 years for females; the total fertility rate (number of children per woman) was only 1.6 (i.e below replacement level of fertility) and the contraceptive practice rate among currently married women was 79.4 per cent.

In India we have made a mess of the family planning programme which is monopolised by an unimaginative bureaucracy not equipped to handle the task of social transformation of a traditional rural agricultural society into a modern industrial urban society. And yet Department of Family Welfare goes on making tall claims about the millions of births averted, the high couple protection rate and doles out fancy figures about the progress of the family welfare programme. In contrast note what the official country statement of the Republic of Korea (Presented at the United Nations ESCAP Fourth Asian and Pacific Population Conferences held at Bali, Indonesia, in August 1992) has to say:

"The overall responsibility for planning and implementing the national family planning program is delegated to the Ministry of Health and Social Affairs. The success in family planning programs in Korea can mainly be attributed to the contributions made by non-governmental organisations. The Planned Parenthood Federation of Korea (PPFK) has been mainly responsible for the information, education and communication activities; the Korea Association for Voluntary Sterilization has worked with the training programs for physicians and follow-up services for surgical contraceptive methods, and the Korea Institute for Health and Social Affairs has conducted evaluative studies on family planning. The Saemaul Women's Association, a voluntary non-government organization, has worked to raise the family planning acceptance level and to improve the level of family planning welfare in the villages throughout the country."

It may be noted that the overall population policy goals in Korea are set by the Economic Planning Board (EPB) in consultation with the concerned ministries. The ministries concerned with population policies, draft a set of detailed programs and measures, which is reviewed and approved by a cabinet level Population Policy Coordinating Committee (PPCC), chaired by the Deputy Prime Minister, who is also the Minister of Economic Planning.

Interestingly enough, Korea like India is facing the problem of son preference. According to a survey in 1991, son preference continues to be strong; while 70 per cent of the couples with two sons adopted sterilisation as a method of family planning , only 35 per cent of couples with two daughters took to sterilisation. In fact, the vital registration system shows ''a significant increase in son preference''. In 1982, for the fourth child and beyond, there were 114 boys for 100 girls in this category. It is certainly a disturbing phenomenon. Obviously, sex determination before birth is being increasingly resorted to in Korea (a practice which is spreading in India too). The country statement on Korea has the following to say about the increasing son preference:

"These increases suggest that a couple without a son would continue to have children until they have a son. To discourage such preference, the medical laws were amended in 1987 to heavily penalise those physicians rendering services relating to biased selection of a child."

Table 5.1: Demographic Indicators, Republic of Korea

	1960	1970	1980	1990
Total Population (in million)	25.0	32.2	38.1	42.9
Density (person per sq. km)	254	328	385	432
Birth rate (per thousand)	42.1	29.9	23.4	15.6
Death rate (per thousand)	12.1	9.5	6.7	5.8
National Increase rate(per cent)	3.0	2.04	1.67	0.98
Mean age at first marriage (years)				
Male	NA	26.7	26.4	27.8
Female	NA	22.6	23.2	24.8
Life Expectancy at birth (years)				
Male	NA	59.8	62.7	66.9
Female	NA	66.7	69.1	75.0
Per cent of urban				
Population	28.0	41.2	57.3	74.4
Contraceptive practice				
rate (per cent)	20.1	44.2	70.4	79.4
	(1966)	(1977)	(1985)	(1991)

Source : *Country Report of The Republic of Korea* for the Fourth Asian and Pacific Population Conference, August, 1992, Bali, Indonesia.

$\boxed{6}$

Lessons from Indonesia

It is in the fitness of things that the fourth Asian and Pacific Population Conference was held in the beautiful island of Bali in Indonesia (August 19-27). This Conference series sponsored by the United Nations ESCAP (Economic Commission for Asia and the Pacific) started with the first conference in New Delhi (1963) followed by the second conference in Tokyo (1972) and the third in Colombo (1982).

I had the honour of participating at all these three conferences. The present conference was sponsored by ESCAP and UNFPA (United Nations Population Fund). The main theme of the Conference was "Population and sustainable development; Goals and strategies into the twenty-first century." The growing concern for population in relation to environment is fully reflected in the venue of the conference--Bali island with the unpolluted sea around, the ever green vegetation, the magnificent flowers and fruits and above all, the graceful and peaceful people of Indonesia and the legendary charm and beauty of the people of Bali (which incidentally is predominantly Hindu and the people are known as Bali Hindus). There are Hindu temples all around in a country which is predominantly Muslim and the harmony of the people living together and professing different religions certainly adds to the quality of life.

The venue of the conference also reflects the tribute that the international population experts and agencies wish to pay to Indonesia for its outstanding performance on the family planning front. Family planning administrations all over the world are familiar with the pioneering role of the National Family Planning Co-ordinations Board (whose Indonesian acronym is BKKBN), headed by the President of Indonesia, reflecting the strong political commitment at the highest level. But not many are aware that Indonesia is perhaps the only country in the world which has a Ministry of Population and Environment.

The concern for environment on the part of population experts, planners and policy makers is of recent origin. It is therefore quite remarkable that Indonesia thought of

Appeared in *Financial Express*, 1 September, 1992

linking population directly with environment about a decade back when the Ministry of Population and Environment was formed. In fact, the Fourth Asian Population Conference was inaugurated by Dr. Emil Salim, State Minister for Population and Environment (who is also a professor of economics), and Dr. M. Alwal Dahlan, Assistant Minister in the same Ministry was elected as the Chairman of the senior officials meeting at this conference (he is also a professor of economics).

It is worth noting that in April 1992, the Parliament of Indonesia passed an Act (Number 10 of 1992) concerning "Population, Development and Development of Prosperous Family". According to this Act, "the Government formulates policies to regulate the quantity of people" as well as "policies to implement the enhancement of quality of the people". The Act emphasises that the formulation of such policies is based on "the principles of harmor.y, comparability, and balance between the number of people and environmental carrying capability, as well as the condition of social economy and social cultural development" (Article 10). The "elucidation" of the Act points out that "the principal target of long-term development is to improve the quality of people and the quality of the Indonesian society" keeping in mind the "balance of the relationship among individuals, between individuals and the society and between individuals and the environment and obedience to God Almighty".

Dr. Nafis Sadik, Executive Director of UNFPA in her opening statement rightly observed: "Indonesia is now able to offer technical assistance to other countries in the Asia-Pacific region setting an excellent example of co-operation between countries". She had in mind Indonesia's outstanding success in population programmes.

According to the 1992 ESCAP Population data sheet, Indonesia's population in mid 1992 was 184 million, with an annual growth rate of 1.6 per cent. In contrast, India's population is estimated at 880 million with an annual growth rate of 1.9 per cent. It may be recalled that the 1991 Census of India recorded a growth rate of 2.1 per cent during 1981-91. The current birth rate in Indonesia is 25.2 per thousand compared to India's 29.3 with the death rate is 8.8 per thousand compared to India's 10.2.

It is worth noting that the birth rate of Indonesia was as high as 48.4 per thousand in 1971 and even in 1980 it was 36.2 . There has been a dramatic fall in the birth rate in recent years, thanks to the success of the family planning programme.

Mr. Haryono Suyono, Chairman of the National Family Planning Co-ordinating Board of Indonesia (BKKBN) in his paper on the Indonesian Experience of the family planning programme points out: "Quantitatively, the largest amount of motivating is done by village volunteers, and the largest amount of service delivery is done by the staff of the Department of Health's nationwide health facilities. But many others are also involved. They include other government units, such as the Department of Agriculture, the Department of Religious Affairs, the Armed Forces, the Department of Information, non-governmental organisations, such as the Women's Welfare Movement (PKK), religious leaders in their mosques and churches and temples and political or administrative leaders ranging from the President of the Republic, the Governors of the 27 provinces, and the intermediate level leaders, namely the district and sub-district heads down to the chiefs of all the 62,000 villages of Indonesia".

It is also important to note that because of religious opposition, the Indonesian Family Planning Programme has not included any type of sterilisation in its official programme.

Mr. Suyono points out that "When it first began, BKKBN discovered that most of the religious leaders opposed the use of IUDs (Intra Uterine Devices). BKKBN spent almost 10 years talking with the Ulemas (religious leaders) and only in 1983, when the National Ulema Conference finally approved. was BKKBN able to incorporate IUDs in its programme."

What are the lessons for India? The Indonesian prescription in brief is based on a strong political commitment, effective implementation (though called co-ordination) by the Family Planning Board, respect for religious views and patient and careful tackling of religious leaders, involvement of government functionaries right from the President to the village chiefs, and the effective involvement of NGOs. All these factors are missing in India. Time and again, it has been suggested by international donor lobbies that India should set up a Population Commission headed by the Prime Minister. I have opposed the idea on the ground that setting up an apex organisation in New Delhi will not improve things as long as Primary Health Centres and sub-centres throughout the country do not function properly. As for religious factors, there is a world of difference between Muslims being the majority community as in Indonesia and being a minority community as in India. The army is not involved in India's Family Planning Programme (except to the extent armed personnel are encouraged to adopt Family Planning) and there is no network of NGOs throughout India.

I have therefore grave doubts if the Indonesian model will work in India. This is not to belittle the Indonesian model but to face the harsh reality of the Indian scene and admit the poor performance of the Department of Family Planning (Welfare) for the last 25 years. After a first hand study of the Indonesian model, I am more than convinced that the Department of Family Welfare (running a vertical programme from New Delhi) should be abolished and the family planning programme should be merged with the Department of Health to ensure effective delivery of health services (which should automatically include reproductive health and MCH) at the grassroot level.

Time and again, Indian leaders indulge in the empty rhetoric of making family planning a "people's movement". My field studies have convinced me that there is absolutely no chance of any such people's movement surfacing in India in the coming decades. We have got into a sterilisation trap and to my mind the only way to get out of the sterilisation trap is to link population to environment and generate a people's movement to make our masses conscious of the intimate link between population and the eco-system (of course, we must look beyond tigers and forests and think of drinking water, sanitation, and basic needs of the people in relation to our limited resources and worsening environment).

What we can learn from Indonesia is the convergence of population and environmental issues. Our Prime Minister should give serious thought to the creation of a new Ministry of Population and Environment which he could himself head. This is not to say that Family Planning should take a backseat but to move with the times and realise that as we enter the 21st century, we must banish the inertia and obsolescence which have overtaken us. The challenges ahead are indeed daunting.

7

Globalising Family Planning

The world's best luminaries in family planning were in New Delhi in the last week of October, 1992 to celebrate the 40th anniversary of the International Planned Parenthood Federation (IPPF) which was formed in Bombay in 1952. More than 450 delegates from over 130 countries converged in the glittering Convention Hall of a five star hotel to discuss a theme of profound importance to mankind: "Family planning: Meeting challenges, promoting choices". Judging by the high quality of speeches and interventions and the technical papers presented at this Conference, it was more than clear that it was serious business and not just a glittering international celebration. The World Health Organization (WHO), the United Nations Population Fund (UNFPA) and the US Agency for International Development (USAID) joined hands with IPPF in organising this conference.

To give a little bit of history, IPPF was formed as an outgrowth of the International Committee on Planned Parenthood established in 1948. The initiative was taken by four brave and angry women: Margaret Sanger of the USA, Elise Ottesen-Jensen of Sweden, Shidzu Kato of Japan, and Dhanvanthi Rama Rao of India. In subsequent years, Avabai Wadia of India became a key figure and her total dedication to the cause of family planning in India and round the world, made her an international figure and she became the President of IPPF (1983-89). She still continues to be the President of the Family Planning Association of India (FPAI) which was founded in 1949. Her pleasing personality, eloquence and sustained work of a lifetime have contributed very substantially to the family planning movement in India and all over the world.

The current President of IPPF is Dr. Fred Sai, a distinguished medical scientist from Ghana. He stole the show at the New Delhi Conference by his eloquence, his sense of humour and above all, his humaneness. He is at his best when he discusses ethical dimensions of family planning and population issues. The Secretary General of IPPF--

---

Appeared in *Financial Express*, 3 November, 1992

Dr. Halfdan Mahler was formerly the Director General of the World Health Organization. He regards India as his second home as he worked for ten years in India with the National Tuberculosis Programme. He is a powerful speaker and a great champion of family planning as a basic human right and a staunch supporter of the feminist movement and the concern for the health and welfare of mothers and children. Fred Sai and Halfdan Mahler were undoubtedly the two star performers at this Conference but it was India's Dr. Karan Singh who received the most thunderous applause for his concluding address. His charm and eloquence overpowered everybody (there were more women than men in the audience).

Dr. Attiya Inayathulla from Pakistan is a well-known figure at international conferences and she impresses everybody by her sincerity and youthful energy. She is currently the chairperson of IPPFs Central Council. The most prominent lady at this conference, also from Pakistan but based in New York, was Dr. Nafis Sadik, Executive Director of UNFPA, a highly competent administrator. She is a great friend of India and has her roots in Jaunpur in Uttar Pradesh. She gave the keynote address on the first day, followed by a very enlightening lecture by Professor Mahmoud Fathalla from Egypt, on the impact of family planning on health.

Another highly competent speaker was Mrs. Usha Vohra, the new Secretary of Family Welfare, Government of India. She made no attempt to soft-pedall India's family planning programme or indulge in the usual government propaganda but put the cold facts with convincing logic. Dr. Ishrat Hussain, formerly from Lucknow and currently the head of a division at the World Bank in Washington, made an excellent presentation on water resources in the context of population and environment. She used the most modern techniques of visual presentation. A very useful but boring lecture on the fertility impact of family planning programmes was given by Dr. John Bongaarts, a famous demographer from the Population Council, New York. In contrast, the lecture by Dr. Rustom P. Soonawala of India on the Indian experience of family planning was lively and instructive. An excellent overview of the Asian situation was given by Dr. Nibhon Debavalya, Chief of the Population Division of ESCAP, Bangkok.

Space does not permit me to refer to many other distinguished speakers from all over the world. One theme which recurred again and again was the issue of unmet family planning needs. It has been estimated that 300 to 500 million women are wanting to use some method of family planning and yet they have no access to family planning services. It therefore follows that if only the family planning programmes could expand their services, the challenge of population explosion could be met easily. Of course, all the speakers emphasised the need for improving the quality of the service offered to the acceptors of family planning.

Another theme which came up quite prominently for discussion was the issue of abortion. It did seem to me that the overwhelming majority of the participants at this conference were for abortion and were not impressed by the arguments against abortion. The passion with which the doctors and family planning workers spoke on the plight of women dying because of quackery in the name of abortion and the high maternal mortality rates in the developing countries of the world, made one sit up and think afresh about the whole issue of abortion. As Fred Sai put it, life is more important than potential life.

Incidentally, there were arrangements for simultaneous interpretation in four languages at this conference: English, French, Spanish and Arabic. All the speeches were recorded and IPPF will publish all the papers as well as the proceedings. Thanks to the highly efficient secretariat and in particular, the excellent logistical work of Air Vice Marshall (Retd.) E.S. Lala, the Secretary General of FPAI, this conference was run even better than most United Nations conferences. There was perfection and an ambience of femine grace everywhere.

On the negative side, one must point out that attending this conference, one got the feeling that contraceptives will ensure *nirvana* for humanity and what the world and in particular, the developing countries of the world need most is access to contraceptives. One heard very little about social and economic condition of the people, the ramifications of international politics, the role of multinationals and powerful drug lobbies, the international politics of family planning and a host of allied issues. Perhaps it was thought that these subjects were outside the scope of the Family Planning Congress.

Table 7.1: Prevalence of contraceptive methods

	Developing world	*Developed word*
Female sterilisation	33%	10%
Male sterilisation	12%	5%
Pill	12%	20%
Intra-uterine device	24%	8%
Injectible	2%	-
Condom	6%	19%
Vaginal barrier methods	1%	3%
Rhythm	5%	13%
Withdrawal	3%	20%
Other methods	3%	2%

Nevertheless the message of the Congress was clear: Family Planning is a basic human right and a vital health measure. Therefore, all couples should be offered advice and access to a full range of methods, to help them choose the timing, spacing and number of their children. Over 300 million married women in the reproductive age group want to plan their families but do not have access to modern methods of contraception. This figure could be as high as 500 million if young (presumably unmarried) people are included. In the context of the growing menace of AIDS, family planning methods become even more important not only for married people but also for the unmarried people. There is no doubt that AIDS introduces a new dimension to the demand for contraceptives and in particular condoms.

In spite of the powerful advocacy of contraceptives at this conference, I am still not convinced that in a country like India, flooding the market with contraceptives will bring down the birth rate unless we successfully tackle the more important issue of motivation and liquidation of illiteracy, issues with which medical doctors are not directly involved. Given the poor track record of India's State-sponsored family planning programme, I am still not convinced that more and more money should be ploughed into the family planning programme in order to make a dent on the birth rate. In my view, most of this extra money will go into the budget sub-head of salaries and will only enlarge an inefficient bureaucratic apparatus without benefiting the people. International donor agencies are sold on the idea that all we need to solve the problem of population explosion is to double the funding of agencies like UNFPA and introduce new technologies like the norplant. To me it is perverse to think that millions of men and women can be kept illiterate and the basic needs denied to them because there is no money and yet money has to be found to double up the family planning budget. I am also not convinced by the international lobbies pleading for political will for family planning. What they mean is the power of the President or the Prime Minister to enforce family planning. In my view, politicians should be kept out of family planning. What credibility do our politicians have when for forty years, giving safe drinking water to people remains a political slogan?

Has contraceptive technology alone brought down the birth rate in the Western countries? I wonder if the delegates to the Family Planning Congress understood the implications of a statistical table distributed in the Fact Sheet based on the latest WHO report. The table shows that in the developed world, the folk method of "withdrawal" accounts for the highest percentage (along with the pill) of contraceptive use. This underlines the importance of motivation and not contraceptive technology *per se*.

[**8**]

Issues in the 21st Century

What are the population issues--the continuing chronic ones as well as the new and emerging issues--as we enter the 21st century? Are the population issues in India different from those in other countries and the rest of the world? What are the population issues in powerful industrialised countries like Japan, Germany and the USA? What are the population issues in Africa and in the least developed countries?

These and numerous other questions will be raised and their answers sought in two forthcoming international conferences, the four-yearly conference on population convened by the International Union for the Scientific Study of Population (IUSSP) at Montreal in Canada, in August 1993; and an international conference on population and development sponsored by the United Nations at Cairo in Egypt in 1994.

As a member of the International Organising Committee (IOC) of the IUSSP Conference, I helped in screening the papers submitted to the 47 scientific sessions slated for the week-long conference at Montreal, where more than 1200 population experts from all over the world are expected to participate.

High on the agenda of the IUSSP conference are sessions on population pressure and environment; comparison of population and development in China and India; demographic consequences of structural adjustment programme; social, economic and demographic consequences of aging of population; health impact evaluation; mega cities and social and economic aspects of international migration, refugee problems and issues.

Some of the new topics are HIV transmission and AIDS; bio ethical implications of births and deaths; minorities; demographic size and power strategies; religiosity, secularism and fundamentalism; impacts on demographic behaviour and policy; the use of geographical information systems in demography. The concern for regional demography is reflected in sessions on components of population growth in Africa; population history of East Asia; and demography of polar regions.

Appeared in *Financial Express*, 30 December, 1992

The new topics will not overshadow the standard content of demography, comprising five groupings as follows: (i) fertility and family planning (ii) health, mortality and morbidity, (iii) migration and minorities, (iv) society and population, and (v) methodology and statistical measures.

There are several countries where the census is considered redundant, given the excellent registration system (e.g. in Scandinavian countries). Then there are countries (e.g. USA and Germany) where the census is being constantly challenged in law courts on the ground that the census violates privacy by asking personal questions. Even in India, it has been argued that census taking will be almost impossible in the decades to come (considering the quality of data). We continue to rely on a vast army of unpaid enumerators drawn from the ranks of primary school teachers and petty revenue officials, who get no financial incentives to get involved in the complex task of census enumeration. In short, frustrated, unwilling and unmotivated enumerators cannot deliver the goods. A census is much more than a head-count.

An important issue is the ''content error'' and not merely the "coverage error" of the detailed data collected through an elaborate questionnarie covering every single man, woman and child in the country. And we have to count more than a billion persons in the Census of 2001. In spite of all our efforts, we do not have a worthwhile system of registration of vital events like births, deaths and marriages. Our vital statistics collected through the civil registration system are hopelessly unreliable, except in a few parts of India. The Sample Registration System (SRS) gives fairly reliable estimates of birth and death rates on a yearly basis but because of the sample size, no generalisations are possible at the district level. We cannot, therefore, answer a simple question: what is the birth rate or death rate or infant mortality rate in any particular district, say in Uttar Pradesh? We have estimates for the whole of UP but this does not satisfy anybody.

We cannot, therefore, monitor the family planing programme at the district level and see what is happening to the birth rate. The only data we get at the district level are family planning performance statistics dished out by the Department of Family Welfare; data which are highly exaggerated and therefore unreliable. If we do away with the census, there will be a statistical disaster. The Government of India must take up this vital question of restructuring census, SRS, and the Civil Registration System (CRS) in earnest and it is not too early to start this work. The Government should not wake up only in 1998 after they appoint a new Census Commissioner for the census of 2001.

Unfortunately, the census department is under the Ministry of Home Affairs in India, which gives it a low priority and funds are never available to meet the increasing demands made on the census by planners and policy makers. How is it that we can allocate Rs. 6,500 crores for family welfare (largely a non-performing sector comparable to the sick public sector of India) in the Eighth Plan and we have no money for the census and CRS?

My strong recommendation is that the entire cost of the census, SRS and CRS should be debited to the family welfare budget for the next ten years. This will strengthen the much needed demographic data base which is essential for sound planning and policy-making.

Coming back to the IUSSP conference, one of the most delicate aspects of our organisational work concerned the issue of "geographical balance" and "gender equality" while choosing organisers and chair-persons for various sessions. At the same time, we had to choose persons known for their technical competence and specialisation in the subject matter under consideration. This was a hard task indeed considering the fact that IUSSP has more than 2000 elected members in 120 countries of the world. So the whole world was our canvas. We found that Africa was inadequately represented and there were not enough women organisers and chairpersons. We also had to consider travel costs and per diem. Fund raising, always a difficult task, has become even more difficult in the face of continuing recession in the developed world. A new trend is that donors are rather reluctant to put money in conferences--they care more for projects. We had also to ensure that because of financial constraints, the Montreal Conference does not end up by becoming a North American population conference!

To sum up, some of the major population issues in the 21st century as visualised by the IUSSP conference are (1) the nexus between population and environment, both in developed and developing countries, (ii) the ramifications of international migration (legal, illegal, refugee, etc.) and the consequent ethnic issues of social tension, both in developed and developing countries; and (iii) the socio-psychological and economic (even political) implications of aging population, both in developed and developing countries. In the developed countries, the proportion of the elderly population is constantly rising which in the developing countries (particularly in China and India) even a small proportion of the elderly means a staggeringly large absolute population of the elderly.

The cost of health care in general and particularly of the elderly has become a challenging issue for governments all over the world, and particularly in the USA. It is a disturbing thought that in the US, there are 37 million citizens without medical insurance, even though a fairly high proportion (13 per cent) of the GNP is spent on health care. The figure would be around 18 per cent by the year 2000.

I cannot help observing that the ease with which the President-elect, Mr. Bill Clinton handled the Economic Conference shows his latent talent as a professor, apart from his superb public relations capability. While writing this I paused to have a look at the New York Times (16th December) which I just received. The editorial said; 'The two-day economics seminar in Little Rock led by Professor Bill Clinton...". I do hope Mr. Clinton will do a good job on the health front and he would be called Dr. Clinton next time!

9

*Bali Declaration on Population and Sustainable Development**

I. Preamble

We, the members and associate members of the Economic and Social Commission for Asia and the Pacific (ESCAP), having convened at the Fourth Asian and Pacific Population Conference in Bali, Indonesia from 19 to 27 August 1992, have reviewed the population situation and outlook and noted the substantial progress achieved by the countries of the region in responding to the Asia-Pacific Call for Action on Population and Development adopted by the Third Asian and Pacific Population Conference held at Colombo in 1982. We express concern that population issues remain among the most pressing challenges facing the region and, in addressing the theme of the present Conference, "Population and sustainable development: goals and strategies into the twenty-first century", we

Recognize that :

(a) *Population factors play a decisive role in all human endeavours, especially in safeguarding the environment and the pursuit of sustainable development. Accordingly, population considerations must be fully integrated into all aspects of planning and policy-making;*

(b) *Sustainable development as a means to ensure human well-being, equitably shared by all people today and in the future, requires that the interrelationship between population, resources, the environment and development should be fully recognized, properly managed and brought into a harmonious, dynamic balance;*

(c) *Full consideration of population concerns is crucial to any strategy to achieve sustainable development and to give future generations an environmental legacy better than that received by the present generation;*

(d) *An integrated approach incorporating population, resources, the environment and development elements must be pursued, although understanding of the*

---

* *Issued by United Nations, 1992 (ST/ESCAP/1195).*

complex interrelationships between these elements is still at an early stage. To do otherwise would endanger the attainment of sustainable development and narrow the options available to future generations;

(e) Measures to improve the status, role and participation of women must be given high priority, both because women have a fundamental right to enjoy equality with men in all aspects of life and because women play a critical role in, and must fully participate in, the sustainable development process;

(f) The alleviation of poverty is fundamental to the achievement of sustainable development;

Emphasize that:

(a) Population problems have local, national, regional and global ramifications and must therefore be addressed at all these levels;

(b) Every country has its own specific array of population problems and policy objectives and has the sovereign right to pursue its own population goals, policies and programmes respecting the goal of global sustainable development;

(c) Dealing with population problems requires strengthening of social policies as well as regional and international cooperation; and

(d) Rapid population growth and the consequent changes in demographic structure and uneven population distribution are crucial factors that impose pressures and constraints on economic development efforts, the environment and natural resources as well as social conditions. However, these factors are often neglected in environmental and economic development strategies that regard population as a neutral factor rather than a dynamic variable requiring policy intervention;

Affirm that:

(a) In showing concern for human well-being, population policies should recognize that individuals are members of the family, community, society, State and global community, and they possess rights within those contexts;

(b) Population size, growth, distribution, structure, composition and mobility should be considered at all levels of planning and in the formulation of comprehensive population policies;

(c) Resolution of population concerns is central to achieving equitable and efficient development of human resources and alleviation of poverty;

Note with appreciation:

(a) The efforts and progress made by the countries of the Asian and Pacific region in demographic, social, economic and development spheres and the leadership exhibited by political leaders and parliamentarians in the formulation and implementation of national policies and programmes dealing with population and development issues and problems;

(b)   The invaluable contributions of United Nations organizations, especially ESCAP and the United Nations Population Fund (UNFPA), and other intergovernmental organizations and multilateral agencies in providing technical and financial support for population programmes in the Asian and Pacific region;

(c)   The contributions of donor countries through bilateral development assistance programmes;

(d)   The pioneering and significant contributions that non-governmental organizations have made to population efforts in the region;

Keeping in mind:

The provisions of the World Population Plan of Action adopted at Bucharest in 1974; the recommendations of the International Conference on Population, held at Mexico City in 1984; the Call for Action on Population and Development adopted at the Third Asian and Pacific Population Conference, held at Colombo in 1982; the Amsterdam Declaration on a Better Life for Future Generations adopted at the International Forum on Population in the Twenty-first Century, held at Amsterdam in 1989; Agenda 21 and the Rio Declaration on Environment of the United Nations Conference on Environment and Development, held at Rio de Janeiro, Brazil in 1992; and the deliberations of the Fourth Asian and Pacific Population Conference, held in Bali, Indonesia in 1992;

Urge that:

(a)   All members and associate members of ESCAP make a firm political and financial commitment to incorporate population and environmental concerns fully in all national efforts to achieve sustainable development;

(b)   All members and associate members of ESCAP establish a set of population targets in line with sustainable development goals, and initiate and implement policies and programmes to achieve those targets;

(c)   The ESCAP secretariat accord high priority and take appropriate action to assist members and associate members in implementing their population, environmental and development policies, programmes and strategies;

(d)   UNFPA strengthen its programme support and mobilize the needed resources to help the members and associate members of ESCAP in implementating their population policies, programmes and strategies;

(e)   Other United Nations organizations, international agencies and non-governmental organizations support the members and associate members of ESCAP in implementing their population, environmental and development policies, programmes and strategies;

Adopt:

The following goals and recommendations for population and sustainable development into the twenty-first century.

II. Population goals

Within the overall objectives of sustainable development, the goals of population policy should be to achieve a population that allows a better quality of life without jeopardizing the environment and the resource base of future generations. Population policy goals should also take cognizance of basic human rights as well as responsibilities of individuals, couples and families.

The population of countries and areas in the Asian and Pacific region amounted to 3.2 billion in mid-1992. Although there has been a significant decline in the rate of the population growth over the past two decades and the current annual growth rate of 1.7 per cent is expected to continue to decline steadily, it is projected that 920 million people will be added to the region's total by 2010. The bulk of the increase will occur in South Asian countries and least developed countries, where annual population growth rates are not expected to fall much below 2 per cent. It is in these less developed countries that the problems of poverty are most acute, and pressures on the education, health and employment sectors are greatest.

Fertility, as measured by the total fertility rate, currently averages 3.1 children per woman in the Asian and Pacific region. However, there are substantial variations between and within the subregions of Asia and the Pacific. Fertility is lowest in East Asia, at 2.1 children per woman. It is highest in South Asia, at 4.3 children per woman. A similar marked disparity is exhibited in subregional levels of mortality. For example, infant mortality in South Asia, at 90 per 1,000 births, is more than three times the rate in East Asia, where it is 26 per 1,000 births.

In many countries of the Asian and Pacific region, urban populations are expanding at three or four times the rate of the national population. The region will witness a significant increase in the number and size of urban areas, particularly of "mega-cities" and other large metropolitan areas. Furthermore, new issues, such as environmental degradation, ageing, imbalanced population distribution and international migration, are emerging and require priority consideration.

To help reduce high rates of population growth, countries and areas should adopt strategies to attain replacement level fertility, equivalent to around 2.2 children per woman, by the year 2010 or sooner. Countries and areas should also strive to reduce the level of infant mortality to 40 per 1,000 live births or lower during the same period. In countries and areas in which maternal mortality is high, efforts should be made to reduce it by at least half by the year 2010.

III. Recommendations

A. Population, environment and development

Issues

Among the ultimate objectives of sustainable development are to achieve a balance between human needs and aspirations in balance with population, resources and the environment and to enhance the quality of life today and in the future. There is an urgent need to bring into balance population dynamics, socio-economic development, the use of natural resources and environmental quality. Special attention should paid to decreasing the demand for natural resources that is generated by unsustainable consumption and to using those resources efficiently, to minimize depletion and reduce pollution. Although consumption patterns are very high in certain parts of the world, the basic consumer needs of a large section of humanity are not being met.

In many countries and areas, high rates of population growth and concentration have caused environmental problems, such as land degradation, deforestation, air and water pollution, threats to biological diversity from habitat destruction and rising sea level due to the greenhouse effect. In some countries, calamities and associated loss of life have followed the extension of human settlements into marginal and vulnerable areas, especially along rivers, coasts and foothills.

Recommendations

(1)   More research needs to be undertaken to improve understanding of the complex synergy between population, resources, environment and development. Moreover, this knowledge must be used in formulating policies and strategies for sustainable development. The conceptual framework and appropriate analytical tools and indicators need to be developed further.

(2)   A comprehensive data collection and information system on key aspects of population, development and resource linkages that have implications for environmental quality must be developed to support planning, implementation and management, and evaluation of, as well as research on, population and sustainable development programmes.

(3)   Governments should formulate policies and strategies and implement programmes regarding appropriate technologies, keeping in view the interaction between population and environment, as well as their long-term susceptibility. Such policies could include development of environmentally friendly technology, reforestation, improvement of the quality of air and water, waste recycling and the phasing out of environmentally harmful technology. Furthermore, countries should formulate enforceable measures to promote greater harmony between population, resources, environment and development so as to achieve improved quality of life on a sustainable basis.

(4)   There is a need for appropriate interdisciplinary programmes to develop information, education and communication (IEC) activities, human resources, and environmental and population-related educational materials for all groups in the community. In this regard institutions at all levels, governmental and non-governmental, formal and informal, private and public sector, should be involved and supported.

B. Urbanization, internal and international migration

Issues

Population movements in countries and areas of the ESCAP region have greatly increased in scale and complexity. Voluntary population mobility has become an option to improve the life chances and opportunities of a much wider group of people in the region than ever before. This increased potential for significant population mobility within and between countries has major social, economic and environmental implications. In particular, increasing demand for overseas workers in countries and areas of the ESCAP region in which the demographic transition has been completed will become of increasing policy importance.

The gender selectivity of migrants is gradually changing as more and more women in the ESCAP region are migrating independently. This phenomenon has opened considerable opportunities to improve the role and status of women. However, growing numbers of migrant women work and live in situations that in which they are vulnerable to exploitation.

The increasing tendency for people to concentrate in large metropolitan cities in the region presents a number of new and important management challenges for policy makers and planners.

Recommendations

(5)   Governments should reassess policies relating to urbanization and seek to implement policies that recognize that urbanization is inevitable. These policies should stress human resources development and be concerned with the environment and sustainable development and improvements in the quality of life in cities and the countryside, particularly in slums and other disadvantaged areas.

(6)   Linkages between rural and urban areas are of such strength and significance that rural and urban development should not be undertaken in isolation from each other, and therefore comprehensive planning should be undertaken.

(7)   Spatial implications and environmental consequences of major sectoral policies should be fully assessed as part of the national development planning process.

(8)   Sectors in which there is either labour shortage or labour surplus need to be identified to facilitate the development of policies to achieve a better matching of the distribution of job opportunities on the one hand and labour supply on the other.

(9)   In view of the importance of the informal sector in absorbing large numbers of migrants and other workers in many countries and areas of the region, measures should be taken to improve the living standards of workers in the informal sector in a manner that is consistent with the principles of sustainable development.

(10) Measures should also be taken to protect the rights of migrants, particularly women and children, and to improve their access to services and working conditions.

(11) Recognizing the importance of decentralization for sustainable development, more decision-making power and resources should be transferred to regional and municipal bodies. Local communities need to have more involvement in planning, management and revenue collection. The complexity of management, services and infrastructure in large urban agglomerations necessitates greater cooperation between various administrative areas and levels.

(12) Policies need to be developed to involve the private and public sectors in adequately accommodating the growth of mega-cities and to create opportunities in rural areas and smaller cities to divert migration away from mega-cities. To cope with rapid urbanization government should create a favourable climate for private sector investment in smaller towns and cities and provide the required support mechanisms, such as physical and social infrastructure, and favourable fiscal and monetary policies.

(13) Existing data sources for the study of urbanization, migration and development at the national and international levels should be fully utilized. Research that seeks explicitly to measure the costs and benefits of rural-to-urban migration should be undertaken. Migration impact should be studied in greater detail. Data collection systems to obtain better information on forms of short-term migration or circulation within national boundaries as well as international movements need to be developed. Governments should strive to adopt more consistent and comparable data collection systems on international movements and develop measures to share the data and information.

(14) Further steps should be taken to monitor adequately trends in international migration and to develop appropriate policies to accommodate and plan for future needs.

(15) There should be greater cooperation among countries and areas of the region to ensure that the rights of international migrants under the International Labour Organisation (ILO) Convention concerning Migrations in Abusive Conditions and the Promotion of Equality of Opportunity and Treatment of Migrant Workers are protected and their working and living conditions safeguarded.

(16) Steps should be taken to develop policies and programmes to prepare for and accommodate people displaced by environmental calamities.

C. Family planning and maternal and child health

Issues

Family planning and maternal and child health(MCH) programmes have played an important role in influencing population growth and improving the quality of life and human resources development in the countries of Asia and the Pacific. The success of family planning and MCH programmes is closely associated with the improved role and status of women; lower infant, child and maternal mortality rates; better birth-spacing and breast-feeding practices; and the delivery of services by trained personnel. Nevertheless, much remains to be done. There is a pressing need to strengthen programmes and adopt innovative approaches and strategies. To a large extent the success of programmes depends upon empowering individuals, families and communities to plan and decide for themselves, as well as to design and implement, programmes based on their own needs.

Recommendations

(17) Family planning and MCH programmes should undertake comprehensive and critical reviews of existing policies and programme strategies:

(a) In countries where the programmes have not yet achieved the desired objectives, priority should be given to strengthening policy development and related processes as well as to expanding and streamlining delivery systems of family planning and MCH within the primary health care framework, to adopting innovative management and multisectoral approaches, and to encouraging wider community and intersectoral participation in programme implementation efforts;

(b) In countries where fertility has been reduced to a low or acceptable level, programme strategies should aim to build upon achievements made so far with a view to attaining susceptibility.

(18) Efforts should be made to improve the accessibility and utilization of family planning and MCH services for men as well as women, taking into account the changing preferences and needs of clients and rapidly changing technologies. There is a particular need for women-centred and women-managed facilities to ensure that women and their family planning and MCH needs are fully taken into consideration. Counselling and information on the use of all MCH services and methods of family planning should be freely available. Resources should be allocated to upgrade and improve the quality of services and prevent attrition among skilled workers. Governments should develop the skills of service providers and improve the accessibility and logistics of family planning and MCH services.

(19) Reproductive health care should be improved considerably in the region. Policies and programmes should strive to incorporate the totality of reproductive health care and aim at reducing maternal morbidity and mortality, induced abortion, sterility, childlessness, sexually transmitted diseases (STDs) and spread of the human immunodeficiency virus (HIV) and acquired immunodeficiency syndrome (AIDS).

(20) Special attention should be focused on countries with high fertility and high population growth rates, especially the small island nations of the Pacific and Indian oceans.

(21) Family planning and MCH programmes should encourage healthful birth-spacing and breast-feeding. They should always make available and offer birth-spacing methods of family planning.

(22) Sustained efforts should be made to increase the involvement of males in family planning and to promote the use of family planning methods designed for males. Specific IEC strategies should be developed to inform and educate men about family planning and fertility regulation.

(23) There should be population IEC programmes and services specifically designed for youth and adolescents to minimize the incidence of unplanned adolescent pregnancies and associated health risks.

(24) There is a need to upgrade management information systems (MIS) so that they can provide timely and good quality information and to adopt appropriate strategies, such as rapid and independently conducted low-cost surveys, for the proper monitoring and evaluation of programmes. There is also a need to train MCH service providers and programme managers in the use of such information for these purposes.

(25)   There is an urgent need to incorporate family planning in the syllabi in medical, nursing and other health-profession training institutions and in other in-service training programmes for health and family planning personnel.

(26)   Concerted efforts should be made to undertake relevant research studies and to translate the findings into action through their incorporation in ongoing policies and programmes.

(27)   Factors relating to problems of integrating family planning and MCH programmes should be determined and studied in order to formulate and implement such programmes in line with the socio-cultural, political and administrative conditions in each country.

(28)   Non-governmental organizations should continue their roles in support of national programmes. Governments should collaborate with, and enhance the potential of non-governmental organization by: (a) involving them in the development of innovative programmes, especially for vulnerable segments of the population; (b) ensuring that through their flexibility they are able to offer a greater variety of client-responsive services; (c) encouraging them to strengthen their grass-roots networks and community participative strategies; (d) putting to best advantage their advocacy function; and (e) enhancing their role as good quality services providers.

D. Population and human resources development

Issues

People are the most important and valuable resource that any nation possesses. It is crucial, therefore, that countries ensure that all individuals be given the opportunity to make the most of their potential. Such a policy, as noted in the Jakarta Plan of Action on Human Resources Development in the ESCAP region, will result in the enhancement of social and economic development of the community as a whole.

It is recognized that demographic factors are strategically important in human resources development because of their interrelationships with employment, education, skill and capability development, health and nutrition, and the status and role of women.

Recommendations

(29)   Governments should recognize the key role of human resources in national development and give strong emphasis in national planning and policy-making to the development of human resources. Where this has not yet been done, policy and planning bodies for human resources development should be established at a high level to ensure that human resources development is given appropriate recognition.

(30)   Human resources development planners should recognize that individuals value education, health and other human resources investments as important elements in the quality of their life. Therefore, programmes of human resources development should be linked to the strong interest of people in availing themselves of these important elements of welfare.

(31) More attention should be given to the formulation of policies to cope with the socio-economic consequences of the change in the number of persons in certain age groups, as well as overall growth in number, on fields such as education, employment, food and nutrition, housing, and health and welfare services.

(32) Governments should improve human resources development programmes, especially vocational and occupational training in both rural and urban areas, to open up a wider range of employment options for people living in areas characterO by a surplus of labour. Efforts should be made to promote training in a variety of contexts including the work place, the family and the community.

E. Women and population

Issues

Women's status, as reflected in their legal rights, education, health, employment, position in the household and family decision-making power, affects demographic behaviour such as age at marriage, fertility, and infant, child and maternal mortality. These in turn have an impact on the improvement of women's status and their participation in the development process.

In recognition of the importance of women's contribution to development and the need to improve the status and role of women, many countries have begun to formulate policies and implement programmes. Despite some progress, women in many countries still do not enjoy equal status with men, have only a limited role in national socio-economic development and remain unaware of their rights. For the achievement of sustainable development, the full and unfettered participation of women is essential, especially in the formulation and implementation of population policies and programmes, because they have as much, if not more, at stake as men in whatever action is taken in these areas.

Given that women play an important role as managers of resources and in maintaining environmental quality, they must be involved in all decision-making relating to population and sustainable development.

Recommendations

(33) Governments are urged to adopt and implement national policies and programmes to ensure equal opportunities for females in all sectors of social and economic development as well as political participation. Gender concerns should be incorporated in national development planning. Specific guidelines should be drawn up for the integration of women in all sectors of national development with a view to supporting their productive and reproductive roles and their equal partnerships in national development. Appropriate mechanisms should be developed or strengthened so that the needs of woman at all levels are reflected in national population and development policies and programmes.

(34) In order for females to benefit from the opportunities resulting from the elimination of discrimination, efforts should be intensified to improve their health status, especially in the field of reproductive health and nutrition, and to ensure equal access of

girls and women to education, training and employment as well as credit and other supportive services for promoting self-employment, particularly among the poor. Concerted efforts should be made to reduce constraints and to facilitate the participation of women in the mainstream of social and economic activities.

(35) In line with the recommendations made by the Asia-Pacific Regional Assembly on "Women and Environment: partners in life", held at Bangkok in 1991, women should be empowered with greater decision-making authority and their viewpoints should be considered at all levels to enable better management of resources and protection of the environment.

(36) Governments should ensure that women are neither restricted from participating nor forced to participate in the labour force for reasons of demographic policy or cultural tradition. Furthermore, the reproductive role of women should in no way be used as a reason for limiting women's right to work. Governments should take the initiative in removing any barriers to the realization of that right and, in cooperation with the private sector, should create opportunities and supporting facilities so that activities outside the home can be combined as appropriate with child-rearing and household activities. Efforts should also be made to ensure greater involvement of men in all areas of family responsibility. Women's productive and reproductive rights should be fully recognized by Governments and supported by society at large.

(37) Governments should strengthen national capabilities in collecting, analysing and monitoring gender-specific data and information to facilitate better integration of women's concerns in development planning and implementation.

(38) All forms of discrimination against women, legislative and otherwise, should be abolished.

F. Population and Poverty Alleviation

Issues

There is a complex interrelationship between rapid population growth and poverty. Some developing countries in the region have improved the living conditions of their peoples appreciably, but in many developing countries, the numbers of the poor, hungry and illiterate have increased. Poverty is very closely interrelated with environmental degradation.

Population growth rates are faster in the least developed countries and areas where poverty is severe and there is less access to education and health services. At the micro-level, the poor usually have large families and are less aware of, and have less access to, social services such as family planning and MCH; this contributes to high infant, child and maternal mortality. Among the poor, children and women are especially vulnerable to exploitation.

Although rapid progress in the provision of social and health services in developing countries has occurred during the past decade, the services are unevenly distributed among urban-rural areas and socio-economic groups.

Recommendations

(39) Governments should formulate more effective strategies and measures to alleviate poverty. These should include :

(a) Implementation of integrated population and development policies and programmes, including family planning and MCH strategies, that will slow population growth and produce faster income growth as well as reduce family size, improve education and productivity, and provide better life chances;

(b) The provision of adequate and efficient basic social and health services and facilities to improve well-being and increase human capital and skills among the poor, so that they can respond rapidly to income-generating opportunities and gain access to social programmes such as education, basic health care, improved sanitation, good quality nutrition, food subsidies, family planning and housing, and thus help to improve their living conditions and alleviate poverty;

(c) Equity in the allocation of resources and access to services should be important elements of national policy.

(40) Governments should design policies and strategies to ensure that the benefits of development are shared by wide spectrum of the population. This would help to break the poverty-population-growth cycle.

(41) Governments should formulate long-term policies and programmes to tackle population growth and poverty jointly because of their complementarities and strong synergy. The policies and programmes should be responsive to poor people's needs, particularly in education, training, and family planning and MCH programmes.

(42) When economic restructuring occurs, Governments need to take steps to minimize its adverse impacts upon the poor and underprivileged.

(43) Priority should be given to research on the linkages and interactions between poverty, population dynamics, resources and the environment. The results of such research can be used in the design of policies and implementation of strategic programmes.

G. Mortality and morbidity

Issues

Mortality has declined significantly in most Asian and Pacific countries and areas. In some countries of the region, however, the expectation of life at birth remains below 55 years. Even in countries where mortality has declined, there are subregions and subgroups exposed to high levels of mortality and morbidity. Infants and children, and women in the reproductive ages remain particularly susceptible. Mortality and morbidity patterns are expected to change in the future in a number of countries and areas owing to the increasing incidence of STDs and HIV/AIDS, with grave consequences for the health, well-being and productivity of the people. This would also hamper the reproductive potential of the population. In addition, the incidence of degenerative diseases is increasing in the developing countries of the region.

Further reductions in mortality and morbidity will depend upon improvements in the quality of health services delivery, implementation of programmes targeted at the most disadvantaged groups, and the achievement and maintenance of a higher quality of life.

Recommendations

(44) In countries where infant, child and maternal mortality continues to be high, the factors responsible need to be identified in order to formulate policies and implement appropriate programmes for the further reduction of such mortality.

(45) Governments should strengthen their basic health infrastructure and manpower, and ensure the provision of equipment and supplies for improving affordable health-services delivery.

(46) In view of the rapid spread of HIV/AIDS in the region and its increasing cumulative prevalence, countries and areas should initiate IEC programmes to educate their populations about the prevention of HIV/AIDS infection; such information should be included as an element in family planning programmes. Governments should collect data to monitor the trend of HIV/AIDS infection and design strategies and implement programmes to control its spread.

(47) There is a need for Governments to strengthen research on the levels and patterns of morbidity and mortality changes associated with changes in the environment, life-styles and occupations as development proceeds. Health and medical service programmes should be modified to take account of these changes in patterns of mortality and morbidity.

H. Ageing

Issues

Population ageing is closely interrelated with the dynamic processes of demographic and socio-economic change, with implications for the family, community and nation. With significant and rapid fertility declines and improvements in mortality, population ageing will assume greater importance in the future. The majority of the elderly have considerable potential for both self-reliance and making contributions to their families and communities. They have a right and a responsibility to make those contributions. The family is still the principal source of support for the elderly. However, with rapid industrialization, urbanization and the increasing frequency of both spouses engaging in full-time paid work, traditional family support systems for the elderly will be placed under considerable strain.

Recommendations

(48) Governments are urged to formulate long-tern development strategies that take into consideration the changing age structure of the population, in particular the implications of population ageing for economic and social development. Development policies and programmes must take into account the characteristics of future cohorts of

older people, their potential for involvement in the process of development and the role of the family and community in caring for the elderly.

(49)   Comprehensive programmes that aim to increase the support and contributions of the elderly should involve all sectors and levels of government, as well as non-governmental organizations, the private sector and unions.

(50)   Efforts should be made to develop policies and programmes at the local level to bring the active elderly into the mainstream of economic and social development to enhance their contribution to their families and communities. This may include lifelong education programmes.

(51)   The family support system should be strengthened by providing economic incentives, such as tax exemption and special privileges, to families taking care of their elderly members.

(52)   It is important to recognize the differing needs of the rural and urban elderly in developing countries, particularly in those lacking social security systems.

(53)   Communities should be encouraged to form voluntary and mutual aid organizations to provide support for the elderly and their families.

(54)   Broad information and educational programmes should be introduced to create awareness and understanding of the issues of ageing and to instil moral and social values related to the support of older people. Such programmes should be targeted at families and the general public with special emphasis on the younger generation.

(55)   Appropriate training programmes should be developed for caregivers such as medical and paramedical staff, residential care providers, community and social workers and family members, keeping in view the perspectives of both the caregivers and the elderly.

(56)   Research is needed on the interrelationship among changes in family patterns and structure, cultural and traditional changes and ageing, the findings of which would promote effective integration of the elderly into the mainstream of economic and social development, and the formulation and implementation of appropriate policies and programmes.

I. Population data, research and information dissemination

Issues

While considerable progress has been made in information and database development within the region during past decades, there remains an urgent need to improve the content, quality and timeliness of data and to upgrade national skills for research, policy analysis and the development of integrated management information systems. Furthermore, small-area data sets need to be developed for decentralized and local-level planning.

Recommendations

(57) Governments are urged to strengthen methodologies for collecting quality data and to improve efficiency in the processing and analysis of data for policy formulation, strategy development and programme implementation. Countries should devote more effort to upgrading analytical skills in the areas of policy analysis, monitoring evaluation. In particular, national census, vital registration and survey organization capabilities should be strengthened and enhanced.

(58) The creation of computerized databases, both numeric and bibliographic, at the national, regional and subregional levels should be encouraged for the more efficient dissemination and sharing of population data and information. In particular, there is need to develop small-area databases for local and community area planning.

(59) Governments should give priority to the application of modern information technologies and to the development of the human resources and skills needed to mange them in order to maximize the utilization of data and information at the national level.

(60) National population information systems should be strengthened and should follow the framework of the Population Information Network (POPIN).

(61) Coordination among national, subregional and regional information centres and networks representing various social and economic sectors should be strengthened to foster increased intersectoral networking, thereby assisting in the more complete integration of population with other aspects of development.

(62) Governments are urged to attach high priority to population research, both for its continuous contribution to population policy formulation, programme implementation and evaluation and as a means to fill gaps in knowledge. Countries should establish, strengthen and maintain population research centres.

(63) In support of this effort, regional and international organizations should establish standards related to database development, such as data format, structure and software, to promote the compatibility of database created by national information centres and their utilization at the national and regional levels.

J. Resource mobilization

Issues

Over the years, population programmes have become more diverse and complex. National-level population programmes have been established in many of the countries of the region and have achieved varying degrees of success. Nevertheless, much remains to be done, requiring large amounts of resources, both human and financial. The need for mobilizing additional resources is greater today than ever before.

Recommendations

(64) The International Forum on Population in the Twenty-first Century, held at Amsterdam in November 1989, called for a doubling of resources by the year 2000 to support population programmes. It is estimated that around $US 9 billion per year will be

required to support core population programmes around the world, a substantial proportion of it in the Asian and Pacific region. Towards this end, the option of allocating 4 per cent of official development assistance to population programmes could be considered. In this regard, the important role of UNFPA in mobilizing the needed resources should be recognized and countries are requested, as appropriate, to increase their contributions to UNFPA.

(65) A central challenge all nations face today is to mobilize additional resources to support broad-based population programmes. The Fourth Asian and Pacific Population Conference urges all Governments, inter-governmental and non-governmental organizations, the private sector and external donors to make every effort possible to increase, on a regular basis, their financial commitment so as to attain their targets by the year 2000.

(66) Over the past decade, several members and associate members of ESCAP have successfully formulated and implemented population policies and programmes. The experience and knowledge gained in the process are very valuable and can be shared with members and associate members still striving to attain their desired population goals. Those successful members and associate members are used to allocate resources for the transfer of knowledge and skills — through the exchange of expertise, the sharing of information and knowledge and the facilitation of training — to countries that are in the process of attaining their demographic goals and objectives. Such technical cooperation among developing countries (TCDC) should be encouraged. Within the framework of existing institutions, appropriate mechanisms need to be identified to facilitate TCDC in the region and with other regions.

(67) The emerging population issues in the region will become more diverse and complex during the 1990s, requiring flexible and innovative approaches to sustain the achievements made in the last three decades. UNFPA should provide the needed financial assistance to enable ESCAP to play an enhanced role in assisting the Governments of developing countries in the region in shaping their future population policies and programmes. In addition, UNFPA is requested to provide programme support and financial assistance to countries for the design and implementation of their population policies in accordance with national priorities, working closely with government officials to ensure effective coordination and harmonization of population activities, and to develop fully the national capacity for self-reliance.

SECTION II

INTERNATIONAL MIGRATION

$\boxed{10}$

Migration Between
Asian Countries

The general perception of international migration is in terms of emigration to developed countries like the US, Canada, UK, Germany and Australia. There was a time when the phenomenon of brain drain from developing countries to developed countries dominated any discussion on international migration. In the seventies, a new phenomenon emerged: the Gulf oil boom led to massive migration of skilled and unskilled workers to the Gulf countries. In the eighties, the vagaries of international oil prices influenced the flow of migration to the Gulf countries. Military operations in Kuwait and Iraq affected adversely the flow of migrants from Asian countries. In the nineties, there is every possibility of increasing migration between Asian countries.

In this context, the question of clandestine or illegal migration (the polite expression is "undocumented migration") is drawing increasing attention from Governments in Asia. If such migration is just a small trickle, it does not attract any attention. In fact, almost every country has some illegal migrants. The US with all its strict regulations about visa has not been able to eliminate illegal migration from Mexico.

In India, the quantum of immigration is small in relation to the total population of the country which is massive but in absolute terms, the number of immigrants-refugees as well as non-refugees (who are often called "economic refugees") is by no means small. The real problem is that nobody knows the precise number of illegal migrants. . The census does collect data on place of birth as well as the place of last residence but obviously, illegal migrants would not record that they are illegal migrants. They would give misleading data to claim their status as Indian citizens or they would just not get themselves enumerated. The situation gets complicated because India has an open border with Nepal and there are no visa restrictions whereas this is not true in the case of other neighbours like Pakistan, Bangladesh and Sri Lanka.

Appeared in *Financial Express*, 2 March, 1993

The partition of India in 1947 saw one of the largest movements of displaced persons in the history of the world. The Census of India in 1951 as well as the Census of Pakistan in 1951 had a special question on displaced persons and refugees. Subject to the limitations of census data, one could get a fairly good estimate of the quantum of refugee migration in both these countries. In the newly carved state of Punjab in Pakistan and Punjab in India, there was almost an exchange of population of Muslims on the one hand and Hindus and Sikhs on the other but this was not true of West Bengal and East Pakistan. The migration of Hindu refugees from East Pakistan became almost a "normal" feature and in 1971, there were about 10 million refugees (Hindus and Muslims) from Bangladesh who had crossed over to India. The 1971 war and the surrender of Pakistan's army paved the way for the return of most of these war victims. Nevertheless, migration from Bangladesh to India continued. In Assam the question assumed an explosive dimension and led to the agitations over the foreigners issue. The 1981 Census enumeration could not take place in Assam because of disturbed conditions. In the eighties, it was noticed that Bangladeshi migrants, Hindus as well as Muslims, were found in sizeable settlements in several states of India, including the capital of India. This was not any more confined to Assam and West Bengal. The issue gets highly politicised when the voters lists are prepared. It has been alleged that several political parties have even encouraged illegal migration from Bangladesh because of the prospect of getting block votes. It has also been alleged that several political leaders of stature have in fact encouraged such illegal migration on grounds of religious affinity. Fundamentalist forces have further complicated matters. There are clear indications that the issue of Bangladeshi illegal migrants will be politically exploited in the years to come.

Is it possible to have a scientific discussion on the whole issue and overcome the politically surcharged, atmosphere ? Jerrold W. Huguet of the Population Division of United Nations ESCAP Office has pieced together a lot of useful statistical material on international migration within Asia, though he does not discuss the question of illegal migration from Bangladesh into India. His focus is no intraregional labour migration. He, however, refers to two types of migration that have significant political implications. As he puts it: "The magnitude of refugee movements is the most difficult to predict but an optimist can foresee in the near future political solutions to problems in Afghanistan and Cambodia that would greatly reduce the number of refugees in Asia. Another type of intraregional migration may be considered density driven. An example is the migration of Bangladeshis to the Assam region of India".

It may be mentioned in passing that Bangladesh has one of the highest densities of population in the world, namely, 776 persons per sq. km. The comparable figure in India is 274. West Bengal has the highest density (767) followed by Kerala (749), according to the 1991 Census of India. Density driven migration is caused by poverty and religion may have very little to do with it. Thus the migration of Bangladeshis to India (most of which is illegal) is not a religious phenomenon but an economic phenomenon though one could argue that such migration is facilitated if in the host country certain religious communities help the process of such migration by giving them shelter on their arrival. In this sense, religion may be a facilitating factor but religion cannot be the cause of such migration (the context here is not refugee migration on account of religious persecution, law and order problems or natural disasters). Language is another facilitating factor.

Density driven migration is a demographic phenomenon and should be understood as such. In an official document of the 1961 Census of India, the Census Commissioner had made an estimate of the "infiltration" from East Pakistan, on the basis of data on population growth rates in several bordering districts of East Pakistan, Assam and West Bengal. It is possible to make such estimates on the basis of the recent Censuses of India and Bangladesh. One requires a good grasp of census data in order to make such estimates. It is also necessary to collect data through special sample surveys, etc. to estimate such migration. In population matters, the concerned department is the Family Welfare Department in the Ministry of Health and Family Welfare which unfortunately cannot see beyond family planning and as a result, no Population Research Centre funded by this Ministry would really be in a position to take up a scientific study of illegal migration from Bangladesh. Even in other ministries, the subject is considered "sensitive" and left out. No wonder, only foreign scholars show interest in such studies. The Institute of Strategic Studies and Defence Analysis should give serious thought to this problem of "demographic invasion" from Bangladesh.

Labour migration in Asian countries (and this is true of other countries in the world) is stimulated by large wage differentials in the countries of origin and destination but Huguet points out that "although Japan has the highest per capita income in Asia, it is the only developed country in the world that has not relied on foreign labour to offset labour scarcity in its industrial growth." It has been estimated that long-resident Koreans   and Chinese and unregistered workers constitute only 0.3 per cent of the labour force in Japan.

Interestingly, Malaysia and Thailand which have much lower levels of economic development than Japan, send a large number of workers to the Middle East but they also attract a large number of workers from poorer Asian countries. (Malaysians also go to Singapore, Taiwan and Japan for employment.)

The 1985 Census of the Lao People's Democratic Republic enumerated 3.6 million persons while the United Nations projected a figure of 4.1 million. Huguet observes that "even with a generous assumption of error in the census and projection, it appears that upwards of 100,000 of the Lao population had disappeared into Thailand, where they speak virtually the same language as northeastern Thais."

Given the bonds of language and religion, one may ask: How many million Bangladeshis can disappear in India ? Should the task of checking illegal migrants be entrusted to the border police alone ? Does the problem not call for diplomatic and political solutions ? Above all, should we not look for economic solutions in terms of regional economic cooperation at least between India and Bangladesh?

$\boxed{11}$

International Migration—Guest Workers or Economic Refugees?

There was a time when migrant workers in Europe were referred to as guest workers. With rising unemployment, this polite expression has been replaced by a rather derogatory term—economic refugees.

Many years back, at a seminar on international migration, an American demographer observed in jest: "Round the world, more than 600 million economic refugees are ready with their suitcases to migrate to the USA!" After the breakup of the USSR and the turmoil in Eastern Europe, this number would probably be larger, especially when we consider the vast human reservoir in India, Pakistan and Bangladesh. If one talks to young men and women anywhere in the developing countries of Asia, Africa and Latin America and also in the former USSR and China, one does get the impression that for the young, salvation lies in migration to the developed countries.

The International Labour Organistion (ILO) is quite well-known all over the world. Another excellent organisation also based in Geneva which is not so well-known is the International Organization for Migration (IOM). In 1951 IOM was established to deal with the surplus population in European countries. After the Second World War and throughout the 1950s, IOM assisted the flow of migrants from Western Europe to Australia and Canada. Then came up the refugee crisis in Hungary in 1956 and IOM helped the Austrian government to resettle 180,000 Hungarians in Austria and Yugoslavia.

In the 1960s, IOM helped a large number of migrants in distress who were not necessarily refugees. For example, Belgians in Congo, Armenians coming into Lebanon from Bulgaria, Romania and Egypt. In the 1970's IOM initiated a programme called Return of Talent to encourage professional Latin Americans to return to their homeland after studies and technical training in the developed countries.

Appeared in *Financial Express*, 16 June, 1992

IOM is also involved continuously in refugee migration programmes, in close co-operation with the United Nations High Commissioner for Refugees (UNHCR). For example in 1972, An IOM team was sent to Uganda to organise evacuation of over 5000 Asians who were expelled from that country.

In 1989 IOM received a global mandate to extend its activities throughout the world. In fact, its earlier name of Intergovernmental Committee for Migration (ICM) was changed to IOM. The focus of IOM was no more on Europe. For example, IOM was entrusted by the United Nations Disaster Relief Coordinator (UNDRO) to organise the repatriation of foreigners stranded in the Gulf Region, after the invasion of Kuwait by Iraq.

International migration is a fascinating subject. There are, however, not many experts in this field (India has none). Things are oversimplified when we identify political refugees and asylum seekers and put the rest of the migrants in the category of economic refugees, who are mostly from the poor countries trying to get rich quickly by working in the developed countries. But it would be wrong to assume that economic refugees migrate from poor countries only to rich countries.

What should we call the endless stream of migration from Bangladesh into India ? India is not a land of milk and honey but things are certainly better than in Bangladesh and hence this migration, much of which is illegal. On the other hand, the migration between Nepal and India is all legal because we have an open border and no visa restrictions.

India has also her share of refugee migration: for example, the Tibetans in India. We have also the problem of expatriates from Sri Lanka, Burma and other countries.

Talking of emigration, we have a fairly large labour migration to the Gulf countries and selective migration of professionals to USA, Canada, Western Europe and Australia. India thus is an excellent human laboratory for the study of international migration.

One of the world's leading authoirities on international migration is Professor Reginald T Appleyard from the University of Western Australia at Perth. I recall that when I visited him at his University I was impressed by his aristocratic style in everything he did. I had asked him whether he knew about his ancestry. He replied: "Mr grandfather in England had stolen a goose (not an apple). He was tried and deported to Australia". Professor Appleyard invited me to give an after dinner talk in Canberra at an international seminar on migration. I recall having said: "Going round the world, you cannot help observing that all the dirty menial work is done by migrants whom I shall call international *shudras* (the lowest caste among Hindus). Like the *shudras* these migrants are needed by the developed countries but not always tolerated".

In a recent visit to Germany, I could see for myself the resentment among German youth, after unification, against foreign workers (Germany is full of Turkish workers). The common belief (though not justified) is that given the high rate of unemployment, there is no need for migrant labour from abroad. This assumes that the unemployed youth are a perfect substitute for skilled migrant labour, an assumption which is not always warranted.

Any serious study of international migration has to be multi-disciplinary. The racial overtones of such migration cannot be ignored. One has also to reckon with the political ramifications of such migration. Then we have the problem of collecting reliable data. This is especially true of illegal migration (called undocumented migration by ILO). Nobody will admit to a census enumerator that he is an illegal migrant. So indirect estimates have to be made of such migration.

For example, the 1961 Census Commissioner (Asok Mitra) compared the census data of India (in particular States like West Bengal and Bihar) with the census data of Pakistan (particularly for East Pakistan, now Bangladesh) and made an estimate of illegal migration from East Pakistan. Such an exercise can be repeated on the basis of the recent censuses of India and Bangladesh. There is clear evidence that there has been substantial migration of persons (Hindus as well as Muslims) from Bangladesh into India and this has been so ever since 1947 and the partition of India.

There are countries like Japan which have fairly reliable estimates of illegal migration. The Justice Ministry of Japan reported recently (June 8, 1992) that a record number of 32,908 foreigners were arrested in Japan in 1991 for working illegally (most of them were deported). The countries involved in such illegal migration of workers were South Korea (9782), Iran (7700), Malaysia (4855), Thailand (3249) etc. The Ministry official, however, observed that "this is the tip of the iceberg because a much larger number of foreigners are staying illegally." As of November 1991, there were 216,399 illegal immigrants in Japan (which was 35 per cent more than in the previous six months). Given the extreme labour shortage in Japan, one can understand this level of illegal migration.

Professor Appleyard who was commissioned to write a monograph on "International Migrations; Challenge for the Nineties" (published by IOM. Geneva.1992) raises fascinating questions for the future. Suppose China relaxes its highly restrictive family planning policy as well as migration policy, what will be the impact on international migration?

Appleyard rightly observes that "raising immigration barriers alone is no durable solution for, in the absence of a development strategy, income differentials would continue to widen and emigration pressures increase." He quotes another international expert on migration, Professor Georges Tapinos from France who says: "The impact of international co-operation as an alternative to emigration, at least has the merit of high lighting the fact that the problem of migration is secondary to that of development." In the long term, development is the only alternative to stem massive migration from the South to the North.

Appleyard gives the latest data on international migration in his monograph. In Table 11.1 we present the figures for immigration to the United States in 1989 by country of last residence. It will be seen that only one million people were lucky enough to find a home in USA compared to the 600 million people wanting to emigrate to that country (a figure which we mentioned at the beginning of the article.

In Table 11.2 we give data on refugee populations in Asia in 1989. It will be seen that Pakistan tops the list: that is because there were some 3.6 million refugees from Afghanistan in that country. The break-up for India shows that there are only 96,000 refugees from Bangladesh. This figure will be challenged by many. A recent newspaper survey put the figure of refugees in India at 17 million but this obviously is a guestimate.

Table 11.1: Immigration to the United States: 1989
(Selected country of last residence)

Mexico	**405,660**
Central America	**101,273**
South America	**59,812**
Others	**105,894**
Western Hemisphere	**672,639**
Philippines	66,119
Korea	33,016
India	28,599
China	39,284
Hong Kong	15,257
Vietnam	13,174
Other	100,971
Asia	**296,420**
United Kingdom	16,961
Germany	10,419
Italy	11,089
Portugal	3,861
Other	52,008
Europe	**94,338**
Grand Total	**1,063,397**

Source: INS Statistical Yearbook 1989: Demetrios Papademertriou, (UNFPA/ECE paper) p. 13A. Fig.1), considers the figures an overview"... 'heavily contaminated' by partial data..."

Table 11.2: Refugee Population in Asia
1989

Country of Origin	Nos
Pakistan	3,647,000
Thailand	436,500
India	294,300
Malaysia	103,700
Hong Kong	57,000

Source: World Refugee Survey, US Committee for Refugees as reported in *The Economist*, 23 December, 1989.

Table 11.2: Refugee Population in Asia
1989

Country of Origin	Nos
Pakistan	3,847,000
Thailand	498,300
India	254,300
Malaysia	108,700
Hongkong	57,000

Source: World Refugee Survey, US Committee for Refugees as reported in The Statesman, 22 December 1990.

SECTION III

POPULATION PLANNING IN INDIA

[**12**]

Jawaharlal Nehru
on Population Planning

Jawaharlal Nehru more than any other Prime Minister of India, was fully conscious of the need for population control. It was his vision of India which made him incorporate population planning as an integral part of social and economic planning in India, especially in the context of the very First Plan (1951-56), launched under his chairmanship.

Before independence, Nehru was greatly concerned about mobilising the tremendous manpower of India, for giving the people education and technical skills and upgrading them, for getting them out of mass hunger and poverty. He was all for population control and even went against Mahatma Gandhi and pleaded for modern methods of contraception. But basically Nehru's concern for population planing was reflected in his concern for manpower planning, what we call today, human resource development.

In his presidential address to the 34th Indian Science Congress on January 3, 1947, Nehru said: "The First thing that we must realise is the energy of the people. Secondly, we must provide opportunities for them to train themselves. There would be a tremendous amount of wastage unless people are trained".

Inaugurating the International Conference on Planned Parenthood in New Delhi in February, 1959, Nehru said: "We have to come to grips with this problem of population. We have to plan in terms of food, clothing, housing, education, health, work, etc., and we realise that some kind of limitation of the rapidly growing population becomes an urgent matter for us.. It is a matter of some gratification that the Government of India is the only Government which has, officially as Government, taken up this matter.. Our approach to this question is not, if I may use the expression, a *purdah* approach. At the same time, we realise the difficulties of the problem. It does not matter how far you go and how much you succeed in evolving feasible, simple and cheap methods of birth-control if the hundreds of

<hr>

Appeared in *Financial Express*, 17 November, 1992

millions of our people do not make good in other ways, economically and educationally. In order to achieve wide-spread success, family planning has to go hand in hand with the general economic and social advance in the country... the movement of family planning becomes a part of the larger movement for raising the standard of living of the people."

While inaugurating the First Asian Population Conference in New Delhi in December, 1963, Nehru said : "I confess that we have not succeeded (in tackling the population problem) and the growth of population in this big country is rather alarming.. as population grows, it rather overwhelms the efforts we make towards economic growth. However much we may try, as we do try, to increase the pace of economic growth, the fact of population growing even at a reduced pace comes in the way of any marked improvement".

Gunnar Myrdal in his classic study, "Asian Drama" (1968) devotes two lengthy chapters to population prospects and population policy and quotes at length from Nehru's writings and speeches. Myrdal had a mature understanding of Nehru's views on population. He sums up his assessment of Nehru thus: "Nehru's pronouncements on the population issue was a clear recognition that continued high rates of population increase can prevent any very substantial rise in the level of living. That the situation was desperate Nehru never admitted. Even the 'Marxist' idea that there is no real population problem was not totally absent from Nehru's thinking."

Myrdal also quotes from Tibor Mende's "Conversations With Nehru" (1956) and this quotation to my mind is the essence of Nehru's thinking on population. Nehru said: "The enthusiasts for family planning think that you can ignore everything else and just go out and meet this menace of the rising population. But this menace cannot be met just by large-scale propaganda. That, I think, is a wrong approach. In fact, it is a totally ineffective approach. I think that, at the moment, economic progress is more important than even family planning. The two of course, should go together, as far as possible."

I think that Nehru's views are absolutely valid even today. We have made a mess of our minimum needs programme. Giving drinking water to our people is still an election slogan, after 45 years of independence. Effective health care is till eluding our rural masses in spite of the beautiful international slogan "Health For All By 2000".

Nehru was certainly right in emphasising economic growth. But, looking back at the history of planning in India, one cannot say that our progress has been spectacular. The historical evidence suggests that, in recent decades, Asian countries which have done well in sharply reducing the population growth rate have either done it under conditions of rapid economic growth as in Japan, Taiwan, Hong Kong, South Korea, Thailand, and/or under varying degrees of authoritarian regimes as in China, Singapore or Indonesia. In India, both these conditions are missing—both unhappily and happily. One could of course point out that the authoritarian regimes in Pakistan and Bangladesh leave us as the soft states only in the Indian sub-continent.

In this context, the experience of Sri Lanka and the state of Kerala in India has received special attention from demographers. Among other factors, sizeable investment on health and education has brought down the birth rate substantially. But unfortunately the economic condition is far from statisfactory. Kerala, for example, has the highest unemployment rate and, but for migration to the Gulf countries, things would have been dismal in Kerala. There are limits to what a reduced birth rate could do. But undoubtedly the message from Kerala which is loud and clear is the importance of a high literacy rate, both male and female.

Nehru did recognise the over-riding importance of education but, it seems to me that perhaps the most striking failure of Nehru was his failure to implement compulsory primary education . Our failure on the family planning front is a reflection of our failure on the education front. Nehru does admit, in his letter to the Chief Ministers in September 1958, the difficulty of enforcing compulsory primary education:

"Our Constitution laid down that within a period of ten years there should be universal, free and compulsory education for all children until they complete the age of 14 years. It is manifestly beyond our capacity to fulfil this directive principle of policy within that period. We have made a good deal of advance in primary, secondary and university education, but we are very far from the objective laid down in Constitution".

Before I conclude, I must refer to the five volumes of Nehru's Letters to Chief Ministers (1947-1964) so ably edited by Mr G. Parthasarathi (published in 1985). I do not think Gunnar Myrdal had access to these letters. Going through Nehru's fortnightly letters, I cannot but admire his scholarship, his sense of history, his sincere efforts to know the intricacies of economic planning and, above all, his great desire to carry the Chief Ministers with him, keep them abreast of national and international events and even educate them. In spite of his preoccupation with foreign affairs, Pakistan and China, Nehru devoted considerable space in his letters to economic and social planning.

In January 1953, Nehru wrote to Chief Ministers: "More and more, I think of solving our national problem in terms of employment." He reminded them that a welfare state "must necessarily mean gainful employment for all" He was quick to assert that "We cannot produce this by magic or by some sleight of hand, but every policy that we pursue must keep the question of employment in the forefront."

In August 1957, Nehru wrote to Chief Ministers: "Both countries (India and China) have huge populations which are predominantly agricultural.. there is a great deal of manpower in both as well as unemployment and under-employment. Heavy industry is essential to form the basis of industrial development..."

In January 1960, Nehru wrote to the Chief Ministers: "Implementation of big social and economic programmes must necessarily have the active co-operation of the great mass of our people.. The Chinese increased their production greatly because they could take advantage of their huge manpower and they put practically everyone to work hard. There was no choice about it and the methods were coercive. We cannot and do not wish to function in that way."

Nehru in his wisdom put family planning under the rubric of health—it was a sub-system of the health delivery system. Nehru's primary concern was for women and children. Being a democrat, Nehru did not interfere with the policy laid down by the first

Health Minister - Rajkumari Amrit Kaur, a princess, a Gandhian, a Christian and a spinster, by no means the best combination for one to take charge of family planning. She opposed modern methods of contraception (as Mahatma Gandhi did) and the foreign expert invited to advice us was told in clear terms that he would be shown the door if he advocated any method other than the rhythm method.

13

Indian Census Enters the Electronic Age

A modern census must rely heavily on the electronic computer. But paradoxically enough, the first results of the 1991 Census of India were released by the Census Commissioner with lightning speed on the 25th March, 1991 (i.e. within three weeks of the completion of the census enumeration) with the help of manual tabulation and not on the basis of complete computerisation which would have taken much more time. But there are limits to manual tabulation.

In earlier censuses, the detailed tables and the Primary Census Abstract (PCA) took several years for preparation and it took several more years for the tables to be actually published. Users of census data constantly complained about the inordinate delay in the availability of such data. In short timeliness was a victim of the obsolete method of manual tabulation which, over the years, was supplemented by computerisation. Even the 1991 census data tabulation scheme is not wholly dependent for tabulation on the electronic computer and manual tabulation still plays a role.

The massive task of tabulating the 1991 census data at the village level and ward level for individual cities was entrusted to the National Information Centre (NIC) under the leadership of Dr. N. Seshagiri, Director General, NIC. At an impressive ceremony in New Delhi on the 14th January, 1993 Mr. Pranab Mukherjee, Deputy Chairman of Planning Commission released on the NIC network (called NICNET) the Primary Census Abstract which gives the following information for each district, separately for rural and urban areas: area, number of occupied residential houses, number of households, total population, population in the age group 0-6 years, population of scheduled castes, population of scheduled tribes, number of literates, number of workers: main and marginal and also non-workers; the main workers classified into the following nine industrial categories: (i) cultivators, (ii) agricultural labourers, (iii) livestock, forestry, fishing, hunting and plantation, orchards and allied activities, (iv) mining and quarrying, (v) (a) Manufacturing, processing, servicing and repairs in household industry, (b) Manufacturing, processing, etc., in industries other than household (vi) Construction,

---

Appeared in *Financial Express*, 26 January, 1993

(vii) Trade and Commerce, (viii) Transport, storage and communication, and (ix) other services.

All tables present data separately for males and females. As already mentioned, the rural/urban breakdown is given for all tables. The massive material contained in the PCA should be of immense help for micro-level planning because data are now available in such detail for every village, town and city in India.

All users of census data would indeed be grateful to Mr. A.R. Nanda, Census, Commissioner and Dr. N. Seshagiri, Director General of NIC (under Planning Commission) for this collaborative effort. NIC was set up in 1976 as a computer-based informatics network for supporting Government Departments in decision-making processes. NIC operates a countrywide satellite-based computerised communication network called NIC-NET. It connects 60 Government departments, 32 states/UTs and 450 district centres. NIC has a mainframe computer (NEC-1000) at its headquarters in New Delhi, super mini-computers (ND-550) at state capitals, and super PC/ATs at the district headquarters.

For the first time in India, the census PCA data have been computerised by NIC and stored at its headquarters on the NEC computer under the GISTNIC scheme (General Information Service Terminal of NIC). The PCA data will be accessible on all terminals of NEC in New Delhi, State Capitals and district headquarters. A major improvement in the 1991 Census is the decision of the Registrar General to make available floppies giving statewise and districtwise data at the office of the director's of census in each State. Another improvement in the PCA tables is the presentation of data for the age group 0-6 years separately, to facilitate the calculation of the literacy rate as per the 1991 census definition of literacy.

Let us now have a quick look at the final population total released by the Registrar General on the January 14. It may be recalled that the provisional figure of India's total population (including the estimated population of Jammu and Kashmir where the 1991 census operation did not take place) was 843.93 million (as announced on 25th March, 1991). The final population figure is 846.30 million. In other words, the final population figure is slightly higher (by 2.37 million) than the provisional figure. The Registrar General has yet to announce the results of the Post-enumeration Check (PEC) which gives an estimate of the undercount. If adjustment is made for the undercount, the population of India would be even higher.

Table 13.1 : Salient Demographic Features of India, 1991

Area (sq. km)	:	3.06 million
No. of households	:	152.01 million
No. of occupied houses	:	147.01 million
No. of villages	:	627,434
(i) inhabited	:	580,702

(ii) uninhabited	:	46,732
No. of districts	:	452
No. of blocks	:	5,774
No of towns	:	4,615
No. of urban agglomerations	:	3,699
Total population	:	846.30 million
Scheduled castes pop	:	138.22 million*
Scheduled tribe pop	:	67.76 million*
Literate population	:	359.28 million*

* excluding Jammu and Kashmir

Table 13.2 Distribution of Main Workers
(excluding Jammu and Kashmir)

Industrial Category	Population (million)	Per cent of total workers
Cultivators	110.70	38.7
Ag. Labourers	74.60	26.1
Livestock, etc.	6.04	2.1
Mining, etc.	1.75	0.6
Household ind.	6.80	2.4
Non-household ind	21.87	7.6
Construction	5.54	1.9
Trade & Commerce	21.30	7.5
Transport etc.	8.02	2.8
Other services	29.31	10.3
Total workers	285.93	100.0

It may be noted that in India as a whole (excluding Jammu & Kashmir), there were 28.2 million marginal workers and 524.4 million non-workers.

The detailed data on scheduled castes indicate that the proportion of these castes is more than 10 per cent of the population in the following States: Punjab (28.3%),

Himachal Pradesh (25.3%), West Bengal (23.6%), Uttar Pradesh (21.0%), Haryana (19.8%), Tamil Nadu (19.2%), Rajasthan (17.3), Karnataka (16.4%), Tripura (16.4%), Orissa (16.2%), Andhra Pradesh, (15.9%), Bihar (14.6%), Madhya Pradesh (14.6%), and Maharashtra (11.1%).

Likewise, the following States have more than 10 per cent of the population of scheduled tribes: Mizoram (94.8), Nagaland (87.7), Meghalaya (85.5), Arunachal Pradesh (63.7), Manipur (34.4), Tripura (31.0), Madhya Pradesh (23.3), Sikkim (22.4), Orissa (22.2), Gujarat (15.0), Assam (12.8), Rajasthan (12.4).

The overall percentage of scheduled castes in India was 16.3 of the total population while that of the scheduled tribes was 8 per cent.

$$\boxed{14}$$

Population Crisis
Committee's Report

Population Crisis Committee (PCC), "a private, non-profit public interest organization" based in Washington has just issued a report titled **India's family planning challenge: From rhetoric to action.** It is a lucidly written, beautifully printed document running into 63 pages, with a 16 page executive summary issued separately. The report has been written by two women—Shanti R. Conly and Sharon L. Camp, Ph.D. The cover of the report is very feminine—a sari design, described in the report as "traditional Indian textile".

The first thing which strikes the reader is that the report has been written with great tact and politeness and avoids hysteria, so common with American commentators on India's population explosion. The report is critical of India's family planning programme and yet the report will not annoy anybody, not even the family planning department. Though, there are several 'key references' to authors who have written on population issues, nowhere is there a direct quote. Instead, the authors have a harmless style of saying "population experts advocate ... expert opinion favours..., Indian experts readily acknowledge ... Some experts have suggested ... experts believe ...''. It is not possible to make out which expert said what: I am somewhat embarrassed by the acknowledgement which says: "A special mention is due to those colleagues who patiently reviewed and commented on an earlier version of the text: Prof Ashish Bose .." The report does support my diagnosis of India's population problem in terms of the dominant role of the Bimaru states (Bihar, Madhya Pradesh, Rajasthan and Uttar Pradesh), referred to in the report as "the large northern states". But there is no evidence that the report took note of my criticism of the draft.

Let me first summarise the report very briefly, using excerpts from it.

"Population stabilization is not yet on the horizon. Yet the Indian family planning programme is by no means a failure."

Appeared in *Financial Express*, 6 October, 1992

"Low female literacy, high infant mortality and weak administration of family planning efforts have all contributed to the slow progress in fertility reduction in the North.

"On paper, India has a model population policy ... but a substantial gap exists between the rhetoric of official policy and actual programme implementation.

"In reality, the family planning programme at the field level has been characterized by a single minded focus on sterilisation, poor quality services and an inflexible, overly centralized approach to resource allocation and management".

The report then goes on to say that "Successive governments have recognized these problems but have proved incapable of effective action to address them. Weak political will has undermined efforts to reorient family planning efforts."

This perhaps is the harshest sentence in the whole report. To overcome this harshness, the report begins by saying: "Beginning in late 1991, a newly elected Government in India assumed national leadership on population and family planning, reversing a decade and a half of faltering political commitment following the sterilisation abuses that contributed to the fall of Indira Gandhi Government in 1977."

Obviously the Population Crisis Committee wants to be on the right side of Narashimha Rao Government. As a professional researcher, I cannot help observing that the present Government has yet to score on the population front. All that has happened so far is that under the leadership of the Prime Minister, the National Development Council (NDC) appointed a Sub-Committee on Population under the Chairmanship of the Kerala Chief Minister. A well meaning secretary in the Department of Family Welfare spent several months in finalising a Plan of Action for revamping the family welfare programme. All that we know is that the Secretary was recently transferred to the Department of Chemicals!

Let me come back to the India report. The solution to the present miserable state of the family planning programme offered by the Population Crisis Committee is as follows: "Doubling of funding ... private sector programmes ... external assistance ... international experts especially the US population assistance community ... more open attitude to international collaboration ... increased donor resources".

The report has done an excellent public relations job for foreign donor agencies and, in particular, for World Bank, USAID and UNFPA. The report has also done well for the contraceptive lobby of private companies. To quote the report: "With proper training and supervision, private physicians, pharmacists and nurse-midwives could play an important role in making oral contraceptives, injectibles, implants and IUDs more widely available. Assistance to private health providers could take the form of training, financial incentives and provision of equipment or contraceptive supplies."

I shall now give my comments on the report. To me, the major drawback of the report is that it is silent on the adverse impact of fancy foreign ideas. At best, second rate foreign experts on India's family planning programme were active in the 1960s when foreign influence was at its zenith. All that the report admits (though this is not in the abridged report) is that "Indian critics have tended to blame early failures of the Government programme, with some justification on foreign advice and assistance."

Why talk of early failures ? The tragedy is that the misguided foreign advice given to us in the early years (i.e. in the 60s) is very much ingrained in our continuing programme. What is the guarantee that in the years to come, the "early failures" caused by foreign advice will not be repeated ? I have coined an Indian expression (Sanskrit) to described such advice - KUBUDDHI (literally, bad intelligence). Let me give examples:

Under foreign advice, a separate Department of Family Planning was carved out in the Ministry of Health in 1966. This led to channelling large funds to family planning . Health was neglected, and now we talk of reducing high infant mortality rate and child survival strategies which will ultimately help family planning. Jawaharlal Nehru in his wisdom had put family planning as a sub-head of health. In our eagerness to bring down the birth rate without bringing down the infant and child mortality rate, we have failed both on the child mortality front and the family planning front.

Under foreign advice, we started giving money to acceptors of sterilisation. Initially it was called compensation money (for loss of wages) but soon it became incentive money. The cash amount was increased and incentives in kind were also introduced. The motivators were paid money, the doctors were paid money, and , of course the acceptors of sterilisation were paid money. Since there was no money for other methods (except a very small amount for IUD which the accepters rarely got), it was inevitable that sterilisation would emerge as the dominant method and this is precisely what happened. In the craze to make money, doctors and motivators never bothered about the "eligible couples". The concern was only for sterilisation cases. The result was that the decline in the birth rate was marginal though the increase in the sterilisation cases was phenomenal.

Is it fair, therefore, for the Population Crisis Committee to blame the Indian programme because it is sterilisation-centred? It looks very reasonable to argue that India should now emphasise spacing methods. On the basis of extensive field work I can assert that under conditions of mass illiteracy, it is very unlikely that specing methods would succeed. These are methods which require sustained motivation.

Why should we not do the obvious thing first, namely, tackle the problem of illiteracy. The PCC report does mention, though somewhat casually, that the female literacy rate in India is only 39 per cent compared to 97 per cent in USA. But we are being constantly told that "time is running out ... population is growing... we cannot wait for millions of people to be made literate." Therefore, the formulae is; *Contraceptive technology + financial incentive + IEC + external assistance + foreign experts = population stabilisation.*

Lest you ask, "How do you motivate illiterate masses". there is a ready answer: "through IEC—information, education and communication". It is most unfortunate that foreign donor agencies are wasting money on IEC which to me stands for "incompetence, extravagance and corruption." What "information" can we give to illiterate masses? I would seriously urge all donor agencies to diver IEC funds to programmes for liquidating illiteracy in the shortest possible time. To me, "I" stands for illiteracy—eradication and not information. Foreign, experts have a right to ask: "Why should there be foreign assistance for getting rid of illiteracy? Is it not the Government's responsibility?" I would then ask: "Why should foreign agencies be more interested in a contraceptive programme than a literacy programme?"

Under foreign advice, the Department of Family Planning introduced a rigid system of monitoring based on targets and achievements for different family planing methods. This led to widespread corruption, exaggerated figures for performance and therefore achievement rate which obviously was not reflected in the data for birth rate published by the Registrar General every year. This led to the absurd situation where the Couple Protection Rate (CPR) indicating the practice of family planning was constantly going up while the birth rate stagnated. The credit for hauling up the Family Welfare Department for this state of affairs goes to Rajiv Gandhi who as soon as be became Prime Minister, monitored on his computer all sectors of Indian economy and rightly asserted that family planning was a non-performing sector.

Again, it was under foreign advice that we pinned all our hopes on technology and neglected the basic problem of motivation and awareness. There was a time when our foreign friends asserted that India's population problem would be solved in no time through the extensive use of IUCD (popularly called Lippy's loop) but this method misfired. After some years, we were told that it was high-tech laparoscopy (female sterilisation) which would revolutionise India's family planning programme. This too misfired. Now the Western contraceptive lobbies are ardently advocating Norplant—a controversial method.

[15]

Towards Demographic Liberalisation

Economic liberalisation and privatisation is an accepted policy of the Government of India. Even key sectors like steel, energy, oil and minerals are open to privatisation. But a key social sector like family planning remains the exclusive domain of the Department of Family Welfare in the Central Ministry of Health and Family Welfare. The Ministry will not readily admit that it is running a massive monolithic family planning programme which is 100 per cent centrally financed, directed, monitored and controlled, though the actual implementation of the programme is left to the states. A massive exercise in target setting is done in Nirman Bhavan in New Delhi, and detailed figures are set out for the practice of family planning by specific methods like sterilisation, IUD, conventional contraceptives (condom) and oral pills. In short, human reproduction is equated with production of steel or cement and quotas are fixed for each method of family planning for each State in India. Not, even in the erstwhile Soviet Union, with a totalitarian regime, would such targets fixed by a Central authority have worked. And even in China, the family planning targets are not set in Beijing. These are set at the local level. In any case the Chinese model can be copied by India at a grave risk, namely, the prospect of the fall of the Government. It happened in 1977. It can happen again. In my last visit to China, I was told by some Chinese scholars: "We cannot push our family planning programme any further. We know what happened to the Indira Gandhi Government."

The Central Ministry of Health and Family Welfare maintains that targets are not set in New Delhi: the states are consulted. The National Development Council (NDC) comprising all the Chief Ministers endorses the population directives and the targets. I have a fairly good knowledge of what is happening in the states. Most of the states do not know how to set the family planning targets even if they are asked to do so. In any case, they are more interested in getting the Central Government funds in the name of family planning rather than in the programme.

Appeared in *Financial Express*, 16 March, 1993

The Central Government is sadly mistaken if it thinks that ceremonial meetings of state health ministers and state health and family welfare secretaries amount to decentralisation of the family planning programme. I am not aware of any State, not even Kerala, where the State Government really feels that the family planning programme is its own programme. Things are much worse at the district, block, primary health centre (PHC) and sub-centre (SC) level. Everybody is harassed by the family planning targets: the medical bureaucracy is hostile to the higher level authorities in state capitals and in New Delhi for humiliating them, the health functionaries all along the line resent the autocratic imposition of family planning targets, which if not fulfilled, would lead to different forms of punishment like withholding of their salary, transfer to remote areas, etc. The worst part of the story is that the health functionaries at the grassroot level feel helpless: They have nothing to offer to the people except the monetary incentive (which by no means is an incentive these days, given the price level) while the revenue department functionaries promise (which is rarely fulfilled) loans, right to landholdings and other facilities which attract the rural people. In the month of March, many health functionaries including the hapless ANMs (public health nurse) have to shell out money from their pocket to entice some women to undergo sterilisation. The other escape valve is just to cook data, falsify records and show highly exaggerated performance figures, particularly of IUD insertions, oral pills and condoms. The picture is indeed pitiable.

Even then, the official figures of family planning performance are bleak. It was reported in leading newspapers recently that a review of the family planning programme between April and November last year has shown that in 15 states, IUD insertions have declined by 7.6 per cent, the use of conventional contraceptives by 3.5 per cent and of oral pills by 14 per cent. To me these are meaningless figures. The easiest way to show good family planning performance is to fudge the figures for condoms, IUDs and oral pills. The Central Government or for that matter, the State governments just can't check these figures. Anybody who has done field work in India (and I have done it for the last 30 years) will testify this, if he is truthful. The unfortunate fact is that the family planning programme has reached a deadend. The endless change of Family Welfare ministers and secretaries has made the situation even worse.

Surprisingly, the Eighth five year Plan has the following to say about the programme: "The family welfare programme has also suffered on account of centralised planning and target setting from the top... Monitoring mechanism under the programme has been reduced to a routine target reporting exercise incapable of identifying roadblocks and applying timely correctives." (Vol II, p.333).

The Economic Survey for 1992-93 presented by the Finance Minister in Parliament the other day admits: "In spite of massive efforts, budgetary support and infrastructure development, the performance of the family welfare programme has lagged behind in the northern states of Bihar, Madhya Pradesh, Rajasthan and Uttar Pradesh which continue to be characterised by high birth and total fertility rates." (p.201).

The international donor agencies are also disillusioned by India's family planning programme. They too are opposed to the continued bureaucratic stranglehold. Therefore, there is a growing advocacy of non-governmental organisations (NGOs), but alas, there are very few NGOs doing family planning work. Can NGOs deliver the goods? Undoubtedly there are a few NGOs who have idealists and dedicated workers at the helm who inspire grassroot workers but not all NGOs can claim such a record. Most of the NGOs are tied to the apron strings of foreign funding agencies and would collapse if foreign funds are withdrawn. And some NGOs are so bureaucratic that they put to shame the Government bureaucracy. Should we then turn to panchayats? Traditionally, panchayats do not view family planning as a domain of their legitimate activity. There are, however, states like Gujarat where panchayats have done good work in the field of health and family planning. But what about the private sector? Private doctors, hakims, vaids, private and charitable hospitals and nursing homes? Why are they not involved in family planning work?

Why is not demographic liberalisation and privatisation on the family planning agenda? Why not hand over a big chunk of the health infrastructure at the PHC and Sub-Centre level to competent and dynamic private doctors? It is not true that rural masses are always looking for free medicines and free contraceptives. They are spending quite a lot on quacks and chemists. What they are looking for is reliable and safe health care including sterilisations (male and female) which the Government medical outfit is not able to provide. Why not give the private sector a chance? In the urban areas where there are numerous hospitals and nursing homes run by the private sector, family planning work can be entrusted to them selectively and suitable income tax concessious given to them. They would do a much better job that the Government functionaries. Family planning will succeed in this country only when people consider it worth-while to pay for family planning services (that shows true motivation) instead of the present system of people collecting money from the Government for practising family planning.

I am reminded of my experience during field work in a backward district of Madhya Pradesh. The PHC doctors complained that they could not possibly achieve the sterilisation target set by the Government, as people were not coming forward for sterilisation. I asked a group of villagers if this was true. Their reply was: "Of course this is true. The Government wants to pay us only Rs.160 for a sterilisation case. This is not fair. We are willing to help the Government but they must give us at least Rs. 2000 (rupees two thousand) per case.'' The people were convinced that they were obliging the Government by offering to undergo sterilisation! So much for the IEC (Information, education, communication) programme of the Government! I must hasten to add that even if this money were paid, the men would not come for sterilisation: they would send their wives, on the plea that men are breadwinners and what would happen to the children, if the breadwinner dies? If the wife dies, a man can take a new wife. So much for status of women!

In fairness to the Ministry of Health and Family Welfare, I must put on record that Mr. B. Shankaranand, the Union Minister for Health and Family Welfare did call some senior persons working in the field of family planning, to give him advice. The only advice I could give was: "Please remove all family planning targets from 1st April, 1993. They have become counterproductive." In my view, the Prime Minister should declare family planning as a sick social sector like a sick public sector undertaking and open the gates to the private sector. The Department of Family Welfare is a prisoner of its own targets.

SECTION IV

FAMILY PLANNING

[16]

Registrar General's
Report on Vital Rates

In the absence of a reliable civil registration system in India, the only source of information on the annual birth and death rates is the Sample Registration System (SRS) under the Office of the Registrar General. The main limitation of SRS data, however, is the absence of any estimate at the district level, because of the constraint of sample size. The district is the basic unit of administration and the monitoring of various plans and programmes depends to a large extent on district level data. In fact, the Planning Commission has been demanding and rightly so, block level data. As far as the family welfare programme is concerned, it may be pointed put that the Department of Family Welfare gives estimates of the couple protection rate (CPR) to indicate the practice of family planning, for every district in India on an anual basis. Unfortunately, these data cannot be matched by the SRS data on annual birth rates and death rates beause the SRS does not go beyond state level estimates. Block level estimate is a far cry.

Several years back, a Technical Committee on SRS data was appointed under the chairmanship of the Director General of the Central Statistical Organisation (CSO) to explore the possibility of generating at least district level data through the SRS. I was a member of this Committee. We went into the details of the sample frame, the size of the sample, the sampling error and other statistical aspects. We also did selective field work in villages to get a first hand report of the field situation. But when it came to administrative and financial matters, we got stuck. If the estimates are needed at the district level, the size of the sample had to be vastly increased. This meant a much bigger field staff, more supervisors, more training programmes, and above all, more money. An earlier attempt to ask for more money for the SRS was turned down by the Finance Ministry and it seems even the Cabinet Secretary had noted that the civil registration system should be improved instead of spending more money on SRS. This was very discouraging to the Office of the Registrar General. Our Technical Committee, therefore, decided to be more pragmatic and recommended that in large states like UP, data should be generated at least for each Division comprising several districts.

Appeared in *Financial Express*, 26 October, 1992

Another important aspects to which the Committee applied its mind was in regard to data on marriages and annual estimates of the marriage rate in India on which no data exists. Several of us thought that the SRS was the best agency to collect data on marriages along with data on births and deaths. Several others felt that SRS should not be loaded with any more work. We decided to go to the field. I recall that along-with the Director General of CSO (Mr. G. Sardana), I had gone to several villages in Gujarat and discussed the matter with the SRS field staff as well as the people. We were convinced that there would be no special difficulty for the SRS to collect data on marriages on an annual basis, provided a little more financial backup and some incentives were given to the field staff. Our report was submitted to the Government. I do not know what exactly the Governemnt decided. As far as I know, nothing was done and the status quo is maintained.

It should have dawned upon our planners and policy-makers long back that in a country like India, in any family planning strategy, the first intervention should be in regard to the age at marriage. Over the years, the clinically-oriented Department of Family Welfare has done practically nothing about raising the age at marriage. In fact, it can do very little about such a social phenomenon. Besides, the programme has been commercialised by giving incentive money to acceptors of sterilisation. As a result, undue importance is given to sterilisation and an important intervention strategy like raising the age at marriage is relegated to the background. This is more so, as there is no incentive money for raising the age at marriage. But before we launch an ambitious programme for raising the age at marriage, the least that we could do is to make registration of marriages compulsory. The recent incident in Rajasthan where a social worker was assaulted because she was trying to prevent a child marriage should highlight the absolute necessity of compulsory marriage registration to enforce the Child Marriage Restraint Act. No doubt it is a difficult proposition but how long can we live on rhetoric and avoid doing the hard things?

Coming back to SRS, it must be pointed out that SRS cannot meet the requirements of compulsory marriage registration because by definition, SRS relies on a sample, whereas under marriage registration, every married couple must have documentary proof of registration. In short, marriage registration has to be universal. It has legal implications. But the objective of collecting data on marriages on a sample basis was to have an idea of the marriage rate on a yearly basis. This could be a valuable input to the family planning programme. Thus we need both compulsory registration of marriage and SRS data on the marriage rate. It would be valuable if such data are available at the district level. This subject deserves the most serious consideration from the Ministry of Finance and the Ministry of Home Affairs.

These improvements apart, let us have a look at the latest annual Report on the Sample Registration System, 1989, just published by the Registrar General. It is a valuable report and gives a wealth of data on the fertility and mortality pattern in the rural and urban areas of all the States and Union Territories of India.

In Table 16.1, we present data on crude birth rate at two periods of time, 1981-83 and 1987-89, based on the SRS report. The states are arranged in order of the rate of decline in the birth rate.

According to SRS, three-yearly moving averages are more reliable than yearly figures. Table 1 is based on three-yearly figures. It will be seen that during the six years under study, the decline in the birth rate has been fastest (i.e. more than ten per cent) in the States of Kerala, Tamil Nadu, Gujarat, West Bengal, Rajasthan, and Andhra Pradesh. It must be noted that Rajasthan's initial figure of birth rate was very high. Surprisingly, the so-called "good" states of Maharashtra and Karnataka have not performed well at all.

Table 16.1: Average Crude Birth Rate for India and Major States

CBR (per 1000)

State	1981-82	1987-89	Per cent change during the period
INDIA	33.8	31.4	-7.0
Kerala	25.6	20.7	-19.1
Tamil Nadu	27.9	23.3	-16.5
Gujarat	34.3	29.7	-13.4
West Bengal	32.5	28.8	-11.4
Rajasthan	38.5	34.2	-11.2
Andhra Pradesh	31.2	27.8	-10.9
Orissa	33.5	31.1	-7.2
Himachal Pradesh	32.3	30.1	-6.5
Assam	34.0	32.1	-6.1
Punjab	30.3	28.5	-5.9
Haryana	36.4	34.5	-5.9
Madhya Pradesh	38.2	36.3	-5.0
Bihar	37.9	36.1	-4.7
Uttar Pradesh	38.9	37.3	-4.1
Maharashtra	29.3	28.9	-1.4
Karanataka	28.4	28.5	+0.4
Jammu & Kashmir	31.4	31.4	0.0

The Registrar General also publishes a six-monthly Bulletin on the Sample Registration data. In the latest Bulletin which has just been released, the annual birth and death rates as well as infant mortality rate for the year 1990 have been published. Table 16.2 summarises the picture for India as a whole.

Table 16.2: Vital Rates for India, 1990 (Per 1000)

	Birth rate	Death rate	Natural Growth rate	Infant mortality rate
INDIA : RURAL	31.7	10.5	21.2	86
INDIA : URBAN	24.7	6.8	17.9	50
INDIA : COMBINED	30.2	9.7	20.5	80

It is distressing to note that even as late as 1990, the rates of natural increase in population has been of the order of 2.05 per cent per year. It is somewhat encouraging to note that the infant mortality rate which was 91 per thousand in 1989 has come down in 80 to 1990. In seems likely that the increased investment and activity in regard to the MCH (mother and child death) programmes is makng an impact. Nevertheless, it is distressing to note that the infant mortality rate is a high as 122 in Orissa and 111 in Madhya Pradesh. In fact, in Orissa, according to SRS yearly data, the infant mortality rate has gone up from 121 in 1989 to 122 in 1990. This increase cannot be explained in purely statistical terms. The case of Orissa needs indepth investigation. For too long a time, the Governemnt has been bragging about the low birth rate of Orissa. In the face of such a shockingly high infant mortality rate, where is the welfare in the family welfare programme?

17

Ritual, Rhetoric
and Rising Population

Every year, on July 11, we observe the World Population Day with considerable official enthusiasm. This has become almost a ritual and we Indians are particularly good in observing rituals. It comes naturally to us. But unfortunately nothing much happens for the rest of the year.

As usual, on the World Population Day this year also, we were showered with messages from the President of India, the Prime Minister, the Union Minister for Health and Family Welfare, and the State Minister for Health and Family Welfare. The Secretary of the Department of Family Welfare wrote a long article on the action plan for revamping the family welfare programme. There were panel discussion on All India Radio and Delhi Doordarshan. A leading newspaper brought out a special supplement on the World Population Day. All this is very encouraging for the Government of India. Where do the people come in? How do they ''observe'' the World Population Day?

In a country where millions of people cannot count beyond 20, what do the population projections mean? Can they comprehend a billion people? According to the latest United Nations projections, the world population is estimated to be 6.3 billion in the year 2000 and 11.2 billion in the year 2100. Everybody is fond of quoting these figures but do they make any sense to our illiterate masses?

Things are slightly better when we say that china has done much better than India in regard to population control. The masses understand the message when we tell them that at the rate we are going, India's population will be more than China's population by the year 2050. But then China is very remote and the year 2050 is even more remote. How do we then communicate with our illiterate masses on the population question? Most communication experts, both Indian and foreign, have failed in this field.

Appeared in *Financial Express*, 28 July, 1992

Powerful international population lobbies and donor agencies think they have the answer: It is more and more of IEC or information, education and communication that we need in the field of family planning. Under conditions of mass illiteracy, how do we go about giving information to the people and that too on a subject like family planning? And what sort of "education" are we planning for the illiterate people, without first ensuring 100 per cent literacy? And do our western experts know how to communicate with illiterate masses, especially with illiterate rural women in North India?

In my 30 years of field work in different parts of rural India, I have found that much of the money meant on IEC is wasted. The situation has not improved over the years. I am not against slogans and catch words. I cannot think of a more powerful slogan in India than Mahatma Gandhi's "Quit India". This slogan worked due to a variety of historical and political factors. Indira Gandhi's slogan "Garibi Hatao" was also a powerful slogan but it did not quite work. The war against poverty has to be fought relentlessly and over a long period.

I cannot think of any family planning slogan which makes sense to the people. For example, when I asked village women about the slogan: "A small family brings health and happiness", the answer was: "Only God can give us happiness and not the Ministry of Health and Family Welfare." When I asked about the two-child norm, the answer was: "It depends whether the two are boys or girls. How can you have only two girls? Will you look after us in our old age?" The tragedy is that we want to impose an urban middle class norm of two children on the illiterate, landless poor in the rural areas and the urban slums, without improving their lot, wihout changing their material condition, without giving them any security but at the same time, depriving them of the inbuilt security of a large family.

To say this is not to argue against having a vigorous programme of family planning which we desperately need. The question is: Are we on the right track? On the World Population Day, the Union Minister of Health and Family Welfare was asked in a TV interview: "Has our family planning programme been less than successful?" His candid reply was: "The programme has been marginally successful."

Interestingly enough, the Minister talked of getting rid of the "tyranny of targets". I have been campaiging for several years for the removal of the bureaucratic family planning targets set in Nirman Bhavan in New Delhi in meticulous detail, specifying the number of couples who would adopt different methods like sterilisation, IUD, etc. I have said that the Ministry of Health and Family Welfare is suffering from a new disease--Targetitis. There is nothing wrong with targets as a monitoring tool and a management device but everything goes wrong when the target becomes an end in itself and figures are extensively falsified to show that the targets have been more than fulfilled. I am happy, therefore, to note that the concerned Minister recognises the failure of a programme which gets stuck in family planning targets.

The Secetary of the Department of Family Welfare did spell out the details of a new action plan for the family welfare programme. This however, did not impress Dr. Karan Singh, a former Minister of Health and Family Welfare, who claimed in his recent TV panel discussion that in the 1976 population policy statement drafted by him and adopted by Parliament, all this was said. I had the unfortunate task of pointing out during this discussion that this policy was adopted during the Emergency and it contained a controversial enabling clause which said that state governments may go ahead with compulsory sterilisation if the facilities are available to meet the requirements of compulsory sterilisation. It was not neceesary for me to point out that the fall of Indira Gandhi Government had a lot to do with allegations regarding forced sterilisation, particularly in the northern states.

If we must have targets, I would start with a target of 100 per cent litercy rate in every district of India within the Eighth Plan period. It is not enough to have 100 per cent of near 100 per cent literacy for males alone. We must also ensure that 100 per cent of the females are literate. There can be no better input to the family planning programme than 100 per cent literacy of females. If this target is fulfilled family planning targets will have a real chance of getting fulfilled.

I would also urge the World Bank, UNFPA and all other donor agencies to divert all funds earmarked for IEC to the fulfilment of the target of 100 per cent literacy rate for females in rural areas and urban slums. The talk of making family planning a people's movement is empty rhetoric.

Finally, a word about our ever rising population. According to the latest United Nations long-term projections (1992), China's population in absolute terms will decrease after the year 2025, while India's population in absolute terms will continue to increase till the year 2050. It may also be noted that in 1950, China claimed 22.1 per cent of the world's population, while India's share was 14.2 per cent. By the year 2050, China's share will come down to 15.2 per cent while India's share will go up to 17 per cent. In sharp contrast, Europe's share of the world population will come down from 15.6 per cent in 1950 to only 4.9 per cent by 2050.

Taking a long view, if the projections prove correct (I hope they do not) demographically speaking, India will dominate the world. It is no doubt a terrifying prospect. In the last four decades, we have added 500 million people, roughly the population of two USAs but not a fraction of their resources.

┌─────┐
│ 18 │
└─────┘

Rise and Fall of the
Red Triangle

Everybody knows the red cross. It has universal acceptability and so much credibility. An Indian family planning administrator, aided by an American expert on communications, thought of a red triangle to symbolise familly planning. This was more than two decades ago. Today, a big cemented red triangle adorns Nirman Bhavan in New Delhi, from where the Ministry of Health and Family Welfare runs India's family planning programme spread over 630,000 villages and 4,000 towns and cities.

Unfortunately for the Ministry of Health and Family Welfare (family planning was renamed as family welfare after the emergency debacle), the red triangle inspires nobody, not even the bureaucrats in the Department of Family Welfare. As for the masses, the red triangle is yet another symbol of oppression. At the grassroot level, the lower level bureaucrats and the health workers are perpetually tormented by the rigid and unattainable sterilisation targets set by Nirman Bhavan.

Twenty years ago, I was asked to lecture on population in an orientation course on development journalism. This was when the red triangle was at its zenith. I had told the class that the three sides of the red triangle stood for massive Indian inertia, obsolete British bureaucratic rules and fancy American ideas!

By way of example, I pointed out that the average age at marriage of girls had increased very slowly in the past 70 years, the caste system still persisted, the dowry system had a new lease of life--thanks to increasing consumerism--society as a whole was as stagnant as ever in spite of some islands of modernisation (rather westernisation).

The impact of the British bureaucracy was all pervasive in India. The British in their wisdom did not introduce birth control in India but when we launched a state sponsored family planning programme after independence, the rules we adopted were the same as those in the Public Works Department! The programme was judged purely by the number

Appeared in *Financial Express*, 2 June, 1992

of sterilisations performed, like the PWD counting the number of bricks supplied. The result was that nobody was interested in issues like raising the age at marriage. This was also because there was no money in it (for sterilisation there was no money for acceptors as well as for motivators). Further, no importance was given to literacy, education, infant mortality and allied factors which depress the birth rate.

As for fancy American ideas, the example I gave was the novel idea of a foreign expert who bought an elephant and paraded it all over India with a red triangle on it. This was supposed to convey to India's illiterate millions that the population problem was of an elephantine nature. When I was asked to comment on this innovative communication strategy by students in the USA in 1969, I had said: "I cannot think of a more assinine solution of an elephantine problem." To complete the record, the elephant bought by the foreign expert met a tragic end due to starvation after some years. The foreign expert did not know that in Indian mythology, an elephant stands for rain and prosperity. Besides, an elephant scares nobody in India.

One should not dramatise the ignorance of an expert. But what does one say when under foreign advice, a separate department of family planning was carved out in the Ministry of Health and Family Planning in 1966 on the reasoning that family planning needed a special boost (but not health, as a decline in the death rate only adds to the population problem, so ran the perverse argument). Jawaharlal Nehru had the right vision when he put family planning under health. He knew the masses and Indian psychology. He also knew that family planning as such would not be readily acceptable to Indian masses and so he put it as a sub-system of health which was a crying need.

Putting family planning in a separate basket was a disaster. Another fancy idea was to set rigid family planning targets from New Delhi and make the programme a vertical programme with a vengeance, Centrally funded, directed and monitored but implemented by the states. The result was that most States regarded the programme as an imposition from New Delhi but as there was money in it, they accepted it but no serious attempt was made to run the programme as a priority programme, barring a few exceptions.

In all international conferences, one invariably talks of integrating family planning with various development programmes. Is it not a contradiction that within the Health Ministry itself, there is no integration between health and family planning and we demand a much wider level of integration? For example, the Director General of Health Services has nothing to do with family planning.

As Professor D. Banerji, the foremost critic of India's family planning programme has rightly observed: "Health has been hijacked by family planning, the way the programme is run at the grassroot level." Because health workers are judged wholly by the number of sterilisation cases, there is all round neglect of primary health care. In fact, health was hijacked by family planning but the plane crashed, ruining both the health and the family planning programme!

It was Dr. Karan Singh, the leader of the Indian delegation to the world Population Conference in Bucharest (1974) who gave the famous slogan: "Development is the best contraceptive", while the Americans tried hard (though unsuccessfully) to sell the idea of setting rigid family planning targets in all the developing countries.

It is therefore rather comical that Mr. Robert S. McNamara of World Bank vintage should be saying the following in his first Rajiv Gandhi Memorial Lecture (May 23, 1992): "India has failed to give adequate attention to other factors which also affect fertility: in particular, the age at which women marry; and the status of women, specially as reflected in their educational levels.... population control in India has been narrowly identified with family planning".

But who advised us to make a frontal and direct attack on high fertility by launching a massive sterilisation programme? Who is promoting laparoscopes? Who is pleading for Norplant 6? Who asked us to commercialise the programme by paying money for accepting sterilisation? Looking back, Sanjay Gandhi was mainly responsible for the fall of the red triangle during the emergency and since then successive governments have made no serious attempt to fly the flag high again. The red triangle today has no acceptability, no credibility and no respectability. Private companies selling condoms ensure that the red triangle is nowhere on their packages.

The Department of Family Welfare boasts of an ever-increasing figure of couple protection rate, and dishes out figures of couple protection rate, and million of births averted and such other hypothetical and spurious statistics. The family planning programme has failed to make any worthwhile dent on the population growth rate. For more than ten years the birth rate has stagnated around 32 or 33 per thousand.

A careful study of India's family planning programme will indicate that the programme is both conceptually and operationally unsound. The foreign donor agencies have contributed in no small measure to the failure of our family planning programme. Even now we are receiving misguided advice from our foreign well-wishers. For example, only last month, a leading British medical scientist, Dr. Maurice King from England, argued in a public lecture in New Delhi that UNICEF and India should go slow in implementing child survival programmes so that India could come out of the demographic trap! In short, he was arguing that the infant mortality rate should remain high.

Another piece of advice we are receiving lately from foreign donors is that in order to achieve intersectoral co-ordination, India should appoint a Population Commission. Invariably the example of Indonesia is quoted. One may ask what happened to the foreign sponsored Population Council in Egypt? Was it not a failure?

In his recent lecture also, McNamara recommended setting up a National Population Council. Do we need an apex organisation in New Delhi to run the family planning programme when we talk of making family planning a people's movement? There is no doubt that the foreign donors will offer to fund adequately the proposed Population Council. There is also no doubt that they will try to field their Indian henchmen as members of the Council who will fly the flag of contraceptive technology high.

Table 18.1: Outlay on family welfare programme in five-year plans of India
(in million rupees)

===

First Plan	
1951-56	6.5
Second Plan	
1956-61	50
Third Plan	
1961-66	270
Annual Plan (3 years)	
1966-69	829
Fourth Plan	
1969-74	3300
Fifth Plan	
1974-79	4974
Sixth Plan	
1980-85	10100
Seventh Plan	
1985-90	32560
Eighth Plan	
1990-95	65000

===

In figure I we show the increase in India's population between 1951 and 1991 and in figure 2, we show the increase in the expenditure on family planning in different Plan Periods, (from the first to the Eighth Plan). Much more than population explosion there has been an explosion in the expenditure on family planning. To use bureaucratic jargon, the expenditure on family planning programme has not been commensurate with the performance of the programme.

We are loaded with a huge but largely nonperforming staff which consumes most of the money in salaries, a staff which cannot be disbanded. This year's Budget alone provides for about Rs. 10,000 million for family welfare. We have reached a deadend and the red triangle has become a red flag!

19

Couple Protection Rate or Community Participation Rate (CPR)?

There is nothing more endearing to the Department of Family Welfare than the magic figure of Couple Protection Rate (CPR). The curve of CPR is everrising. For those not familiar with this demographic jargon, it may be pointed out that CPR refers to the protection rate against the risk of pregnancy. In simple language, it shows the level of family planning practice. In technical terms, it refers to the number of couples who accepted family planning in the current year as also those who accepted it in previous years, minus those who dropped out because of mortality or widowhood, married women crossing the age of 45 years, removal or expulsion of intra-uterine device (IUD) and failure of different methods of family planing. The annual attrition rates are calculated and the figures are worked out per 100 couples, which give the effective couple protection rate. In the absence of detailed data, various assumptions have to be made. The CPR is also calculated for different methods of family planning. These elaborate statistics are the exclusive domain of the Evaluation and Intelligence Division of the Department of Family Welfare, Ministry of Health and Family Welfare, Government of India.

The Sample Registration Division (SRS) of the Office of the Registrar General, Ministry of Home Affairs, presents annual figures for birth and death rates, separately for rural and urban areas for individual States and Union Territories.

There is lack of consistency between the rise in CPR and the fall in the crude birth rate (CBR). In other words, the Registrar General's data do not reflect the progress claimed by the Department of Family Welfare.

For twenty years, I have challenged the methodology of CPR and the data dished out by the Department of Family Welfare, on the basis of my field work in different parts of India. Interestingly enough, it was Rajiv Gandhi, who as Prime Minister challenged these

Appeared in *Financial Express*, 19 May, 1992

figures (on the advice of his computer boys who were outside the bureaucratic system). I had also challenged the cash award of Rs.2.5 crores for the best performance in family's welfare, which incidently was given to one of the worst performing states in India. But the worst part of the story was that the Family Welfare Department itself was evaluating its own work! I suggested to the Prime Minister that the least that the Government could do was to entrust the evaluation work to organisations like the Indian Council of Medical Research (ICMR), Operations Research Group (ORG), etc. This recommendation was accepted and the evaluation done by these agencies did not bring glory to the Department of Family Welfare.

An activity which went unnoticed even by the Prime Minister's Office concerned the so-called Area Projects under the Department of Family Welfare. These projects involving hundreds of crores of rupees were supposed to be comprehensive health and family welfare projects. The donor agencies involved were (and still are) World Bank, UNFPA, USAID, ODA (UK), DANIDA (Denmark), NORAD (Norway), SIDA (Sweden) UNICEF, WHO etc.

On the basis of field work I found that much of this money was wasted in the name of the people. The major chunk of the expenditure was on construction (rather sub-standard construction) of buildings for the Primary Health Centres (PHCs), Sub Centres and quarters for doctors and nurses. The philosophical basis of these area projects was that Indian rural masses were not getting proper health care because there were not enough doctors and nurses in rural areas and this in turn was because there were not enough residential quarters for doctors and nurses in rural areas. So why not create this much-needed infrastructure, get the money from donor agencies and in this process earn foreign exchange also? Such reasoning shows ignorance of ground reality, rural conditions and medical ethos in this country. My finding was that the so-called Area Projects were in fact PWD (public works departments) projects, notorious for their corruption. No foreign exchange was needed to deliver health services to the rural poor. And foreign exchange is not a sacred cow.

My ideas received the support of the Prime Minister and his advisers. A high powered Steering Commitee was appointed to oversee the foreign aided Area Projects (I was included as a Member). The donor agencies quickly changed their strategy. They suddenly realised that training was the most important thing and what India needed most was training in IEC--information, education, and communication. I retorted by saying: IEC stands for inefficiency, extravagance and corruption!

In passing, it may be mentioned that in 1989-90, the amount of external assistance received by the Department of Family Welfare was of the order of Rs. 2160 million, accounting for 27.6 per cent of the total expenditure on family welfare.

Where are the people in this game? Everything is being done in the name of the people but have we consulted them? Why does the Government repeat like a parrot that family planning should become a people's movement? Is it not a contradiction that the family planning targets are set by bureaucrats in Nirman Bhavan in New Delhi in meticulous detail specifying each method of family planning, and at the same time we talk of a people's movement? One has to do field work (which is different from Government inspection with all the accompanying *bandobast*) in different parts of India and talk to the people in order to understand how the credibility of the health and family planning programme has been eroded by the tyranny of targets.

Many eyebrows were raised when I observed in a recent seminar on family planning that the CPR was almost zero in most states of India. By CPR, I meant community participation rate and not couple protection rate.

There is a new wind blowing in the Department of Family Welfare. A well-meaning Secretary, aided by three dynamic joint secretaries is trying to revamp the family planning programme. In the Planning Commission, we have a medical scientist who is in charge of Health and Family Welfare. Though a clinician, he understands community health. He had advised Sheikh Abdullah, the then Chief Minister of Jammu and Kashmir to introduce an innovative rural health scheme involving school teachers. One can hope that under his leadership, the village Health Guide Scheme will be revived and rejuvinated. If there is one scheme in the field of health and family planning which is closest to the people and gives a chance to the people to have their own local person involved in health activities even marginally, it is the Village Health Guide Scheme which, unfortunately has been maimed by the bureaucracy and in particular, the medical bureaucracy ever since it was launched on the 2nd October 1977.

We hope that the Prime Minister and the National Development Council which will meet shortly will not rubber stamp the ten point Action plan to revamp the family welfare programme which says, *inter alia*, "The possibility of the (VHG) scheme to make it more effective or alternatively of *disbanding it* would be examined further taking into account the varied implications including from the legal angle". The Prime Minister should not be a party to such indecision. In village after village, I was asked by innocent people: "We understand that the *Sarkar* does not have Rs. 50 to pay as honorarium to the village health guides. How is it possible?"

My recommendation to our eminent Finance Minister would be to put must of the foreign asistance for family planning in the kitty of the village health guides. In turn, he should be happy with the foreign exchange.

20

India's Growing Demographic Misery: The Irrelevance of Kerala

At the recent Rio Earth Summit, Mr. Kamal Nath, India's ebullient Minister for Environment was cornered by the foreign press when he was asked about India's population problem. According to newspaper reports, he wriggled out by citing the success story of Kerala.

While we should be proud of Kerala's achievements on the social and demographic front (though not on the economic front), the fact remains that Kerala cannot make a dent on India's birth rate as also the growth rate of population because Kerala is not statistically relevant--it accounts for only 3.4 per cent of India's total population and contributed only 2.2 per cent of the net increase in India's population during the 1981-91 decade. This by itself does not discredit the Kerala model. In fact, as argued earlier we have to learn more from Kerala than China.

Kerala does throw light on the impact of literacy and education, on the age at marriage and fertility, on the relationship between status of women and the size of the family, on the role of a high level of investment on health and education in reducing the birth rate, the impact of better access to health care on the mortality rate and in particular, the infant mortality rate and in turn the impact of a low level of infant and child mortality on the family planning programme. There are also other important factors accounting for the success of the Kerala model. For example, the human settlement pattern in Kerala (there is hardly any difference between 'rural' and 'urban'), the large size of villages, the physical accessibility (100 per cent of the villages are connected by road or water) and a higher level of communication (100 per cent of the villages are electrified, the literacy rate is near 100 per cent and Kerala has the largest number of newspaper per capita) are all factors which have contributed to the demographic modernisation of Kerala. We should also not forget historical factors like the enlightened policies of the Maharajas who championed the cause of education and health several decades back, the role of

Appeared in *Financial Express*, 30 June, 1992

Christian missionaries, the positive impact of Marxist land reforms and public distribution system, the beneficial effects of migration to the Gulf countries, the matrilineal system (though of historical interest only today), the higher status of women and a host of other factors which make up the Kerala model. On the negative side, one must mention the high unemployment rate in Kerala which acts as a deterrent to early marriage and high fertility. No amount of Government propaganda can come anywhere near motivating people to accept family planning as the high unemployment rate in Kerala.

In a recent seminar in New Delhi, there was a lot of discussion among population experts on the relevance of spacing methods vis-a-vis non-terminal methods in India's family planning programme. Many eyebrows were raised when I said that IUD will be India's number one family planning method. People thought I was talking of Intra-Uterine Device (Copper T) which has limited success in India. I spelt out that by IUD, I meant INFLATION, UNEMPLOYMENT and DEPRIVATION.

In my view, the real motivation for family planning is the grim economic situation and not so much the prospect of "health and happiness", as the Government posters point out.

Table 20.1: Birth Rate and Death Rate, 1990 (per 1000)

	Total		Rural		Urban	
	BR	DR	BR	DR	BR	DR
Kerala	19.6	6.0	19.6	6.0	19.8	6.1
Uttar Pradesh	35.6	12.0	37.0	12.8	29.3	8.8
Bihar	32.9	10.6	33.8	11.0	24.6	10.2
Madhya Pradesh	37.1	12.6	38.9	13/7	29.3	7.6
Rajasthan	33.6	9.6	34.7	10.1	28.3	7.5

Table 20.2: Infant Mortality Rate, 1990 (per 1000 live births)

	Total	Rural	Urban
Kerala	17	17	15
Uttar Pradesh	99	105	67
Bihar	75	77	46
Madhya Pradesh	111	120	61
Rajasthan	84	88	59

Table 20.3: Total Population and Decadal Growth Rate, 1981-91

	Population (million)	Percent of India's Population	Decadal Growth Rate 1981-91 (per cent)
Kerala	29.0	3.4	14.0
Uttar Pradesh	138.8	16.4	25.2
Bihar	86.3	10.2	23.5
Madhya Pradesh	66.2	7.8	26.8
Rajasthan	43.9	5.2	28.1

Researchers often give complicated explanations of phenomena which are obvious to the common people. For example, in Kerala, I was often told that because of the high unemployment rate, one has to wait for a long time to get a secure job and he cannot possibly get married when he is unemployed (who will marry an unemployed man?) and this pushes up the age at marriage. But then there are economists who ask: "the unemployment rate is high in Bihar also. Why is the age at marriage not high there?" It is a valid question. But why should we analyse each factor in isolation? In Kerala, it is literacy (and education) plus other factors which have brought about a significant demographic change. It is also important to remember that a more appropriate indicator is the female literacy rate (and also educational level) in rural areas. Given the same unemployment rate, the motivation for family planning would be different if the women are nearly 100 per cent *illterate* in rural areas (as in Rajasthan) or nearly 100 per cent *literate* (as in Kerala).

Table 20.4: Birth Rate, Death Rate and IMR in Four Southern States, 1990

States	Population (million)	Birth Rate	Death Rate	IMR
Andhra Pradesh	66.3	26.3	9.1	70
Tamil Nadu	55.6	21.6	8.5	59
Karnataka	44.8	28.0	8.1	70
Kerala	29.0	19.6	6.0	17

Much also depends on the political climate. The political conciousness in Kerala is very high (which can become a minus point also). The impact can be seen at the Primary Health Centre (PHC) level in rural areas: people demand health serivces. If the doctors are absent, the people will physically catch hold of them in their homes Things are totally different in Bihar, for example, where doctors are absent from PHCs for days together and helpless patients just suffer in silence.

One cannot list here all the factors in the Kerala model. But one must note the extent of institutional care during child birth which is very high in Kerala (while it is extremely low in states like Bihar or Uttar Pradesh), the abundance of water, the cleanliness of the people, the absence of son preference (in contrast with the obsession for sons in the northern states, in particular), the social reform movements of Kerala, the successful health cooperatives, the role of Ayurveda in health care, the abundance of colleges and hospitals in rural areas (in sharp contrast with the situation in Uttar Pradesh, Bihar, Rajasthan or Madhya Pradesh), the religious tolerance of Kerala (the higher fertility of Muslims persists but this is not used as political propoganda as in the northern states) and finally, the overall social environment in the state (the quality of life indices take no note of the quality *of society* as such) which is far more satisfactory than in most other parts of India. The people are intelligent, dynamic and have a sense of humour; lacking in most other states of India. The women are intensely feminine and yet are more than a match for the modern aggressive women, fighting for their status.

This in short is the Keala model of demographic modernisation. But alas, this model is not statistically relevant for India. It is the irrelevance of Kerala which makes India's demographic situation so gloomy.

It is my contention that unless we tackled effectively the demographic situation in Uttar Pradesh Bihar, Madhya Pradesh and Rajasthan (my acronym is BIMARU states), India's future is bleak. A recent UNFPA study has unnecessarily added Orisa to these four states (Perhaps for the sake of originality) but Orissa is a special state (with a large tribal population, high incidence of poverty and a high level of mortality and in particular, infant motality). Besides, cultural homogeneity is also an important factor in demographic analysis (Orissa cannot be linked to the four Hindi-speaking states).

In passing it may be mentioned that the SRS data for Bihar are on the low side because of operational problems.

Statistically speaking, the Kerala model is irrelevant because Kerala accounts for only 3.4 per cent of India's population, compared to about 40 per cent in the states of Uttar Pradesh, Bihar, Madhya Pradesh and Rajasthan. These four states contributed over 42 per cent of the total increase in India's population during 1981-91, compared to Kerala's contribution of just 2 per cent.

It is not quite correct to bracket all the four southern states with Kerala (though they are way ahead of the (BIMARU States) as will be evident from Table 20.4.

Tamil Nadu's birth rate is getting closer to Kerala's but in terms of the infant mortality rate, Tamil Nadu is lagging far behind Kerala. We have to look much beyond Kerala to solve India's population problem. Kerala cannot bail out India.

21

India's Family Planning Programme--Getting Out of the Sterilisation Trap

Regardless of government pronouncements to the contrary, reflected in Planning Commission's and Health Ministry's documents, the fact remains that in the eyes of masses of people, particularly in Bihar, Madhya Pradesh, Rajasthan and Uttar Pradesh (BIMARU states), Family Welfare = Family Planning = Sterilisation = Female Sterilisation = Laparoscopy. The health and family welfare functionaries at the state level, district level, PHC level and Sub-Centre level, know that their confidential reports will be written and performance judged by their superiors only on the basis of the number of sterilisation cases, even if the Government says in New Delhi that the emphasis is on the spacing methods. Thousands of workers at the grassroot level will not accept the shift in government policy as long as the 'bring cases' (*case lao*) approach persists. As D.Banerji has rightly observed, "Health has been hijacked by family planning". I might add: "the plane crashed, ruining both the Health and Family Planning Programmes".

MINISTRY, PLANNING COMMISSION AND POPULATION PROGRAMME

I think the Planning Commission has made a sincere attempt in the formulation of the Eighth Plan to get out of this sterilisation trap. The Department of Family Welfare in its Action Plan for Revamping the Family Welfare Programme in India endorsed by the National Development Council (NDC) in 1992 has also highlighted the need for giving adequate consideration to female literacy rate, age at marriage of girls, status of women, position of employment of women, social security and general level of economic development. But in the same breath, the Action Plan also says that these are well beyond the pale of activities of the Department of Family Welfare. Not only this, the document clearly says: "The Family Welfare Department in the Centre and Health and Family Welfare Departments in the State Governments are organisations which should be

Published in the *Indian Journal of Public Administration*, July-September, 1992 essentially viewed as supply departments for making available the family welfare services". This, to my mind, is a correct assessment of its limitations by the Department of Family Welfare. It is only a supply department for providing contraceptive services and its track record so far has been that it is basically a sterilisation department. Now that there is a realisation that there are limits to a sterilisation-oriented Family Planning Programme (FPP), what is the role of the Family Welfare Department ? If, as it rightly says, its role is to supply contraceptive service, this can be done better under the umbrella of health. Reproductive health is also a part of health; the concern for mothers and children is certainly a vital part of the concern for health.

Perception

Jawaharlal Nehru, the first Prime Minister and the first Chairman of the Planning Commission, under whose leadership Family Planning (FP) was incorporated in the First Five-Year Plan, had a clear perception when he put FP under the health umbrella. To quote from the First Plan, "the main appeal for family planning is based on considerations of the health and welfare of the family. Family limitation or spacing of the children is necessary and desirable in order to secure better health for the mother and better care of up-bringing of children. Measures directed to this end therefore form part of the public health programme".

Unfortunately, under misguided foreign advice, family welfare was put in a separate basket and a new Department was created in the Ministry of Health and Family Planning in 1966. In my opinion, this has contributed to a very great extent to the failure of India's FPP. I cannot help observing that in some international circles, there is a mistaken feeling that if we reduce the death rate sharply, the population problem will only be aggravated and therefore it follows that priority should be given to birth control rather than death control. I would like to refer to the views of an eminent British medical scientist, Maurice King, who, in his recent writings and lectures, has maintained that UNICEF and the Government of India should go slow on child survival strategies in order to come out of the "demographic trap".

Urgency

Without going into this controversy, I can say that the Planning Commission as well as the Ministry of Health and Family Welfare have clearly accepted the urgency of safe motherhood and child survival strategies and the need to reduce infant and child mortality rates which are desirable objectives in themselves, apart from their impact on the birth rate. But surely the infant mortality rate does not depend only on the medical services: much would depend on the age at marriage, the age at different pregnancies, the literacy rate and level of education of the mother in particular, the quality of drinking water, the state of sanitation, the level of nutrition and a whole lot of other social and economic factors. The Department of Family Welfare can do very little about such wide-ranging measures which go beyond hospital oriented health care and contraceptive technology. The management solution offered by the Ministry's Action Plan is as follows:

> There is need to have an institutional mechanism at the Centre for inter-sectoral coordination particularly among the Ministry of Health and Family Welfare and the Ministries of Human Resource Development, Finance, Information and

Broadcasting, Environment and Forest, Labour, Department of Women and Child Development and the Department of Rural Development. A suitable institutional mechanism would be evolved at the Central level to achieve the desired level of inter-sectoral coordination and similar mechanism would be developed at the state level.

Such a move has also the backing of powerful international lobbies, foreign donor agencies and some interested groups in India. They have been pleading for the last several years for appointment of a Population Commission. To me, this is just passing the buck and shelving the problem. In any case, we have missed the bus and it is too late to think of a Population Commission or any other apex organisation at the Centre. Ironically enough, the First Five-Year Plan talked of a Population Commission 40 years back. To quote from the plan:

> It would also appear desirable to set up at a later date a Population Commission to assess the population problem, consider the different views held on the subject of population control, appraise the results of the experimenting states, recommend measures in the field of family planning to be adopted by the government and the people.

Hesitant Steps

This recommendation is understandable in the early years of economic planning and the hesitant steps we took in the field of FP in the absence of adequate information and the acceptance or otherwise of the idea of birth control by Indian masses. But after 40 years, to talk of a Population Commission to assess the population situation or achieve inter-sectoral coordination is redundant idea. In any case, it contradicts the other objectives of our planning, namely, decentralisation in our planning efforts. One more apex organisation in New Delhi or similar organisations in the state capitals will only introduce a further layer of bureaucracy and to that extent the chances of the success of the FPP will be further reduced. Such tokenism does not work. I was a member of the National Children's Board headed by the Prime Minister. I could see for myself how ineffective this mechanism was to bring about any worthwhile improvement in the lot of the children. The Board would meet for half-a-day once in six months or a year. The Prime Minister would be too busy to sit through the deliberations and nothing much happened after the Prime Minister left the meeting. Just because we want to give high priority to an issue it does not mean that we should involve the Prime Minister. In any case, health is a state subject under the Indian Constitution and FP is on the Concurrent List. As of now, the ruling parties in Uttar Pradesh, Bihar, Madhya Pradesh and Rajasthan belong to the opposition whereas the Central Government is headed by the Congress Party. This itself creates considerable friction and time and again, the question of centre-state relations crops up. A Population Commission in New Delhi and various state population commissions will only benefit the members of these commissions and not the people in any way. To me, it is a poor management solution. It is comical to see that the mighty secretaries of the Government of India see the role of the Prime Minister as a headmaster, who will discipline the various ministries so that inter-sectoral coordination is achieved in FP work!

People's Participation in the Programme

On the issue of mass involvement of people in population matters my conclusions are as follows:

1. Considering the field situation and the low credibility of the FPP and the urgent need for the Family Welfare Department to get out of the sterilisation trap, it would be desirable to merge the Department of Family Welfare with Health. In other words, *abolish the Department of Family Welfare but surely not the FPP.*

2. In order to go beyond contraceptive technology, I would suggest linking population planning with environmental planning, in order to generate a people's movement at the grassroot level. Health in the eyes of the people and also the government, has a low priority and therefore, linking family planning to health constraints the programme right from the beginning and condemns it to low priority in terms of political and administrative backup. This affects the overall perception of people. In recent years, environmental issues have come to the forefront. Ever since the Stockholm Conference in 1972, the people all over the world have become environment conscious. In India, though our concern for environment started with tigers, we moved on to forests and today we have a much better perception of the problems of environment at the national and state level. Thanks to the growing number of environmental activists and several successful Non-Government Organisations working in the field of environment, our masses have become increasingly environment-conscious. The Earth Summit 1992 at Rio has made us even more environment conscious. I believe that it is high time we get out of the health and FP nexus and relate population issues to the entire eco-system. In other words, consider population in relation to environment. This does not mean that the contraceptive services will be delivered by the Department of Environment. Our proposition of merging FP with health will still hold good. But that is only the servicing aspect. *The motivational aspect which is far more important, should be looked after by a new Ministry of Population and Environment, both at the Centre and in the states.* Instead of appointing a population commission, to my mind, it would be far more desirable to introduce this important change in the working of the government. I must hasten to add that I am not at all suggesting that henceforth, the working of the Family Welfare Department should be looked after by the Ministry of Environment. What I am suggesting is a *paradigm shift* and not an administrative order of the President of India transferring one department from one ministry to another.

3. My next proposal again concerns a paradigm shift in order to make a success of the FPP. Our focus should shift from the currently eligible couples to the *future eligible couples.* The age group, I would like to concentrate upon is 14 to 18 years. Our concern should be for the new generation, who should be imparted literacy, schooling and skills so that they contribute to human resource development in a big way. As of now, we have a fairly good programme for the age group zero to six years, i.e. the ICDS programmes. My proposal is to have an extended ICDS programmes for the age group six to along with formal schooling and a totally new programme for adolescent girls in the age group 14 to 18 years.

To me, this will be the best input to the FPP and would be the surest way of getting out of the 'sterilisation trap'.

BEYOND '*PAPAD AND ACHAR*' SYNDROMEOTARA PROJECT FOR ADOLESCENT GIRLS

Whether we like it or not, India's FPP has become primarily a women's programme. The battery of contraceptives, including the Norplant, are all meant for women. From the operational point of view, therefore, at least in the immediate future, our energies should be devoted to creating a conducive social environment which motivates the masses of our women, both in rural and urban areas, to take to family planning. At the same time, we should make relentless efforts to convert men and involve them in a big way. In a society which is dominated by men, a total reliance on a women's programme will not succeed in delivering the goods.

The FPP is centred round the sterilisation programme. Nowhere in the world, not even in China, do young women opt for the terminal method of sterilisation. There is enough statistical evidence to show that in India, by and large, women in the later stages in their reproductive life with already four or five children, opt for sterilisation and surely, this cannot have much of a dent on the birth rate. Therefore, it is being increasingly recognised that we should cater to younger women and also popularise spacing methods.

Concept Behind the Project

Conceptually, I find that this strategy will not work because *spacing methods require a very high degree of sustained motivation which is not possible under conditions of mass illiteracy*. This is not to argue for the continuation of the present emphasis on sterilisation but to forewarn our planners and policy-makers that they would be sadly mistaken if they are expecting illiterate masses to take to spacing methods, and what is more important, practise these methods effectively. On the basis of the field work in the BIMARU states, I can state that the prospects of the spacing methods under the present socio-economic conditions are far from bright. This does not mean that we should not endeavour to introduce spacing methods in the programme. In fact, the oral pill has a good chance of being accepted by the rural women even in the BIMARU states. It is agreed by everybody that the crucial factor in the FPP is motivation. However, whenever we talk of motivation, we think only of the couples in the reproductive age group. In other words, a commonsense view is taken that FP should be directed only to married couples. But there is no reason why the motivational campaign should also be directed to married couples only. Since children come only after marriage in a country like India, *the first intervention strategy is to raise the age at marriage*. While this has been conceded all along, there is no mechanism in the clinically-oriented Department of Family Welfare or for that matter, in the Ministry of Health and Family Welfare to do anything in this matter. We have faltered in taking the very first step, namely, pushing up the age at marriage. It may be recalled that in most countries (including China and also the state of Kerala in India), raising the average age at marriage of girls has played a significant role in curbing the birth rate.

Age Groups of Beneficiaries

It follows, therefore, that the target group for any intervention strategy for raising the age at marriage is not the reproductive age group but the cohort of unmarried boys and girls, who in course of time will be married couples. From this point of view, *the crucial age group is 14 to 18 years for girls*. The main strategy I wish to advocate is to formulate a sustained programme for girls in the age group of 14 to 18 years (lasting all through the five years).

I have examined the numerous schemes put out by the Central and state governments for women's development, mostly under the initiative of the Planning Commission, the Department of Women and Child Development, the Social Welfare Board, various international agencies and voluntary organisations. These schemes are rightly directed towards development of the girl child, adult women, elderly women, education and training programmes, imparting skills, generation of self-employment, income, etc. There are also schemes specifically directed towards health and nutrition. I am not aware of any scheme which concentrates on the crucial age group of 14 to 18 years in a manner which will keep these adolescent girls occupied during the entire period of five years in sustained manner, so that the age at marriage is pushed up. The only such scheme was put forward several years back by C. Gopalan, an eminent nutritionist but unfortunately, neither the Planning Commission nor the Ministry of Health and Family Welfare took note of the scheme. In my scheme, the focus is on development of skills in the modern industrial sector with the hope of absorbing the girls under this scheme in the organised industrial sector which would ensure a high level of income and prospects for a better life. This scheme even though limited to a small number of girls will have a *multiplier effect* and generate a social environment conducive to the upliftment of women, apart from its limited role in influencing the age at marriage and moderating fertility behaviour. I am not suggesting for a moment that my scheme will solve all the problems of India but it is a scheme which will not depend on the government alone or any international agency or the private sector alone. Anybody, including the government, can sponsor this project. Initially, this project will be started in selected cities and towns, district headquarters and gradually spread over to small towns and even rural areas at the Block level.

The National Institute of Public Cooperation and Child Development has listed numerous schemes for women which are in operation somewhere or other. In a recent study, the Research Centre for Women's Study in SNTD Women's University in Bombay has made an up-to-date list (1992) giving full details about various schemes operating in Maharashtra for assisting women's development.

I am aware that some of the projects for training, employment and income generation for women sponsored by the Norwegian Agency for Development (Norad) are close to my scheme of things. However, I have not been able to see any such programmes in operation in the BIMARU states. I understand that only a beginning has been made in states like Andhra Pradesh.

The basic philosophy of my scheme is that we should help women to overcome the *papad-achar* syndrome and get hooked to modern technology. In this context, I must refer to the creative ideas of Ramprasad, a distinguished scientist from the National Physical

Laboratory, who has been pleading for many years for *technological nurseries* in the hill areas of Uttar Pradesh in order to develop human and natural resources in a manner which would help India to industrialise in a big way as well as utilise neglected human resources in backward hill districts. I had the benefit of long discussions with Ramprasad on his ideas. In the absence of financial backup, his project has not taken off.

Main Elements of the Project

The main elements of my project are as follows:

Name of Agency

TARA stands for technology-oriented adolescent resource development agency, TARA means star in Sanskrit and other Indian languages and is understood by rural masses. it symbolises hope. It is not an English acronym like ICDS and ANM which unfortunately our village beneficiaries have been forced to learn because of lack of imagination on the part of our administrators, who could not think of simple vernacular words. *The proposed agency will be an autonomous independent agency outside the purview of the government.* It will be a consortium where the Government and in particular, the Department of Women and Child Development, the Ministry of Health and Family Welfare, the Ministry of Education and other ministries, as well as organisations like the Central Social Welfare Board can join and to that extent they would be given representation in the Governing Board of TARA but the main funding of these agencies should come from the private sector and in particular, the organised industry. Donations should be free of income tax liability. Any company which sponsors a TARA project would have the right to prefix its name to the centre run by the Agency: for example, if the TATA group of industries decides to run 100 TARA Centres, in the BIMARU states, these centres will be called TATA TARA Centres. If the Uttar Pradesh Government decides to run 500 such centres, these will be called U.P. Government TARA Centres.

Eligibility

1. Girls in the age group of 14 to 18 years (must be unmarried);

2. Level of education would normally be class eighth and above, with relaxation in exceptional cases;

3. Interview by Selection Committee;' and

4. If a very large number of candidates apply, some sort of lottery may be considered.

Stipend

Rs. 100 per month, for the entire duration of five years, with an annual increase of Rs. 50 per year.

Location

The TARA Centres will be located wherever there are big industries or a group of small-scale industries or other service-oriented organisations which requires skilled and semi-skilled labour. Initially, these centres may be located in districts and towns and such other places where there is considerable economic activity, regardless of the size of the town.

The TARA Centres will not be located on *free land* given by people or panchayats on the outskirts of villages. This was done by the various area projects and as result, ANM quarters were built on desolate areas, on land donated by the panchayats. This is not the way to ensure people's cooperation. Ensuring the safety of women is more important.

The TARA project should be located in places which are easily accessible and where the girls do not feel insecure. The buildings of the TARA Centres should have a distinctive architecture which should be simple, elegant and inexpensive. For example, milk booths of the Mother Dairy (under the inspired leadership of Verghese Kurein) have a distinctive arhitectural style which is modern and yet inexpensive.

If the girls come from neighbouring villages, arrangements should be made for a bus to bring these girls, properly escorted by a woman trainer to the place of work. The budget should provide such mobility. In the alternative, girls hostels may be built.

Objectives

(i)   To impart skills to selected girls in the age group of 14 to 18 years for a continuous period of five years so that at the end of the training period, these girls can be employed in the modern organised sector or they will be in a position to be self-employed in the modern sector.

(ii) To ensure that these girls get adequate formal education, on-the job training, population education, sex education, etc., so that when they get married, *after* the age of 18, they become responsible parents and they would have sufficient motivation of their own to have a small family without being given financial incentives for practising FP. Monetary incentives have led to considerable corruption. Instead of paying Rs. 5,000 per sterilisation, as is frequently advocated by some FP enthusiasts, it would be much better to invest money on an adolescent girl, by giving her a stipend of say Rs. 12,000 in five years. This will have a lasting effect on human resource development and reproductive behaviour rather than gimmicks and the advertising approach to generate motivation.

Type of Training

I cannot list here the whole range of modern activities which could be introduced in the training programme at the TARA Centres. An appropriate syllabus should be drawn up. It is important to note that there should be no set pattern for skills to be developed at these centres. Much will depend on the local resources--physical, human and financial. The objectives would be to develop the skills at the local and sub-regional levels. Obviously, the industry, which wishes to sponsor a particular TARA Centre, should be consulted in advance while drawing up the training programme.

TARA Centres should imbibe the spirit of IITs, ITIs, and Women's Polytechnics but the accent will be on socio-demographic modernisation along with learning modern skills.

Budget

I have estimated that the recurring budget of each TARA Centre would be around Rs. three lakhs per year and for the five-year period it should be around Rs. 25 lakhs, allowing for yearly increases. It should be possible for TARA to collect this amount in instalments from various private sector agencies, government departments, international agencies, etc. The non-recurring expenditure would be around another Rs. 25 lakhs. In other words, after five years, the total expenditure would be Rs. 50 lakhs or Rs. 10 lakhs per year. Most of the big industries spend this amount in a few minutes for advertising their goods on TV!

22

Population, PDS and Family Planning in Madhya Pradesh

Judging by the vast expanse of land one sees while travelling through Madhya Pradesh, one would not think that this state is facing a serious population problem. But as one walks to villages and meets the people, the intensity of the population problem unfolds itself.

Madhya Pradesh is the largest state in India, in terms of area. Uttar Pradesh, the most populous state has an area of 294,411 sq. km. compared to MP's 443,446 sq. km. Whenever the population problem is discussed, one talks invariably of Kerala. But not many people know that one district in MP alone has an area larger than that of the whole state of Kerala: Bastar district of MP has an area of 39,114 sq. km compared to Kerala's 38,863 sq.km.

The density of population in MP is only 149 persons per sq. km. compared to Kerala's 749. But this does not guarantee that things are better in MP. Access to health and education depends on the human settlement pattern and the transportation network. In Kerala, one hundred per cent of the villages are connected by road or water. The average size of a village is as large as 15,476. In MP, the average size of a village is only 709. Transportation is a major problem and during the rains, hundreds of villages are isolated.

The vastness of Madhya Pradesh, the lack of adequate roads and the small size of rural settlements make things difficult for policy makers and planners. The 45 districts of MP have 459 community development blocks, spread over 71,736 villages. In addition, there are 465 towns of all sizes. This gives an idea of the tremendous task of effectively enforcing a Public Distribution System (PDS) through fair price shops (FPS).

Let me give a few striking features about the population profile of Madhya Pradesh.

Appeared in *Financial Express*, 8 June, 1993

* MP has the highest birth rate in India (36.9 per thousand).

* MP has the highest death rate in India (12.5 per thousand).

* MP has the second highest infant mortality rate (111 per thousand live births), next only to that or Orissa (123).

* The practice of family planning is one of the lowest in India (Couple Protection Rate: 35.4 per cent).

* MP's growth rate of population during the 1981-91 decade was among the highest (26.8 per cent) in the major states of India. The all-India figure was 23.9 per cent.

* MP's urban growth rate during the 1981-91 decade (44.9 per cent) was the second highest among the major states in India. Kerala's urban growth rate of 61 per cent was more statistical than real. In absolute terms, MP's urban population (15.4 million) is double of Kerala's urban population (7.7 million).

* The literacy rate (44.2 per cent) of MP is one of the lowest in India.

* The female literacy rate (28.9 per cent) is also one of the lowest in India.

* MP has the largest tribal population (15.4 million) in India. Mizoram which has the highest percentage of tribal population (94.8 per cent) has a total population of only 0.7 million, compared to MP's 15.4 million tribal population, though the proportion of tribal population is 23.3 per cent in MP.

* MP has a sizeable scheduled caste population (9.6 million) accounting for 14.5 per cent of MP's population.

* The combined population of SC and ST accounts for 37.8 per cent of MP's population, which is the highest among the major states of India. Bihar, for example, has a combined population of 22.2 per cent of SCs and STs. Insofar as SCs and STs have the highest incidence of poverty, the proportion of vulnerable population is therefore the highest in MP among the major states in India.

* MP has one of the highest proportions of workers in the agricultural sector (76.7 per cent) compared to India's 66.8 per cent, as per 1991 Census data. The figure for UP is 72.9 per cent and for Bihar 81.1 per cent.

These figures give a bleak picture of the poverty-population syndrome in Madhya Pradesh. Nevertheless, Madhya Pradesh has a bright future when one considers the potential for development of natural resources like land, water, forests and minerals. The prospects for industrialisation in the new era of economic liberalisation are indeed promising. The prospects of balanced urbanisation are also bright when one considers the economic momentum in cities like Indore, Bhopal, Durg-Bhilai and Gwalior.

Let me now come to the people and give a glimpse of my recent visit to Madhya Pradesh. On the whole, MP has a good record of the public distribution system, specially in the remote tribal areas. Mr. G.S. Shukla, formerly Principal Secretary, Food and Civil Supplies was quite proud of the record of PDS in Madhya Pradesh. As of January 1993, there were 22,180 fair price shops (3435 in urban areas and 18,745 in rural areas). In addition, the Government runs 94 mobile vans, mostly in tribal areas which function as mobile FPS, visiting weekly markets where foodgrains, kerosene oil, matches, salt and cheap cloth are made available without insisting on a ration card.

Currently, Mr. Shukla is the Principal Secretary for Health and Family Welfare and has to deal with a more difficult subject than PDS, namely, family planning.

Several years back, I had occasion to do some intensive field work in some parts of India, in order to assess the impact of several foreign-aided projects. My conclusion was that most of these projects had failed because these were ill-conceived and showed a poor understanding of the ground reality in India. The implementation was also poor because of India's file-ridden bureaucratic procedures. The city-oriented doctors had no idea of community health and under conditions of mass illiteracy, the family planning programme did not have even a reasonable chance of success.

The donor agencies have now come out with new initiatives and are concentrating on training programme, IEC (information, education and communications), social marketing of contraceptives, increased support to NGOs, etc. Unicef has sponsored a new programme for "child survival and safe motherhood."

In my view, all these programmes are unlikely to succeed unless bold steps are taken to liquidate illiteracy and ensure minimum needs to the people (as spelt out in successive five year plans). Family planning should also be regarded as a basic need and effectively incorporated in the Minimum Needs Programme. I believe that an innovative programme can be launched to deliver family planning service through the PDS.

In the eyes of the villagers, food comes first but food without water is unimaginable. So water also has the first priority. Food has to be cooked on fire. So energy is also first priority. I am therefore not impressed when the Government says that we have enough food. Do we have enough water and energy?

During my recent visit to a village in Madhya Pradesh, a villager asked me: "Can you help us in getting food and water?" It took me some time to realise that he was not looking for a donation from me. He wanted me to tell the Madhya Pradesh Government about the plight of his village in Hoshangabad district. They had sunk many wells in their village but there was no water--not even drinking water.

In another village, I asked about the plight of tribals. The answer was: "How can they make a living? They are not allowed to use the forests where they live. They are starving. Collecting a little honey or making brooms is not enough to sustain them." There is no doubt that Madhya Pradesh's forest resources are getting depleted but what about the depletion of human resources?

In a biggish village, I saw a brand new (Health) sub-centre. I was happy to meet the energetic ANM (public health nurse doing immunisation and family planning work) who was going round the village. But in the very first house (rather a collection of huts) almost adjacent to the sub-centre which I visited, I found numerous children of all ages. I met their 80-Year old grandmother who told me that the "army" which I saw belonged to her. But she did not know how many grandchildren she had. I talked to a teenage girl who informed me that they were 12 brothers and sisters! So much for IEC! The whole village was swarming with malnourished children.

Time and again, our Prime Minister has announced that PDS will be extended to all remote development blocks in the country. The Governor of Madhya Pradesh also in his recent meeting with Commissioners, wanted PDS to function efficiently.

In my scheme of things, PDS offers the best opportunity to introduce a system of Family Register which should pool together the following data:

(a) number of members in the household, their sex and age (as per the present system of ration card);

(b) Health card which will be filled up every time a member of the household visits a primary health centre or sub-centre (this is done even now but not systematically).

(c) Education card which gives details of boys and girls in the age group 6-14 and also records whether they go to school or not (this is not done at present).

(d) Employment card which will list adults looking for employment.

(e) Loan card/Beneficiary card which will list all benefits which the household received under various schemes of the Government.

(f) Old age card which will separately list persons 65 years and above, and

(g) Birth, Death and Marriage Registration card which will record births, deaths and marriages systematically.

To me, all these items consttitute Family Welfare. At present, family welfare means sterilisation!

The Family Register will feed the basic information on a fortnightly basis (ration card holders have to get their supplies every fortnight) to various programme officers operating at the Block level. The convergence of all programmes and their effective co-ordination with the cooperation of panchayats and block development officers will revolutionise both PDS and family planning. I am not suggesting a data collecting mechanism but a true public distribution system which can be monitored at the block level without conducting grandiose statistical surveys and hiring international consultants.

SECTION V

VULNERABLE POPULATION

23

Under the Shadow
of Illiteracy

At the recent Inter-Parliamentary Union's Conference (New Delhi 12-17 April, 1992), a delegate from Finland pointed out that an illiterate person cannot get married in Finland. It was the Finnish way of enforcing universal literacy. It was the sanction of social custom and not the legal sanction which made literacy a prerequisite for marriage.

The IPU Conference was not discussing marriage but the need for education for a better understanding of democratic values. Dr. Eimi Watanabe, Unicef Representative in India, in her special address to the conference emphasised the urgency of universalisation of primary education as a critical investment in socio-economic development and an essential ingradient in promoting democratic values.

Is is unfortunate that India continues to live under the shadow of illiteracy. India is in fact the largest illiterate country in the world today (this is because of the near 100 percent literacy rate of China)

The 1991 Census of India--the last decadal census in the 20th century--records that the great majority of Indian females are illiterate though in the case of males, it is the other way about. Hence, while 64 per cent of the males are literate, 61 percent of the females are illiterate.

The data on literacy is quite shocking if one looks at the detailed tables. The mere fact that in India as a whole, 52 per cent of the population is literate should not cause rejoicing, as it did in the Ministry of Human Resource Development, when the first census results were declared. The Registrar-General makes a cautious comment when he says:

"It will be interesting to mention here that for the first time in the history of census taking in India , the number of literates has surpassed the number of illiterates. In the case of females, however, the trend of more illiterates than literates continues".

Appeared in *Financial Express*, 27 April, 1993

For making comparisons between 1981 and 1991, the all-India tables exclude Assam (where no census was taken in 1981) and Jammu and Kashmir (where no census was taken in 1991).

The figures for 1981 and 1991 are also made comparable by adjusting the age group 7 and above (in 1981 the literates referres to the age group 5 and above while in 1991. they referred to 7 and above)

The literacy data may be summed up as follows:

The overall literacy rate increased from 43.7 per cent in 1981 to 52.2 per cent in 1991.

The male literacy rate increased from 56.5 per cent to 64.2 per cent during this decade.

The female literacy rate increased fom 29.9 per cent to 39.2 per cent during this period.

The overall rural literacy rate increased from 36.1 per cent in 1981 to 44.5 per cent during this decade.

The rural female literacy rate increased from 21.8 per cent to 30.4 per cent.

The overall urban literacy rate increased from 67.3 per cent in 1981 to 73.0 per cent in 1991.

The urban male literacy rate increased from 76.8 per cent to 81.1 per cent during 1981-91.

The urban female literacy rate increased from 56.4 per cent to 63.9 per cent.

Let me now make a few brief comments on the literacy data:

The first shocking fact is that even in 1991 there are more illiterate females (age 7 plus) than literate females.

There were 196 illiterate females compared to 126 literate females.

The number of illiterate females in India increased from 181 million in 1981 to 196 mitllion in 1991, while the number of illiterate males increased from 121 million in 1981 to 125 million in 1991. But in the case of males, the number of literates in 1991 was much higher than the number of illiterate (224 million literates and 125 million illiterates.)

In rural areas, the gap between male and female literacy rates was 27.9 per cent points in 1981; it decreased marginally to 27.4 percent points in 1991.

Analysis of state-wise literacy data indicate that the male literacy rate in 1991 was more than 50 per cent in all the states and UTs but the female literacy rate was less than 50 per cent in the following states and UTs--Andhra Pradesh (32.7), Arunachal Pradesh (29.7), Assam (43.0), Bihar (22.9), Gujarat (48.6). Haryana (40.5), Karnataka (44.3), Madnya Pradesh (28.9), Manipur (47.6), Meghalaya (44.9), Orissa (34.7), Rajasthan (20. 4), Sikkim (46.7), Tripura (49.7), Uttar Pradesh (25.3) and West Bengal (46.6). In Dadra and Nagar Haveli, the literacy rate for females was 27 per cent.

What is surprising is that the female literacy rate is below 50 per cent not only in State like Rajasthan, Bihar, Uttar Pradesh and Madhya Pradesh but also in States like Gujarat, Karnataka and West Bengal which are otherwise considered progressive.

The pride of place goes to Kerala where the male literacy rate is 93.6 per cent and the female literacry rate is 86.2 per cent, according to 1991 census. Since then, literacy rates have improved to near 100 per cent in all the districts of Kerala, thanks to the Literacy Mission.

The male-female disparity in literacy rates can be studied by calculating the sex ratio of literates (i.e. females literates per 1000 male literates). In Kerala, this ratio was 965 while in Rajasthan it was only 338.

The Registrar-General analyses the literacy data at the district level (for 452 districts, excluding Jammu & Kashmir) and concludes that districts with sex ratio of 300 or less (literate females per 1000 literate males) are concentrated in only four States--Rajasthan (10 Districts), Uttar Pradesh (8), Madhya Pradesh (3), Bhiar (2), or 23 districts in all.

In short, these four states deserve the highest priority from the point of view of female literacy. The 1991 Census data on literacy fully confirm my earlier diagnosis of India's population problem, the crux of which lies in the four States of Bihar, Madhya Pradesh, Rajasthan and Uttar Pradesh (BIMARU States).

In my view, India's family planning programme will not succeed unless we make a forntal attack on illiteracy in these four States which account for 40 per cent of India's population.

Using the acronym BIMARU to describe all demographically vulnerable districts, we get the following picture (Table 23.1) from the Registrar General's data.

It my be noted that the proportion of population aged 0-6 years gives and idea of the fertility rate. The Registrar General rightly concludes: "It can, therefore, be safely deduced that female literacy has a direct and strong effect on fertility".

One can notice from the table that about one-third of the population 0-6 years in India is concentrated in 125 districts which claim only 13.5 per cent of the female literates in India. These 125 districts must be tackled on a priority basis. But I doubt if distributing contraceptives would make a dent on the birth rate unless the first step of ensuring near 100 per cent literacy for males and females is taken.

Table 23.1: PER CENT DISTRIBUTION OF FEMALE LITERATES AND POPULATION AGED 0-6 YEARS BY FEMALE LITERACY RATE BY THE DISTRICT IN WHICH THEY RESIDE, 1991.

Range of female literacy rate (per cent)	Districts	Share of country's female literates	Share of country's population aged 0-6 Years
Total	452	100.00	100.00
Upto 25.00	125	13.52	32.41
25.01--35.00	92	14.13	20.91
35.01--45.00	90	18.00	17.04
45.01--55.00	67	20.46	14.00
55.01--65.00	43	16.29	9.27
65.01& Above	35	17.60	6.37

* Excludes 14 districts of Jammu & Kashmir

24

Gender Issues:
Rhetoric and Reality

Preparations for the fourth United Nations World conference on Women have started with the appointment of Mrs. Gerrude Mongella as the Secretary General. She was a Minister and an active politician in Tanzania and lately Ambassador of Tanzania in India. The Conference is scheduled to be held in Beijing in 1995. The main theme of this conference is "action for equality, development and peace".

The Office of UNIFEM in New Delhi organised a lively Workshop (on February 2) involving selected scholars, administrators and activists from NGOs to discuss the agent for the Beijing Conference for a benefit of Mrs. Mongella. "For a long we have discussed women's issues. Every issue is a women's issue and so also it is a man's issue. Let us discuss women's perspectives", thundered Dr. Vina Majumdar, India leading scholar on women and development. Ms. Madhu Bala Nath, Executive Director of UNIFEM guided the deliberations with UN style understatement. Mrs. Padma Seth, a spirited member of the National Commission for Women asserted that woman should use their voting power effectively and in fact, they should vote for women only. In response to this, Mrs. Mongella said: "No, we have to get into every party and make sure that we run it." Madhu Bala Nath summarised the discussion by saying that the Beijing Conference should have as agenda item called "women in politics".

In this context, the most thought-provoking observation was made by Vina Majumdar who said that the 72nd and 73rd Amendments to the Constitution passed by Parliament recently make it mandatory for all local government bodies and panchayats to have 33 per cent of the seats reserved for women. This will give tremendous power to women. In fact, the subject of women and child development has been brought under the purview of the panchayats and to that extent, the Department of Women and Child Development of the Central Government would have to shed much of its powers.

Appeared in *Financial Express*, 10 February, 1993

This is indeed a happy development and the Government and Parliament deserve congratulations on passing these amendments for ushering in Panchayat Raj. But what disturbs me greatly is the shocking state of female literacy revealed by the 1991 Census of India. Can Panchayat Raj be effective with this level of illiteracy? There are only two states in India, namely Kerala and Mizoram where more than 75 per cent of the females are literate but these are small states. On the other hand, in the large states of Uttar Pradesh, Bihar, Madhya Pradesh and Rajasthan, the female literacy rate is extremely low (For details, see Table 2.1).

The level of literacy has a direct bearing on infant mortality rate and birth rate, as also the practice of family planning. Kerala which has the highest literacy rate has also the lowest infant mortality rate and the lowest birth rate (barring Goa which is a tiny state). Most developed countries have an infant mortality rate (IMR) of well below 30 per thousand (the lowest IMR is in Japan, namely, only four per thousand) and an IMR of more than 60 is considered very bad and an IMR of over 100 is considered unacceptable in the modern world. In Orissa, the IMR is as high as 126 while in Madhya Pradesh it is 122.

For many   years, Parliament, the Planning Commission and the Ministry of Health and Family Welfare have adhered to a birth rate target of 21 per thousand for the country as a whole by the year 2000. The actual birth rate in Kerala in 1990 was 18.1 per thousand and in Tamil Nadu it was 20.7. Kerala and Tamil Nadu are the flagships. Sadly enough, the birth rate is higher than 30 per thousand in the large states of Uttar Pradesh, Bihar, Madhya Pradesh and Rajasthan. It is most unlikely that by the year 2000, the birth rate in these states would be 21 per thousand.

The inescapable conclusion is that whether we want effective Panchayat Raj, lower infant mortality rates and lower birth rates, the liquidation of illiteracy among women is absolutely essential. At least for India, high on the agenda of women's development must be the imperative of one hundred per cent literacy in the shortest possible time. At the UNIFEM workshop, Mrs. Ela Bhatt, the celebrated social worker, asserted that "the best contraceptive is education coupled with socio-economic development."

I have been a critic of the IEC (Information, Education, Communication) strategy advocated by foreign funding agencies for making India's family planing programme a success. On the basis of my analysis of census data as well as my field work throughout India, I feel that IEC expenditure is a waste of money. Why not go to the root cause of our malady? I would urge all donor agencies to put their money in a bold and massive programme for the eradication of illiteracy in the next three years. This is a task which is beyond the competence of India's bureaucracy. The KSSP model in Kerala has demonstrated what total mobilisation can do in literacy missions and science jathhas.

Hope lies with NGOs and panchayats. Instead of parrot-like repetition of the need for "making family planning people's movement" (which to me is an illusion under conditions of mass illiteracy), why not we talk of a people's movement for attaining total literacy. Of late, the Department of Family Welfare is emphasising spacing methods and their focus is on younger couples. By definition, spacing methods require sustained motivation and this is not possible under conditions of mass illiteracy. When will the Family Welfare Department realise that spreading education is good for family planning motivation and in the absence of motivation no family planning method would succeed, no matter how good is the contraceptive technology. Obviously, the Family Welfare Department does not consider this to be their legitimate sphere of activity. It is the task of the Education Ministry at the Centre and in the states. That is why, there is so much talk of "inter-sectoral coordination." But these are palliatives. They do not strike at the root of the problem.

For 40 years, we have tried to curb the birth rate significantly to meet the challenge of population explosion and we have failed in our efforts. And yet we are not on the right track. Men have almost abandoned family planning. It is basically a women's programme (IUD, oral pill, norplant, and of course, female sterilisation). Women are the victims of dowry, bride burning and amniocentesis and abortion. Literacy alone cannot solve all these problems but without literacy, women are doomed. And men too.

| 25 |

Women in India's Workforce--
Increasing Feminine Tilt

Women activists and scholars working on women and development have been constantly wanting to know why the Indians census records such low figures for women workers (reflected in the work force participation rate). We all know that women in rural areas work (and work hard) on the farm, in household industries and, of course, at home, but if one were to go by census figures, one would think that our rural women are an idle lot.

Census experts have failed to give a convincing explanation of this phenomenon which is not only true of India but of many other developing countries of the world. And even in the developed countries, there is not enough recognition of the contribution of women to development.

When the preparations for the 1991 census of India were on, women's organisations and several individual scholars approached the Census Commisioner to devise methods to get a more accurate coverage of women workers in the 1991 census. Mr. A.R. Nanda, the Census Commissioner, recognised this problem and wrote detailed instructions in the manual for census enumerators urging them to ask probing questions about women so as to get a proper account of women workers, whether they were "main" (principal) workers or "marginal" (subsidiary) workers. His message was clear: women are not to be automatically recorded as house wives (and therefore, as non-workers) but every effort should be made to ascertain the type of productive economic activity in which they are engaged, apart from their normal household duties. Unpaid work is also work.

To double check, the Census Commissioner amplified the question on work as follows: "Did you work any time at all last year? (including unpaid work on farm or in family enterprise?).. In short, the census questionnaires itself was suitably worded to "net" more women workers.

<hr>

Appeared in *Financial Express*, 21 April, 1992

Another significant development was the keen interest taken by the United Nations Development Fund for Women (UNIFEM). Special posters and short TV documentary films were designed by UNIFEM and made available to the Census Commissioner and Doordarshan. The posters were widely distributed and the national TV network showed short films on the type of women's work which should be recorded in the census enumeration (February-March 1991).

The office of the Registrar General has recently published the first set of provisional tables giving population totals for workers by sex and rural/urban residence (Census Paper 3 of 1991).

Before we proceed further, it is necessary to discuss briefly the basic concepts. "Work" is defined as "participation in any economically productive activity... which also includes unpaid work on farm or in family enterprise". It must be noted that work as defined in the Census does not include non-market economic activities. For example, processing of primary commodities for own consumption is excluded from the purview of economic activities as work.

In spite of the sincere attempt made by the Census authorities to collect reliable data on women's work, it is difficult to know if, in fact, the instructions given by the Census Commissioner were properly followed and if the probing questions were indeed asked, in order to get a more complete coverage of women's economic activities, specially in the rural areas. We must also await more detailed tables giving data for different age groups and also data on unemployment before we can comment with some confidence on these complex methodological issues.

A quick look at the Census tables available so far reveals that the work participation rate (WPR) for females has gone up from 19.7 per cent in 1981 to 22.7 per cent in 1991. In the rural areas, the female WPR has gone up from 23.1 per cent in 1981 to 27.2 per cent in 1991 and in urban areas, the female WPR has gone up from 8.3 per cent in 1981 to 9.7 in 1991 (these figures exclude Assam where no census was taken in 1981 and Jammu & Kashmir where no census was taken in 1991).

In contrast, the male work participation rate has gone down slightly. It was 52.6 per cent in 1981 which came down to 51.6 per cent in 1991. In rural areas, the male WPR declined from 53.8 per cent in 1981 to 52.5 per cent in 1991 while in the urban areas, there was virtual stagnation: the male WPR was 49.1 per cent in 1981 and 49.0 per cent in 1991.

Another way looking at the figures is to calculate the percentage increase in the number of workers during 1981-91. In India as a whole, the percentage of male workers increased by 21.4 per cent during this decade, while the increase in female workers was of the order of 42.3 per cent.

The contrast is even sharper when we consider statewise figures. For example, in UP, the number of male workers increased by 22.2 per cent, while the number of female workers increased by 99.6 per cent during 1981-91. In Kerala, the male workers increased by 21.0 per cent while the female workers increased by only 16.5 per cent.

One would get a better picture when the figures for unemployment are released by the Registrar General. A detailed study of the Statewise and district-wise figures, along with relevant economic indicators is necessary in order to answer questions like the following:

Is the increase in the number of female workers a purely statistical phenomenon because of improvement in methodology?

Does this increase reflect the growing emancipation of women and their greater involvement in economic activity?

Or does it indicate economic stagnation, unemployment, inflation and allied factors compelling women to work?

These are difficult questions to answer. The Registrar General in his comments has not given any explanation for this phenomenon, except to say that "the WPR of females has shown a definite increase by over three percentage points during the last decade. "He does observe, however, that "A part of the increase in the female work participation rate may be attributed to the efforts made to net more female workers in the 1991 census."

The 1991 census tables reveal that out of a total 29.5 million "marginal" workers, 25.2 million were female workers. In the case of "main" workers, out of a total of 285.4 million workers, 66.2 million were female workers. That is to say, 23.2 per cent of the main workers were females, while 85.4 per cent of the marginal workers were females. Thus, marginal work is mainly the domain of females.

It is important to note the census definition of "main" work and "marginal" work: Those who worked for more than six months or more than 183 days were called main workers and those who worked for less than six months or 183 days were called marginal workers. The term "marginal" has been resented by many scholars (Are we marginalising women). The National Sample Survey uses the expression 'subsidary-status workers'.

While considering women's work, we have to consider a number of socio-cultural factors which explain the sharp differences in the work force participation rates in different parts of India. Generally speaking, there is a tendency for married women to report themselves primarily as housewives. This is even more true when the respondent is the male head of the household. It often hurts the male ego of a rural farmer to say that his wife works on the farm. It is very difficult to understand why in rural Punjab only 7 per cent of women in rural areas were recorded as workers whereas in rural Andhra Pradesh, the figure was 43 per cent. What is even more surprising is that in the enlightened State of Kerala, the rural female work participation rate was only 18 per cent. In contrast, in the north-eastern States, the rural female participation rates are high. For example, it was 56 per cent in Sikkim, 48 per cent in Mizoram and 43 per cent in Nagaland.

Much depends on the self-perception of women and their status in society, when the census enumerators seeks to ascertain if a women is just a housewife or a productive worker as well. And, of course, so much depends on the census enumerator and his or her own perception of women's work.

There is no doubt that socio-cultural factors play an important role in reporting women's economic activities. Caste too is an important factor in the rural areas of many parts of India.

B.K. Roy Burman, a noted social anthropologist, observes that a higher participation rate of females in the primary sector in rural areas is indicative of their worsening economic situation and not an improved status.

It is just possible that the increasing feminine tilt in India's work force is really a symptom of economic stagnation and unemployment which are pushing women into the labour force, particularly in the impoverished unorganised sector (reflected in the predominant position of women as marginal workers). On the other hand, one could argue that the increase in the participation rate of women in economic activity is indicative of the impact of urbanisation, modernisation and the movement for the emancipation of women.

We need indepth studies on this complex phenomenon.

26

Child Care and Human Resource Development

The Indian carpet industry has received adverse attention all over the world because of the merciless exploitation of children who are employed in making the carpets. There are numerous other sinister examples of child labour.

The carpet industry is not the sum-total of the woes of child labour in India. There are other dimensions. A new and ingenious definition of child labour was given recently by Dr. C. Gopalan, the famous nutritionist. To quote from his brilliant lecture (John Barnabas Memorial Lecture, New Delhi, 29 March, 1992).

"We witness the sad spectacle of millions of 'children' (girls of 14 to 18 years) compelled to engage in bearing and child-rearing even before they have had a chance to complete their own physical growth and development and attain adulthood. This is 'child labour' at its worst in more senses than one. It is labour which carries far greater risks than some of the other forms of child labour over which there is public outcry".

Dr. Gopalan's thesis goes much beyond the pun on the word 'labour'. He is justified in condemning the labour pain forced by society on adolescent girls giving birth to children thereby impairing the health of both mother and child. The first step in improving the situation is to raise the age at marriage of girls. For many years, Dr. Gopalan has been pleading for imaginative incentive schemes like delayed marriage bonus, delayed maternity bonus, etc. But the Finance Ministry has never given serious consideration to such schemes. The Department of Family Welfare is centred round the sterilisation programme and has been totally ineffective in doing anything about raising the age at marriage.

I have been arguing for years that India's family planning programme is conceptually unsound. It concentrates on the age group of 35 plus women with 5 to 6 children. It should be obvious that this strategy cannot bring about a significant dent on the birth

Appeared in *Financial Express*, 13 April, 1993

rate. Our focus should be on the adolescent girls in age group 14 to 18 years. These girls should be unmarried. The Family Welfare Department understands this logic but they assume that their concern is with *married* women and family planning. Therefore nothing happens and we continue to run an ineffective family planning programme.

Dr. Gopalan makes this point forcefully when he says:

"What we sorely need are imaginative programmes for equipping adolescent girls for good motherhood and productive citizenship, well before they are trapped into marriage and maternity. It is our total neglect of the care of the adolescent that has been responsible for our poor performance in the fields of maternal/child health and family planning."

Of late, 'safe motherhood' and 'child survival' are international slogans for Third World countries and donor agencies are pouring in money for such programmes. It has just been reported that the International Development Research Centre (IDRC) of Canada will provide a grant of Rs.7.2 crores for India's Child Survival and Safe Motherhood (CSSM) project. This ambitious scheme will cover all the districts of India and will be jointly sponsored by the Government of India and UNICEF.

Dr. Gopalan's vision extends much beyond child *survival*. His focus is on child *health* and nutrition. He asserts:

"We must strive for optimal 'child health and nutrition' and not settle for just 'child survival' for 'good motherhood' and not for just as 'a safe' one!" His argument is that the inputs needed for averting deaths are far less than those needed for promotion of health and nutrition.

For Dr. Gopalan, child development is at least as important as Atomic Energy or Space Research. He concludes by saying: "No change can be more important, more prestigious, and more onerous, than the overalls responsibility for the promotion of Nutrition and Child Health in the country. This charge must legitimately belong to no less an authority than the nation's Prime Minister".

Dr. Gopalan makes a case for the creation of a National Resource Centre for Nutrition and Child Development. Obviously he is not satisfied with the National Institute of Public Co-operation and Child Development (NIPCCD). It is unfortunate that institutions like NIPCCD and NIHFW (National Institute of Health and Family Planning) have been rendered by the funding Ministries into subservient secretariats, devoid of bold and creative thinking. The scientists and research workers have been marginalised. Yet, without the backup of independent research, the success of ambitious government programmes will be in jeopardy.

Let me give just one example of the need for sustained research of high calibre to back up government programmes. One of the most disturbing results of the 1991 Census of India, was the totally unexpected decline in sex ratio (females per thousand males) from 934 in 1981 to 929 in 1991. The figure of 929 was based on the *provisional* census count. The *final* figure is even more dismal: it is 927 in 1991. The question one can legitimately ask is: why has the female ratio (sex-ratio) gone down during the last decade--a decade marked by numerous schemes for women and children, and national and international conferences to focus attention on the girl child and the adolescent girl?

Numerous causes have been mentioned for the decline in the female ratio. For example, under-enumeration of girls and women in the Indian census. But this is *not a new* phenomenon. Even in the 1881 Census--more than a hundred years back--this phenomenon was observed. But is it a fact that there is *increasing* under-enumeration of women in the Indian census? In other words, is Indian society becoming more and more regressive? It does not appear to me that under-enumeration can be the real cause of the declining sex ratio.

Another factor which is invariably mentioned is the neglect of the girl child and the higher mortality levels of the girls compared to the boys and also the higher mortality of females up to the age 35 or 50 compared to the males. But this was true even in 1981. Only if the male-female mortality differential increase, will the sex ratio decline. But recent data (SRS) released by the Registrar General do not show this trend

Another factor mentioned is the spread of amniocentesis (sex-determination tests) leading to widespread abortion of the female fetus. But such facilities do not exist all over India, particularly in the rural areas (though of late, in the rural areas of Haryana people have increasing access to ultrasound and amniocentesis facilities) and this is unlikely to be responsible for the decline in the sex ratio all over India.

A totally new factor which has been mentioned of late is the change in the sex ratio *at birth*. In the absence of an effective system of birth registration and a small proportion of births which take place in hospitals, data on sex ratio at birth are very scanty. If *increasingly* more boys are born than girls, and more girls die than boys in early ages, the sex ratio will go down.

The Registrar General has given some data on sex ratio at birth, which show considerable variation but a trend of declining sex ratio at birth. In other words, increasingly more boys are born than girls over the years. It is generally assumed all over the world that the sex ratio at birth remains constant. But this may not be true in India.

The Registrar General points out that the phenomenon of declining sex ratio at birth has been noticed in several other countries also (e.g. China and the Republic of Korea). He too is not able to explain this phenomenon. The quote him: "One of the hypotheses that is being examined seriously everywhere is whether pre-natal sex-determination was widely prevalent".

To analyse this phenomenon, one should have detailed data cross-classified by age groups. The final tables of 1991 census (Census Paper No.2 of 1992) do present data for the age group 0-6 years. This was a priority table in order to calculate the literacy rate for the age group 7 + (as per the new definition of literacy in the 1991 Census).

The distressing fact is that the female ratio for the age-group 0-6 has declined in India (except in 1981) from one census years to another (see Table 26.1).

Table 26.1: Sex Ratio (females per 1000 males) of total population and population aged 0-6 years

State		1961	1971	1981	1991
India	T Pop	943	931	935	927
(excluding Assam	0-6	976	964	962	945
& Jammu & Kashmir)					
Andhra Pradesh	T Pop	981	977	975	972
	0-6	1002	990	992	974
Bihar	T Pop	994	954	946	911
	0-6	988	964	981	959
Gujarat	T Pop	940	934	942	934
	0-6	955	946	947	928
Haryana	T Pop	868	867	870	865
	0-6	910	898	902	879
Karnataka	T Pop	959	957	963	960
	0-6	987	978	975	960
Kerala	T Pop	1022	1016	1032	1036
	0-6	972	976	970	958
Madhya Pradesh	T Pop	953	941	941	931
	0-6	982	976	978	952
Maharashtra	T Pop	936	930	937	934
	0-6	978	972	956	946
Orissa	T Pop	1001	988	981	971
	0-6	1035	1168	995	967
Punjab	T Pop	854	865	879	882
	0-6	894	899	908	875
Rajasthan	T Pop	908	911	919	910
	0-6	951	933	954	916
Tamil Nadu	T Pop	992	978	977	974
	0-6	985	974	967	948
Uttar Pradesh	T Pop	909	879	885	879
	0-6	946	923	935	928
West Bengal	T Pop	878	891	911	917
	0-6	1008	1010	981	967

Source : Census of India, 1991, Series 1, Paper 2 of 1992 **Final Population Totals: Brief Analysis of Primary Census Abstract, p.13.**

As the sex ratio for the States is affected by migration, the figure should be interpreted with caution. It will be seen that the sex ratio for the age group 0-6 years has declined sharply in Rajasthan, Madhya Pradesh and Punjab.

At the end of the story, one is still lost about the real cause of the decline in the female ratio!

27

1993--The Year of Indigenous Peoples

The United Nations General Assembly has declared 1993 as the international Year of the Indigenous Peoples. We in India are always eager or celebrate special days, weeks and years. In an earlier chapter, I commented on the observance of the World Population Day (11 July) in India, marked by ritual and rhetoric.

A Working Group of the United Nations has prepared a "Draft Universal Declaration of the Rights of Indigenous Peoples" which reads beautiful. It is not known whether the Government of India will endorse it when it comes up before the United Nations General Assembly next year. But has the Government examined this "harmless" document?

Professor B.K. Roy Burman, the well-known social anthropologist and a former Nehru Fellow has serious misgiving about the Draft Declaration. In his keynote address to a national symposium "who are the indigenous and tribal people of India" (April, 1992) he observed:

"It would be unfortunate if India, which has played for long a vanguard role in the anti-colonial struggle and espoused the vision of a new international order, remains uninvolved in the universal Declaration of Indigenous Rights because of the absence of clear indication of the differences between indigenous and tribal... The people and the Government of India should take the initiative to get the criteria of determination of the 'indigenous' incorporated in the Universal Declaration of the Indigenous Rights and substantive portions of the Declaration suitably amended."

It is not merely the semantic difference between "indigenous" and "tribal" which should worry us. There are substantial issues which merit detailed study and discussion. For example, the draft Declaration of the Rights of Indigenous Peoples begins with the following sentence: "Indigenous peoples have the right to self-determination, in accordance with international law." Does this imply that they have a right to secession?

Appeared in *Financial Express*, 11 August, 1992

In a country like India, which has a large tribal population and if only the tribal people are equated with indigenous population, what will happen if a number of tribes are persuaded by vested interests to be independent of India and invoke the United Nations Declaration?

It seems that the Chairman of the United Nations Working Group on Indigenous People (which has a weak representation from Asian countries) clarified that "the right of self-determination does not include the right of secession" but Roy Burman points out that this clarification has NOT been incorporated in the draft Declaration, while the reference to international law negates this clarification.

Another disturbing point relates to clause 18 in the draft Declaration which says: Indigenous peoples have the right to special measure for protection, as intellectual property, of their traditional cultural manifestation, such as literature, designs, visual and performing arts, medicines and knowledge of the useful properties of fauna and flora. "Ironically enough, this clause was later revised and the reference to "intellectual property" was deleted. The new version says: "In no case may an indigenous people be deprived of its means of subsistence. The right to just and fair compensation, if they have been so deprived."

India is already a victim of recent moves in the West regarding intellectual property rights. In any case, it is not clear why the intellectual property rights should be removed in the case of indigenous peoples in the draft Declaration when our objective is to ensure a better deal to these people. Roy Burman links up this revision to the refusal of the world Intellectual Property Organisation to recognise the entitlement of the indigenous people.

Another controversial issue concerns the ramifications of international aid, including the role of World Bank, UN Agencies and even multinational companies. Clause 13 of the draft Declaration sounds quite harmless: "Indigenous peoples have the right to adequate financial and technical assistance, from States and through international cooperation, to pursue freely their own economic, social and cultural development...."

Many things can happen in the name of international cooperation. The construction of big river valley dams, the uprooting of the tribal population and the "development' at the cost of the local people are issues which have yet to be resolved as in the case of the Narmada Valley project aided by the World Bank.

In this context, I must refer to an excellent monograph on "Indigenous Vision: Peoples of India--Attitudes to the Environment" brought out by India International Centre in their Quarterly Journal (Spring Summer 1992). In particular, one must read the perceptive interview given by the well-known environmental activist, Medha Patkar to Geeti Sen and Dunu Roy. It may be recalled that Medha Patkar is working for her Ph.D. on "Economic Development and its Impact on Traditional Tribal Societies", at the Tata Institute of Social Science. Today she is the guiding spirt of the *Narmada Bachao Andolan* which is truly a people's movement. She has certainly shaken the World Bank.

Enough has been written on the exploitation of the forests and tribal population in the name of development. Roy Burman points out that recently the Global Environmental Facility (GEF), an ancillary of the United Nations and the World Bank, have been accused of colluding and causing damage to bio-diversity in Congo and robbing the rights of the pygmies.

The move to designate 1993 as the year of the indigenous peoples is no doubt a good move on the part of the United Nations but the member countries must ensure that the proposed Declaration of the Rights of the indigenous Peoples does in fact help these people and not result in creating chaos by encouraging all types of groups operating in the name of tribal communities to invoke United Nations help and also not result in hooking up these communities to multinational agencies in the name of development. These may be exaggerated fears expressed by experts like Roy Burman. Nevertheless, there is a good case for our Prime Minister to take interest in this subject and not leave important issues to officers in the Ministry of Welfare or External Affairs. Time and again, we are confronted with a demand for independent states from various communities. Then there is an unending demand for inclusion of several communities in the list of Scheduled Castes and Scheduled Tribes. We are also too familiar with the demand for reservation by the Backward Classes and the controversy generated by the Mandal Commission report.

The Indian Association for the Study of Population (IASP) had taken the initiative in the past in organising two Regional conferences on Tribal demography, one in Shillong, dealing with North-East India and the other in Bhopal, dealing with Central India. Two volumes on Tribal Demography have been published (edited by Ashish Bose and others). An important methodological point to be noted in this context is the trend towards retribalisation or the attempt by some communities to get recorded as "tribal" to get advantage of the special consideration given to weaker sections of the population in our Constitution. This often results in inflated census figures for certain tribes. Apart from this, there is a demand for inclusion of several communities in the list of tribes and the Government has modified its list from time to time. Another point to note is that a community may be recognised as a tribe in one state but not all over India. Last week, (on 5th August 1992) there was a demonstration by Banjara women at the Boat Club in New Delhi, for inclusion of Banjaras as a Scheduled tribe (Banjaras are recognised as a tribe but not all over India.)

Tribal issues cannot be ignored just because the tribal population of India constitutes less than eight per cent of India's total population. In absolute terms, it means roughly a tribal population of 65 to 70 million. Besides, most of our major national resources are concentrated in areas inhabited by tribals. The 1991 Census figures would be available soon. Please see Tables 27.1 & 27.2 for 1991 Census data on Scheduled castes and Scheduled tribes. Meanwhile, we give the position as of 1981.

Table 27.1: Size and Distribution of Tribal Population, 1981

State/UT	Population	Percentage of Tribal population w.r.t.	
		Total Tribals	Total population
INDIA	51,628,638	100.00	7.76
1. Andhra Pradesh	3,176,001	6.15	5.93
2. Bihar	5,810,867	11.26	8.31
3. Gujarat	4,848,586	9.39	14.22
4. Himachal Pradesh	197,263	0.38	4.61
5. Karnataka	1,825,203	3.54	4.91
6. Kerala	261,475	0.51	1.03
7. Madhya Pradesh	11,987,031	23.22	22.97
8. Maharashtra	5,772,038	11.18	9.19
9. Manipur	387,977	0.75	27.30
10. Meghalaya	1,076,345	2.09	80.58
11. Nagaland	650,885	1.26	83.99
12. Orissa	5,915,067	11.46	22.43
13. Rajasthan	4,183,124	8.10	12.21
14. Sikkim	73,623	0.14	23.27
15. Tamil Nadu	520,226	1.01	1.07
16. Tripura	583,920	1.13	28.44
17. Uttar Pradesh	232,705	0.45	0.21
18. West Bengal	3,070,672	5.95	5.63
19. Andaman & Nicobar Islands	22,361	0.04	11.85
20. Arunachal Pradesh	441,167	0.85	69.82
21. Dadra & Nagar Haveli	81,714	0.16	78.82
22. Goa, Daman & Diu	10,721	0.02	0.99
23. Lakshadweep	37,760	0.07	93.82
24. Mizoram	461,907	0.89	93.55

NB: This table excludes Assam where there was no census enumeration in 1981.

Source: Ashish Bose et al (Eds) **Demography of Tribal Development, IASP,** 1990, P.77.

(PER CENT)

Table 27.2: Growth of Tribal Population, 1961-71 And 1971-81

Region/State/UT	Tribal Population		Total Population	
	1961-71	*1971-81*	*1961-71*	*1971-81*
INDIA	25.3	30.6	25.5	24.3
NORTH-EASTERN	31.1	31.5	35.0	35.4
Assam	38.0	--	35.0	--
Manipur	34.3	16.0	37.5	32.5
Meghalaya	27.4	32.2	31.5	32.0
Nagaland	33.3	42.2	39.9	50.0
Tripura	25.1	29.6	36.3	31.9
Arunachal Pradesh	23.9	19.4	38.9	35.1
Mizoram	20.0	47.4	24.9	48.5
EASTERN	19.6	17.3	23.9	23.0
Bihar	17.3	17.8	21.3	24.1
Orissa	20.1	16.6	25.1	20.2
West Bengal	23.3	18.0	26.9	23.2
NORTHERN	15.8	26.4	23.0	25.4
Himalchal Pradesh	15.8	39.3	23.0	23.7
Uttar Pradesh	--	17.2	--	25.5
CENTRAL	25.6	22.1	28.7	25.3
Madhya Pradesh	25.6	22.1	28.7	25.3
WESTERN	30.8	37.9	28.1	27.5
Gujarat	35.6	29.1	29.4	27.7
Maharashtra	23.2	30.3	27.5	24.5
Rajasthan	32.9	33.4	27.8	33.0
Dadra & Nagar Haveli	25.7	24.9	28.0	39.8
Goa, Daman & diu	--	40.1	--	26.7
SOUTHERN	24.7	84.7	22.9	21.6
Andhra Praesh	25.2	42.7	20.9	23.1
Karnataka	20.4	96.6	24.2	26.7
Kerala	26.6	35.5	26.3	19.2
Tamil Nadu	23.6	15.6	22.3	17.5
ISLAND	27.0	26.2	67.6	55.8
Andaman & Nicobar Islands	28.2	23.5	81.2	63.9
Lakshadweep	26.3	27.8	32.0	26.5

Note: There are no scheduled tribes in Haryana, Jammu and Kashmir, Punjab, Chandigarh, Delhi and Pondicherry as per the census.

SECTION VI

URBANIZATION

28

India's Mega-Cities & Mega Problems: Quality of Life Issues

The United Nations defines mega-cities as cities or urban agglomerations with eight million or more inhabitants. The UN also lists cities with five million or more people. The common concept, however, is of million-plus cities (i.e. cities with population of one million and over).

The 1991 Census Commissioner, in his report on the rural and urban distribution of population (Census Paper No. 2) use the term mega-cities to mean cities with population of five million and over (also called metropolises).

There is no special sanctity about the cut-off point: One million, five million or eight million. Much depends on the context in which one discusses mega cities. Theoretically speaking, one could also work out the optimum size of cities in each country and region but in reality, the optimum size would invariably be much below the actual population. The concept, therefore, is of little operational value unless one is planning for a totally new urban settlement.

Theoretically speaking again, one cannot swear by only one figure for the optimum population of a city because the optimum may not be the same when we discuss the requirements of residential land and housing, water supply, sewarage system, transportation needs, energy, etc. Much depends on answering the question: Optimum from the point of view of what objective? It may sound nice to say that our over-riding objective is to improve the quality of urban life but one must be able to operationalise this concept.

How difficult this task is, was evident from a recent seminar (March 17-21) in Delhi, jointly organised by the School of Planning and Architecture and the Max Mueller Bhavan. A group of Indian and German scholars had a marathon discussion on the quality of life in the metropolis.

Appeared in *Financial Express*, 5 May, 1992

Professor Udo Simonis, an eminent German environmental economist gave a graphic description of the environmental damage caused to the German economy. To give just one figure, it was estimated that in the Federal Republic of Germany, the cost of rehabilitating and conserving the natural environment was around $ 175 billion, an enormous cost even by German standards. Separate estimates have also been worked out in Germany for environmental sectors like air pollution, water pollution, soil contamination, noise, etc.

Simonis argued that conventional economic policy does not take enough note of "ecological economy" and we need a different set of guiding principles, keeping in mind the goal of environmental stability, along with other economic goals. Interestingly enough Simonis observed that the quality of urban life in Germany would improve if people took to bicycles. The new rich in Indian cities, with their craze for Maruti cars, would certainly be amused by this prescription.

Professor E.F.N. Ribeiro, an eminent city-planner and Director of the School of Planning and Architecture, gave his own prescription for improving the physical quality of life in our large cities. On the issue of bicycles, he said "The bicycle remains an enigma. They are pollution free and a cheap form of personalised transport... They have, however, limitation of up to 5 to 7 kms per trip, and are indisciplined on roads due to their instability. Cycle tracks are non-starters in most cities and in a furious competition for limited road space, the cycles lose out as accident statistics show."

Taking a comprehensive view of the state of infrastructure in Indian cities, Rebeiro pointed that the collapse of urban infrastructure is imminent in cities with a growth rate of population of 40 per cent and over in a decade.

Apart from physical infrastructure, there are many other elements which determine the quality of urban life. Leaving apart standard items like literacy rate, infant mortality rate and expectation of life, etc. (the so called physical quality of life indices), one could quantify some other indicators which would perhaps give a better idea of quality of urban life.

In fact, one could challenge the notion that a high figure for the expectation of life adds to the quality of life. The problem of aging population has indeed become very serious in all the developed countries. One could argue that an average expectation of life beyond, say, 75 years generates considerable misery for all including the elderly and strains the social security system (in the absence of family security in most western countries).

In the Indian context, we would plead for the following quantifiable indicators (this is an illustrative list and not a comprehensive list):

-- Capacity of the city to generate employment fast enough to absorb surplus labour from rural areas, so that cities play a generative role and not a parasitic role in the process of economic growth.

-- Ensure the functioning of the land market in a manner that does not price the poor out and force them to take to unauthorised colonies which are eventually "regularised" under political pressure.

-- Capacity of the city administrators, the police and the legal apparatus to minimise landlord-tenant confrontation.

-- The level of corruption in the day-to-day encounter of citizens with various levels of bureaucracy.

-- Number of episodes involving bandh, hartal, student unrest, strikes, lockouts, rioting, curfew, lathi charge, firing, bomb explosions, attacks by terrorists, etc.

-- Safety of women.

The incidence of child labour, particularly in the unorganised sector.

-- House rents, property taxes and other municipal taxes.

-- Pricing and efficiency of public utilities (which tend to be "public futilities") and in particular, the quality of public transportation system, hospitals, banks, post offices, municipal offices, traffic police and the general behaviour of public servants.

-- Road accidents and the care of victims.

-- Cultural life, opportunities for sports and youth activities.

Such a list, however, tends to become an exercise in wishful thinking in the face of the stark reality that 30 to 50 per cent of the population of big cities live in slums and for them the fulfilment of the basic needs takes precedence over any other indicator of quality of life.

Awaiting the development of an adequate data base to study the quality of life in our cities, we may have a good look at the 1991 Census data, keeping in mind the formula of 40 per cent growth rate leading to the collapse of urban infrastructure.

We present three tables which summarise the demographic situation in regard to our million-plus cities. The reader can choose his own cut-off point for determining whether or not a city is a mega-city .

Table 28.1: Number and Population of million-plus cities

Year	No. of M-plus cities	Aggregate population (in million)	Per cent of total urban population	Decadal growth rate (per cent)
1951	5	11.7	18.8	-
1961	7	18.1	22.9	54.1
1971	9	27.8	25.5	53.8
1981	12	42.1	26.4	51.4
1991	23	70.7	32.5	67.8

Table 28.2: Growth rates of old * million-plus urban agglomerations

City	Population in million 1991	Decadal growth rate (per cent) 1971-81	1981-91
Greater Bombay	12.6	42.9	33.4
Calcutta	10.9	23.9	18.7
Delhi	8.4	57.1	46.2
Madras	5.4	35.3	25.0
Hyderabad	4.3	42.7	67.0
Bangalore	4.1	75.6	39.9
Ahmedabad	3.3	45.9	28.9
Pune	2.5	48.6	47.4
Kanpur	2.1	23.5	28.8
Nagpur	1.7	40.8	36.2
Lucknow	1.6	23.8	63.0
Jaipur	1.5	59.4	49.2

*   Old cities are those which were already million-plus in 1981.

Table 28.3: Growth of new * million-plus cities

City	Population in million 1991	Decadal growth rate (per cent) 1971-81	1981-91
Surat	1.5	87.4	64.2
Kochi	1.1	48.8	38.1
Coimbatore	1.1	25.0	23.4
Vadodara	1.1	67.4	42.5
Indore	1.1	47.9	33.1
Patna	1.1	66.7	19.6
Madurai	1.1	27.6	20.5
Bhopal	1.1	74.4	58.5
Visakhapatnam	1.1	66.1	74.3
Varanasi	1.0	25.5	28.8
Ludhiana	1.0	51.3	66.8

*   'New' cities are those which became million-plus in 1991.

29

National Capital Region:
From Hibernation to Hope

For over three decades, the National Capital Region (NCR) has been hibernating. It was in 1959 when the Draft Master Plan of Delhi was ready that town planners thought of diverting the unending migration to Delhi to other cities and towns in the adjoining areas of Haryana, Uttar Pradesh and Rajasthan. The strategy was to develop a number of ring towns, satellite towns, growth centres and countermagnets.

The final Master Plan for Delhi (1962) recommended the setting up of a statutory body called the National Capital Region Planning Board. Strangely enough, it was only in 1985 that the National Capital Region Planning Board Act was passed by the Parliament. During the intervening period, nothing much happened: there was some sort of a high powered Committee headed by the Union Home Minister. The Chief Ministers of Haryana, UP and Rajasthan were also members of the Committee.

At that stage, politicians did not quite understand the concept of the National Capital Region. I recall the then Chief Minister of Haryana proclaming that "Haryana would not part with an inch of her territory." Perhaps he thought that the NCR, like the demand for Greater Haryana, was politically motivated. But perhaps the main reason why the NCR did not take off was the meagre allocation of funds for implementation of the proposed plan of diversifying the migration pattern in the region. Big sums were called for which the planners and policy-makers were reluctant to recommend.

Now there is a ray of hope. The Planning Commission has provided for Rs. 200 crore for the NCR in the Eighth Five Year Plan. This is a quantum jump from the present figure of Rs 35 crore or so. In a recent TV interview, Mrs Sheila Kaul, the Union Minister of Urban Development claimed this as a major achievement of her Minister. It may be noted that she is also the Chairperson of the NCR Planning Board.

When I met the Chief Regional Planner for NCR, Mr. B.N. Singh, he was full of hope. For the last six years, he has worked hard on the regional plan which was ready in 1988

Appeared in *Financial Express*, 14 July, 1992

and adopted in 1989. He was happy that the three Chief Ministers (Haryana, UP and Rajasthan) as well as the Lt Governor of Delhi UT had accepted the plan and the time had come for the take off.

Everybody may not share the enthusiasm of Mr. Singh. The PHD Chamber of Commerce and Industry organised a seminar in Delhi recntly on 'NCR--Need for a Critical Reappraisal'. According to them the NCR "unfortunately has been a non-starter due to a variety of reasons like meagre fund allocation and lack of priority within Government circles.

Mr. Singh's enthusiasm stems from the fact that in regard to the total allocation of funds, the share of the states is 50 per cent. Thus he hopes that for the first time there would be considerable resources at the disposal of the NCR Planning Board.

The objectives of the NCR are indeed lofty. As the preamble to the NCR Planning Board Act (1985) says: "... it is expedient in the public interest to provide for the constitution of a Planning Board for the preparation of a plan for the development of the National Capital Region and for co-ordinating and monitoring the implementation of such plan and for evolving harmonized policies for the control of land-uses and development of infrastructure in the National Capital Region so as to avoid any haphazard development thereof..."

It is too early to comment whether the efforts of the NCR Planning Board will succeed in bringing harmony and avoiding haphazard growth of cities and towns in this region. The most significant demographic feature of Delhi UT is the relentless growth of population at a very high rate during the last *four* decades. The decadal growth of Delhi UTs population during 1951-61 was 52.4 per cent, during 1961-71, it was 53.9 per cent, during 1971-81, it was 53 per cent and in the last decade (1981-91) it was 50.6 per cent. Can Delhi go on like this?

Delhi UT comprises Delhi city and New Delhi, the constituent urban units (called census towns) and a sprinkling of villages. In 1991, urban Delhi accounted for 89.9 per cent of Delhi UTs population. Interestingly enough, the growth rate of *rural* Delhi was 108.6 per cent during 1981-91, compared to 46.1 per cent for *urban* Delhi. This reflects the spillover of urban Delhi. The growth rate of the Urban Agglomeration of Delhi has come down from 57.1 per cent during 1971-81 to 46.2 per cent during 1981-91.

Regarding the population growth rate in the major Delhi Metropolitan Area (DMA) towns and Priority towns in the NCR as listed in the *Regional Plan 2001* prepared by the NCR Planning Board, the demographic picture is quite confusing and must await detailed analysis till the 1991 census tables are ready.

In passing, it may be noted that the NCR plan also identifies a number of countermagnets which are outside the commuting distance from Delhi and could grow independently and not under the shadow of Delhi. These towns are: Patiala in Punjab, Hissar in Haryana, Bareilly in UP, Kota in Rajasthan and Gwalior in Madhya Pradesh.

I shall conclude by asking three questions to the planners and policymakers of this country, in the context of future prospects of the National Capital Region: (1) What will be the impact of the recent liberalisation of economic policies on the investment, employment and migration pattern of NCR? Will there not be a tendency towards *further* concentration of economic activities in the Delhi areas because international investors may still prefer Delhi to Rewari or Hapur which are unliveable. (2) In view of the failure of India's family planning programme even in the urban areas and big cities, will natural increase in population not play a big role in urban growth? Are the demographic projections of the NCR plan valid? (3) Is the recent slowing down of the tempo of urbanisation not indicative of almost all our cities and towns crossing the saturation point, leading to the near callapse of the urban infrastructure? Has the World Bank enough funds to dole out our cities. What should we do then?

Table 29.1: Population and Decadal Growth Rate in Selected Towns in the National Capital Region

Region/Sub-region	Population in 1991 (thousands)	Growth rate (per cent)	
		1971-81	1981-91
HARYANA: *DMA Towns*			
Faribabad Complex	614	169.4	85.5
Guargaon UA	135	76.5	33.5
Bahadurgarh UA	57	45.2	52.6
Priority Towns:			
Rohtak MC	216	33.7	29.4
Panipat MC	191	56.8	38.5
Rewari MC	75	17.5	46.0
Palwal MC	59	30.7	24.9
Dharuhera Census Town	11		new town
Other Towns:			
Sonipat MC	143	75.3	30.7
UTTAR PRADESH: *DMA Towns*			
Ghaziabad UA	520	109.6	80.9
NOIDA	167		new census town
Priority Towns			
Meerut UA	847	41.7	49.1
Hapur MB	147	44.3	42.6
Bulandshahr MB	127	73.8	22.5
Khurja MB	80	33.6	19.8
RAJASTHAN			
Alwar UA	211	45.2	44.8

30

Cities of Hope--
Greater Chandigarh

Over two decades back, when political controversy about Chandigarh first cropped up. I wrote an article for leading newspapers under the caption: "Make Chandigarh a Chartered City." At that time Punjab and Haryana had made an exclusive claim over Chandigarh as their capital, while some suggested that the status quo should be maintained and Chandigarh should remain as Union Territory. There was also a perverse suggestion that Chandigarh should be divided and Punjab and Haryana should get their portion. Indira Gandhi's Chandigarh Award gave Chandigarh to Punjab, along with the transfer of some rural areas of Punjab to Haryana. This complicated matters further and over the years, Chandigarh has become a prestige issue with politicians, denying solution and, therefore, status quo is being maintained.

What I had suggested in my article to give a special status to Chandigarh through a charter or a special Act of Parliament, and endow new economic functions to Chandigarh and make Chandigarh a truly great city, I had also argued that the office of some international agency or United Nations Organisation could be located in Chandigarh. This would make Chandigarh a flourishing city. I gave example of Geneva, Vienna and Bangkok cities which owe a part of their prosperity of UN agencies.

My article was well received and got even editorial support. I learnt later the Home Ministry had given a serious thought to my proposal but instead of asking me what on earth was a "chartered city"! the answer was in the negative and there the matter ended.

I wish to revive my proposal. I strongly condemn any attempt to divide Chandigarh. It is not agricultural land. It is modern city designed by a world famous architect. If Chandigarh goes to Punjab or Haryana, it would cease to be an all-India city and will become a second rate provincial city. Politicians do not normally have the vision of a great city. To my mind, Chandigarh has the potential for becoming a vibrant, modern city of the 21st century. I believe that no other city in India has this potential. My definition of

Appeared in *Financial Express*, 25 May, 1993

Chandigarh covers Mohali in Punjab and Panchkula in Haryana and extends beyond the municipal boundaries of present day Chandigarh, In short, what I have in mind is Greater Chandigarh as a hub of economic activity in north-western India, comprising Punjab, Himachal Pradeshm Jammu and Kashmir, Hrayana, Western UP and Eastern Rajasthan.

I am told that Mr. Khushwant sing described Chandigarh as "a city of white beards and geen hedges" I also get this feeling when I take a morning or evening walk around the Lake in Chandigarh. In am also aware of Madhu Sarin's comprehensive and critical sudy of Chandigarh (Urban planning in the third world: the candigarh ex[erience, London, (1982). It was by sheer chance that during one of my short trips to Chandigarh in Shatabdi Exprcss (I wish all our trains were like this), I was sitting next to Dr. Jurgen Oestereich, an eminent German architect-planner and co-editor of a professional journal called--published from Germany. He has written a very perceptive article on "Chandigarh: Philosophy and implementation" in the latest issue of his journal (1992). Oestereich makes an interesting criticism of Chandigarh, To quote him: "As to the roads, the visitor may be irritated by their colonial width plus additional by-lanes.."

With the advent of Marutis in large numbers, our cities do need broad roads and bylanes for cyclists. Chandigarh, more than any other city in India. can fulfil the transportation needs of the 21st century. My argument, however, does not centre round architectural design and urban planning. I am more concerned with the economics of urbanisation.

Madhu Sarin, in her study on Chandigarh, points out that "Beneath the grandiose ambitions and idealism of the planners lay the bare, socio-economic reality of the future population of the city, the project report included remarkably little information about the economic base of the new town." I agree with her.

Though Chandigarh was meant to be only a Government city, over the years, a whole range of economic activities has cropped up in Mohali in Punjab and Panchakula in Haryana. A new military cantonment has been created near Chandigarh. Not far from Chandigarh is HMT Township and on the border of Himachal Pradesh the new industrial township of parwanoo has come up.

I understand that the Punjab Government is acquiring land near Dera Bassi (16 km from Chandigarh) for establishing a Free Enterprise Zone. In short, Greater Chandigarh comprising the Union Territory of Chandigarh, Mohali and adjoining areas in Punjab and Panchakula, Chandi Mandir and adjoining areas in Haryana, can emerge as vibrant centre of economic activity in North-West India. If the necessary infrastucture is created by the joint efforts of the Government of India, and the State Governments of Punjab, Haryana and Himachal Pradesh, in a co-ordinated manner and a new sub-national Region of Chandigarh formed, a lot of investments will flow into this region. The World Bank and international donor agencies as well as foreign private capital and, more importantly, NRI capital would be attracted to this region.

It should not be forgotten that the green revolution was triggered of in Punjab and Haryana. It is not impossible to usher in an industrial revolution involging a whole range of modern, medium and small scale industries in this region. Chandigarh being a planned city has the best potential to mobilise the forces of economic liberalisation, globalisation and modernisation. It would be tragedy if this opportunity is lost and politics is allowed to overshadow economics. What we need is functional intergration and not division and disharmony. Forming Chandigarh national subregion should not invole any adjustment of administrative boundaries and transfer of territory.

To sum up my argument. I believe that

Chandigarh has the unique advantage of being located in the midst of Punjab and Haryana, two of our most prosperous states with high per capita incomes. Agricultural prosperity will strengthen the economic base of Greater Chandigarh. In short, Chandigarh has the potential for being a rich city, sustained not only by a bureaucracy but, more importantly, by rural and agricultural prosperity of Punjab, Haryana, Himachal Pradesh and Western Uttar Pradesh. In turn, Chandigarh can contribute greatly to the rural prosperity of this region.

If proper planning is done for the Chandigarh Sub-national Region (CSR) like the National Capital Region (NCR), and the necessary infrastructure created, a lot of high-tech pollution-free industries will flock to this area. As it is massive investments are being made in Mohali and Panchkula and, very soon, the whole area will be humming with economic activity. The artificial demarcation between Haryana and Punjab in the surroundng areas of Chandigarh and the uncertain political future of Chandigarh tend to discourage massive investments in this region. Once Greater Chandigarh is given a statutory status (even though Chandigarh remains a Union Territory), enormous capital will flow to this area. The people in this region are known for their good health, hard work and dynamic attitude towards life, In short, there is abundance of good human resource. With peace returning to Punjab, things will look up and Chandigarh can be the hub of a flourishing region of medium and small scale industrial enterprises and other allied economic activities. In course of time, Chandigarh can also emerge as a powerful financial centre.

Chandigarh can also emerge as a first rate educational and medical centre, drawing students from all over India and also from neighbouring Asian and African countries. It can also develop as centre of fine arts, performing arts, and a whole range of cultural activities. Most of all, it can be centre of sports training and activities. In short, Greater Chandigarh can emerge as a pollution-free multifunctional medium-sized city with a good quality of life. Big cities like Bombay and Calcutta are suffering from decay and require enormous investments for development. Chandigarh is a medium-sized city and planned city. If careful planning is done right now, it can avoid the "evils of urbanisation witnessed in most of our cities.

It may be recalled that Le Corbusier himself had visualised that "Chandigarh will be open to all cultural factors in different manifestation, such as teaching, means to express and disperse thoughts, modes of expression and dispersion of the arts, all kinds of reproduction of art-witnesses, diverse kinds of exhibitions, shows, theatres, festivals, and creation of the highest modernity."

According to the 1991 Census, Ludhiana has emerged as a million plus city--the only such city in Punjab. But Ludhiana is struggling with its urban problems and cannot stand out as a 21 century city. No city in Haryana is up to the mark, except perhaps Ambala, but Ambala is no match for Chandigarh. In Himachal Pradesh, the only big city is Shimla. The overcrowding and the extreme shortage of water have downgraded Shimla, at least from the point of view of tourism. Nevertheless, Himachal Pradesh has a great potential for tourism. Chandigarh could develop a corridor with Kashmir and be the entry point (instead of Delhi) for tourists from all over India coming to this region.

Fanally, if the Government of India makes a serious effort in lobbying in powerful international circles, it is quite possible that some UN Agency will locate its regional headquarters in Chandigarh. The necessary infrastructure in terms of a big Convention Centre, modern banking, telecommunication, etc will have to be created to meet the international conferences. There are limits to what New Delhi can cope with. The city of Greater Chandigarh can provide similar facilities, if not better, In fact many would prefer Chandigarh to Delhi because of proximity to nice places for holidays and week ends in Himachal Pradesh.

Chandigarh was built as a Government city. Spelling out the aims for planning Chandigarh, Le Corbusier had said: "It should be the aim of planning to do two things: (a) to prevent the creation of bad semi-urban conditions on the boundaries of the new city, drawing away the strength of the city by unfair competition immediately beyond the area of local taxation and (b) to protect the rural community from degeneration from contact with urban life, and to lead it toward a harmonious partnership."

Le Corbusier had clearly said that "Chandigarh, thanks to its urban and architectural layout will be sheltered from base speculation and its corollaries: the suburbs. No suburb is possible at Chandigarh."

Corbusier's dream has already been shattered by Mohali and Panchkula, as will be evident from table based on 1991 Census.

Table 30.1: Population of Greater Chandigarh

	Population in 1991	Growth Rate, 1981-91 (Per cent)
Chandigarh	575,829	35.9
Mohali (Ropar District)	78,457	140.7
Panchkula (Ambala District)	70,375	525.8

Let us have a new dream of Greater Chandigarh. This goes much beyond appointing a Coordination Committee which the TCPO did in 1975 or prepare a Regional Plan (1984).

31

Slums of Hope: Calcutta's Rambagan Experiment

We are heading toward an urban world in the 21st century. Planners and policy makers accept that urbanisation is inevitable. But are slums inevitable?

This question came up for discussion in a big way at a recent symposium in Calcutta on urbanisation and slums (26-28 April 1993). In the serene environment of the Ramakrishna Mission Institute of Culture at Golpark, the Council for Social Development (CSD) based in New Delhi, brought together a galaxy of scholars, activists, administrators, and representatives of NGOs and funding agencies, At the inaugural session, Swami Lokeswarananda of the Ramakrishna Mission showed his thorough understanding of the problem of slum. He also referred to the slums of Singapore and Shanghai which had disappeared over time. Jyoti Basu, the Chief Minister of West Bengal also referred to the slums in the industrial cities of England which he saw as a student. These had almost disappeared now. But what about the slums of Calcutta? Like in Singapore, Shanghai or San Francisco, will the slums be a phenomenon of the past?

There is no doubt that the problem of slums cannot be considered in isolation. The overall urban context must be understood.

The 1991 Census is a gold mine for the study of urbanisation. The Indian census has at last entered the electronic age. The Registrar General has made available to individual scholars massive data on diskettes for every village, town and city in India. More data are awaited, particularly data on migration streams. In the course of the next year or so, one would have access to the detailed tables on cities generated by the Census of 1991. In the past, the Census made attempts to collect data on slums. The main limitation of such data is that the Census considers only 'notified slums'. This leaves out a large number of other slum settlements. I understand that in 1991, the Director of Census of Maharashtra had taken particular care to collect data on the slums in Bombay.

Appeatned in *Financial Express*, 11 May, 1993

One need not spend much time in considering the various definitions of slums. In Calcutta, the term 'bustee' is quite common while in Delhi one talks of Katras, JJ Colonies and 'regularised' colonies. In Delhi, there are also a number of resettlement colonies, many of which are in fact glorified slums. In a recent meeting, the Lt. Governor of Delhi said that Delhi would emerge as a super slum, the way things were developing. If this can be said about the most pampered city of India, one can well imagine the fate of other cities. A cynic would say that we are heading towards a situation where instead of slums being isolated pockets of concentrated human misery would engulf our cities which will become super slums, with a few isolated pockets of liveable neighbourhoods like civil lines, model towns, etc. In Bombay one invariably talks of Dharavi, which is supposed to be the biggest slum in Asia.

Let me give my definition of slums. I would define a slum as a deprived human settlement, a settlement which is demographically, economically and environmentally vulnerable. Slums are looked down upon. Extreme over-crowding, high density and high levels of mortality and fertility are typical demographic features of slums. A large unorganised sector, low levels of productivity, and extreme poverty are the usual economic features, and the lack of access to basic needs like water, sanitation and clean environment make these areas environmentally hazardous. In my definition, slums include small clusters of pavement dwellers as well as glorified slums like some of the Government sponsored resettlement colonies. I would call any settlement with the above mentioned characteristics and with a population of more than one lakh (1,00,000) as a Super slum.

Prodipto Roy from the Council for Social Development who had conducted a comprehensive survey of slums in Calcutta, in collaboration with the Centre for Research in the Epidemiology of Disasters, Catholic University of Louvain (Brussel, Belgium), painted a somewhat rosy picture of Calcutta slums which he said were not growing. He also found a fairly respectable level of literacy and health condition in the slum households which he had surveyed. Nevertheless he was not satisfied with mere empirical data; he was looking for a theory of slums.

It was left to Dinesh Mehta, Director of the National Institute of Urban Affairs (New Delhi) to propound a theory of slums in the Indian context. His paper centered round the theory of slums put forward by Charles Stokes, an American economist whose model (1962) distinguished between slums of hope and slums of despair and also put forward the concept of two classes of slum dwellers: escalators and non-escalators, In short, according to Stokes, there were four types of slums based on ability and income and also the barriers to entry in the labour market. Mehta sought to extend this theory to take note of other theories of migration and labour and labour mobility. In his view, slums were people as well as commodities. His message was that public housing projects for slum dwellers are bound to fail if enough thought is not given to labour market operation. To quote him: "Often, in the zeal of slum clearance, the entire settlement is demolished; when no alternative location is provided for, such households begin from the transitory stage once again ... when housing becomes a commodity for exchange in the market, the poor households behave rationally in maximising their income through housing."

Now from theory to practice. To my mind, the most useful paper in the entire symposium was presented by Mr. S.S. Chakroborty on "Rambagan Slum Re-housing Project--a case study'. Chakroborty is an activist from Ramakrishna Mission Ashram and has spent a life time working with the people and for the people of Rambagan slum in North Calcutta. According to him, there are three categories of slums in Calcutta: (a) slums where people have been living for generations. Basically, these are poor village settlements which were engulfed by Calcutta; (b) slums dominated by migrants who came to Calcutta to work in the wake of growing industrial and commercial development and (c) slums which comprise refugee migrants from East Pakistan/Bangladesh.

Rambagan slums belong to the first category and is as old as the city of Calcutta. The people there are Harijans and artisans who make a living from tradtional handicrafts of bamboo, cane and paper. They are also painters and musicians but because of their caste (Dom), they are isolated from the rest of the city.

In 1952, an adult education centre was started by the R.K. Mission which culminated in a comprehensive Vivekananda Social Welfare Centre. Currently, the following programmes are run in Rambagan: Adult Education Centre; Vivekananda Nursery School; Junior Basic School; Cane and Bamboo Crafts Training Centre; Weaving/ Tailoring Centre for Women; Three years Training Course in Painting; Social Education Centre for Women; Tutorial Classes; Health Centre; Special Nutrition Programme 330 children are given milk and bread daily); Family Helper Project; Creche, Library Services; Light Engineering Training Centre, etc.

Chakroborty points out that the various welfare and educational activities had made a significant impact on the slum dwellers. The literacy rate went up to 80 per cent, every child in the school going age attended school, child mortality rate came down and the employment prospects heightened considerably. The Mission then took up a housing project which involved construction of modern dwelling units in multi-story apartment blocks. The slum dwellers were involved in the project right from the conceptualization of the project. They raised a lot of funds from their own people. The Calcutta Corporation and the West Bengal Corporation and the West Bengal Government also helped and so also several foreign donor agencies.

I went to see for myself the Rambagan slum, without being escorted by any functionary of the R.K. Mission. It was a pleasure to talk to the people. Everybody knew Sibuda (S.S. Chakroborty). I was escorted by a school teacher to the Office of the Welfare Centre. I was impressed by their ongoing projects. It was indeed a slum of hope.

What are the lessons for the rest of India of the Rambagan experiment? In Chakroborty's words, these are: "(1) No doubt housing is major problem in slums but to solve this problem, the first priority is education and human resource development. The Rambagan project started with the literacy programme, then moved on to vocational training, health, etc and finally to construction of new apartments; (2) the local people were involved in all stages of welfare work through the Jan Kalyan Samity; (3) The experiment succeeded because of the joint efforts of the slum dwellers, Calcutta Corporation, Government of West Bengal, voluntary agencies and Indian and foreign donor agencies; (4) As far as possible, slum dwellers should be rehabilitated on the same site where they live and they should be given temporary shelter near the site of new house construction; (5) the people in the slums must also contribute to the ongoing projects; and (6) Government agencies and the Municipal Corporation must adopt a flexible policy."

The sum up, the Rambagan experiment shows that emphasis on human resource development should precede the physical improvement of the slum.

$\boxed{32}$

Reforms in the Urban Sector

It is rather surprising that in the new economic environment of liberalisation and structural reforms, the urban sector remains untouched. The stranglehold of urban legislation and in particular, the Urban Land Ceilling and Regulation Act of 1976 and the Rent Control Act have played havoc with the urban land and housing market, without helping the poor or generating equity in the urban sector.

It was therefore not a day too soon that the Planning Commission organised a high-powered Expert Group Meeting (March 17, 1993) to discuss the implications of economic reforms for the urban sector. The message of the day-long deliberations was loud and clear: Liberalisation must invade the urban sector. Raja Chelliah, a leading exponent of structural reforms and economic liberalisation and his colleague, Om Prakash Mathur, from the National Institute of Public Finance and Policy, presented the theme paper. They lamented that "the Eighth five-year Plan, published a year after the initiation of the reform process takes no note of the new context and the implications thereof on the urban sector. Indeed, the urban policies as contained in the Eighth Plan are more a continuation of the past than a break from it."

It reminds me of the famous statement by the late Professor Raj Krishna who once said: "The Sixth Plan is the sixth edition of the First Plan!" Interestingly, the present member of Planning Commission, incharge of Urban Development, Dr. D. Swaminadham (who inaugurated the Expert Group Meeting) himself argued that "liberalisation of macro policies may not be enough. It is also necessary that procedural simplification, debureaucratisation and removal of legal bottlenecks are introduced simultaneously to create the facilitating environment for enhancing flow of investment in the urban sector. Many of these changes may be required at the level of urban local bodies with supporting legal and procedural provisions by the State Government."

Appeared in *Financial Express*, 30 March, 1993

The pertinent question is: Who will initiate these reforms in the urban sector? One would have expected that the Ministry of Urban Development, being the concerned Ministry, would take the lead in this direction. But more often than not, this ministry is found napping. The Planning Commission had appointed a Task Force on Housing and Urban Development which produced an excellent series of reports is 1983. But there is no evidence that the Ministry of Urban Development took adequate note of the recommendations of the Task Force. At the instance of Prime Minister Rajiv Gandhi, the National Commission on Urbanisation was appointed in 1986 and the report was submitted to the Ministry of Urban Development in 1988. The Ministry has more or less scuttled this report, though of late, there are some signs that it wants to take note of some of the recommendations.

As was evident from the deliberations of this Meeting that number one priority has to be given to the question of Urban Land Ceilling Act which, by all accounts, has proved counterproductive. The National Commission on Urbanisation had given careful thought to the question of scarpping this Act and finally suggested some important modifications. The majority of speakers at the Planning Commission's Meeting were of the view that the Urban Land Ceiling Act must be scrapped. It has been a bad piece of legislation and has served no purpose. In my intervention, I pointed out that our recommendations should also be politically acceptable and feasible. The is no doubt that the Urban Land Celling Act was a populist measure, hastily enacted during the Emergency. But it is also a fact that no Prime Minister has been bold enough to scrap it. I recall that during the Emergency I had interviewed, for Delhi TV, the Minister for Housing and Urban Development, immediately after the Act was promulgated. It seemed to me that the Minister himself was ignorant about the Act. He was justifying the Act on the ground that there was land ceiling in the rural sector and therefore there was need for similar ceiling in the urban sector.

There was unanimity among the participants that this piece of legislation has been obstructive. Several members argued that MRTP Act has been scrapped. FERA has been modified and in the new era of economic legislation the only worthwhile strategy would be to scrap the Urban Land Ceiling Act. It was left to the representative of the Ministry of Urban Development to point out that this piece of legislation could not be scrapped by the Central Government unless at least 11 state governments passed similar legislation. In his view, this was a constitutional requirement. His observation threw cold water on all the deliberations of the meeting and at the end of the day we were left no wiser. From time to time, committees have been appointed to suggest modifications in the Urban Land Ceiling Act and the Government has sat over the reports. Perhaps this state of affairs will continue.

Another theme paper urging reforms in the urban sector was prepared by Dinesh Mehta, Director of the National Institute of Urban Affairs. He suggested a 20 point programme of which the very first item was removal of Urban Land Ceiling Legislation. It seems to me that the urban experts are not very familiar with the constitutional requirements.

In order to promote equity and access of land for the poor, Mehta had a three-point formula:

(1) Creation of a fund from vacant land tax for purchase of land and housing; (2) fiscal incentives to private developers for EWS housing; and (3) promoting public-private partnerships like land sharing, land pooling, guided development, coloniser licensing for land allocations to the poor.

There was a general agreement that nothing should be subsidised and people must be made to pay for the urban services and public utilities. This is also the World Bank line. But will the poor not be priced out in this process? There has to be some element of subsidy for the poor even in an era of economic liberalisation.

There was quite some discussion on the DDA model which is being replicated in every part of India. Some participants were very firm in their view that all the housing boards should be done away with and the market forces should be allowed to operate. In this context, the high price of transaction cost was mentioned by more than one speaker. In a recent study of towns in North-East India, it was found that the transaction cost was as high as 39 per cent. This is a result of the over-regulation of the urban sector and of course, corruption. All this must change. The urban sector has to be deregulated.

As Raja Chelliah and Om Mathur argued forcefully: "The Indian economy is now on a different path. The export-oriented industrial development, elimination or reduction of subsidies, delicensing of a large portion of the industrial sector and appropriate pricing of infrastructure and services will mean a change in the existing pattern of urban growth and distribution of activities over price. Export orientation could mean growth of different types of cities, particularly the port cities. Similarly, delicensing could mean dispersal of economic activities and consequently a more balanced spatial distribution of population. Such changes will be a natural outcome of new economic policies and will need to be supported and strengthened."

It may be recalled that even before the era of economic liberalisation, the National Commission on Urbanisation had done a detailed exercise to generate a balanced spatial distribution of population in India and had suggested 49 Urbanisation Regions spread throughout the country and 329 GEMs (Generators of Economic Momentum) classified into National Priority Cities (NPCs) and State Priority Citieis (SPCs). Of course, these cities have to be backed up by massive investment on infrastructure. The discussion at the meeting of experts made it clear that one could not bank on the government sector alone for generating these resources. The private sector and the joint sector have to come in a big way. Institutional financing has a key role in this regard. In this context, a reference was made to the National Housing Bank which, according to some, has turned out to be a "monster" and has not served the cause of housing.

Not many ideas were generated in regard to modification in the Rent Control Act. As Abhijit Datta pointed out, the genesis of the Rent Control Act lay in the war-time situation and it was indeed an Emergency measure which, over the years, became a part of the legal system. There is no doubt that the Rent Control Act has obstructed the development of the housing market and has also not really contributed to equity. The Act has in fact let to extreme housing shortage, avoidable litigation, crime and violence and the absurd phenomenon of a large number of vacant houses in the face of a tremendous demand for housing. Some of the participants were in a mood to scrap this Act also, while others suggested some modifications.

My only comment in passing is that in our effort to globalise the Indian economy and generate an atmosphere of market friendly land and housing sectors in the name of urban reforms, it would be a tragedy if we get out of the clutches of the bureaucracy and land in the lap of land speculators!

$$\boxed{33}$$

Urbanisation in the
21st Century

Will cities in the 21st century be spectators of their own future or will they shape their own destinies? Will the marvels of high tech, electronic mail, fax, videophones and computerised banking make city centres and main streets studded with shops and banks an obsolete concept? Will urban poverty occupy a back room or become a central issue in the cities? Will unemployment, ethnic conflicts, and violence make cities unpleasant habitats? These questions are more easily raised than answered.

The homeless in Calcuta and Bombay--the pavement dwellers as we call them--have always attracted the attention of city planners all over the world. I was surprised to see New York Times with a headline on the homeless in New York. A city judge has just ruled that New York City has illegally sheltered 1,200 homeless men in dangerous and overcrowded armories (once used by the army) and ordered the city authorities to cut down the number of homeless. The city officials feel that if they reduce the armory population, they would be unable to shelter all the homeless in New York. The advocates for the homeless plead that the city consider using empty mental hospitals run by the state to shelter the homeless.

In New York, just as in New Delhi or Calcutta, the people look for some source of sustenance rather than housing. And yet in many influential circles including international donor agencies, the concern is for housing, for improvement of slums and so on and it is often fogotten that priority one for a migrant is employment and not housing. This is true all over the world.

Why do the homeless come to the big cities like New York and Washington instead of going to places like New Haven? Obviously because the prospects of making a living are better (at least as perceived by the potential migrant) in the big city rather than in the suburban areas or small towns. But is this the only reason for such migration?

Appeared in *Financial Express*, 13 January, 1993

I asked Oru Bose, architect and city planner in Orlando, Florida about this phenomenon in the West. He said: "Unlike in the cities of India there is a lack of infrastructure or a virtual collapse of the limited infrastructure, the western cities usually offer a large number of facilities for public use (like shelters, public toilets, subways, lobbies of office buildings, etc.) which attract a lot people who drift into the category of homeless because they find they can survive without working. But one must realise that this infrastructure was not meant for such misuse. The easy access to this infrastructure has generated a life style unique to the cities like New York, especially in the last decade. It is for the first time that the American public has suddenly realised that it is not only the Third World countries which are facing the problem of homeless in the cities. There was a time when the average American refused to believe that such a problem even existed in the US. Thanks to the media and the involvement of celebrities in projecting the plight of the homeless, there is today a great awareness of the problem."

When asked, "Is there a difference between the homeless in New York and those in New Delhi." He answered, "The homeless do not belong to one category alone and it would be a mistake to treat them as such. For example, in the lowest rung there are criminals, beggars, drug addicts and other undesirable sections of society, both in India and the US who join the ranks of the homeless in the cities. But this is not primarily a problem of shelter--it is a sociological phenomenon which calls for a sociological solution".

Turning to the more "normal" category of homeless, one finds that a major reason for their being homeless is the non-availability of affordable housing in the cities. It would, therefore, appear that the thing to do is to provide housing or even shelter. But Oru emphasises: " The obvious solution is not necessarily the best solution."

Another point to note is that in cities like New York, the existing housing in poor neighbourhoods has deteriorated to a point where such housing is rendered unliveable. The people in such localities (who are not migrants from rural areas) also join the category of homeless.

What then is the solution? "To my mind, shelter is not the solution", said Oru. He went on, "The real problem is employment and income generation. The benevolent efforts to build more quick shelters only perpetuates the problem instead of facing the basic problem. There are people who believe that modern technology will come to the rescue of the homeless. But this will not work because we are seeking 21st century solutions to resolve 19th century problems. Any solution which envisages subsidised housing and other forms of substandard housing will ultimately create a bigger problem which will invoke more and more welfare programmes. The surest way to help a person is to give him a sustainable source of income."

"What are the prospects of an average American family owning a house?" Oru, who has considerable experience of development in the flourishing region of Central Florida, said: "With rising prices and recession, housing has become increasingly unaffordable to the middle income groups and the younger people (first time buyers). In a consumer driven and profit oriented economy, this leads to a greater emphasis on luxury housing where profit are high. The rising cost of land accentuates this phenomenon. To get out of this impasse one really needs innovative ideas and appropriate technology".

How do we provide affordable housing on a plot of land which is extremely expensive? "Subsidy is not the real solution in a private sector economy. One has to think in terms of creative financing, unorthodox zoning practices, and technological solutions to tackle this problem. The Government no doubt has a big role to play in formulating such programmes. I am not thinking of welfare programmes, land at subsidised cost and so on. We must create a profitable housing industry to take care of affordable housing. In this society, anything that is not profitable does not work. Increasing involvement of the Government may only lead to proliferation of bureaucracy without making a dent on the problem," said Oru.

In Orlando, for example, it is easier to buy a million-dollar house than a hundred-thousand dollar house. In order to create affordable housing, the developers go farther and farther from the core area because of the lower land prices but this is not always the right solution. The problems of utilisation of space, trasportation, energy and social infrastructure (schools, hospitals etc.) crop up in a big way. When you take an overview of the urban situation, you find that in the long run, you are loaded with problems of high-cost infrastructure in the name of affordable housing.

What is true of Orlando, is also true of Indian cities. Only the situation is worse because of the large number of persons involved, the hundreds of JJ (jhuggi-jhopri) colonies, the unauthorised colonies and the political pressure during civic elections to "regularise" these colonies and poor who suffer. Look at a middle class colony like Vasant Kung in South Delhi, facing a constant water shortage. There was a time when only a few cities like Madras and Hyderabad faced the problem of shortage of water. Today almost all our cities are facing this problem. The same is true of energy and transport.

Urbanisation under conditions of rapid population growth creates two sets of problems for cities in the developing countries: the problem of intense population pressure arising out of population growth and migration from rural areas and small towns, and the problem of the collapse of the limited infrastructure of cities and the lack of economic resources.

The cities in the developed countries are not facing the burden of demographic pressure except through the limited migration in the cities. New York, London and Paris are not growing. If at all, their population may go down with increasing suburbanisation. And the marvels of modern technology make decentralised urbanisation a reality in the western cities.

Let us look at a few figures. According to United Nations estimates, there were 13 urban agglomerations in the world in 1992, with more than 10 million persons in each agglomeration. Of these, 7 were in Asia, 4 in Central and Latin America, and 2 in the US. London and Paris do not feature in this list. Tokyo has the largest population (25.7) million, followed by Sao Paulo in Brazil (19.2 million), New York (16.2 million), Mexico (15.3 million), Shanghai in China (14.1 million) and Bombay (13.3 million).

The remaining large cities are Los Angeles (11.9 million), Buenos Aires in Argentina (11.8 million), Seoul in the Republic of Korea (11.6 million), Beijing (11.4 million), Rio de Janerio in Brazil (11.3 million) Calcutta (11.1 million) and Osaka in Japan (10.5 million).

As we enter the 21st century, our perception of the world's great cities in terms of London and Paris and New York will yield place (at least in demographic terms) to Asian cities like Tokyo (fast becoming the financial capital of the world) and Osaka in Japan, Shanghai and Beijing in China, Bombay and Calcutta in India and Seoul in Korea. New York and Los Angeles will still count in the list of the largest cities of the world but according to United Nations projections, the annual growth rate of New York's population during 2005-2010 would be only 0.3 per cent, while that of Los Angeles is 0.4 per cent. (The projected growth rate of London and Paris during this period is zero per cent). On the other hand, Bombay is expected to grow at the rate of 2.7 per cent per year and Calcutta is expected to have a modest growth rate of one per cent per year.

The urban scene in the 21st century will thus be dominated by cities in the developing countries in spite of a much lower level of urbanisation.

According to the United Nations estimates, 73 per cent of the population of more developed regions of the world in 1990 was urban, compared to 34 per cent in the less developed regions (the figure was only 20 per cent in the least developed countries). Let us look at the urban proportion in a few Asian countries. Chinna (26 per cent), India (26 per cent), Republic of Korea (72 per cent), and Japan (77 per cent).

In Mexico, the urban population was 73 per cent, in Argentina (86 per cent) and in Brazil (75 per cent). The urban proportion in USA too was 75 per cent.

Interestingly, in spite of the low level of urbanisation in India, there are more people living in the urban agglomerations in India than in the USA. Thus it is important to consider not only the level of urbanisation but also the urban population in absolute terms. According to the 1991 Census of India, there were 23 cities in India with a population of one million and over.

Looking at the process of urbanisation in India, one is left with a disturbing thought. Is it really urbanisation? Or is it ruralisation of our cities?

There was a time when Bombay was India's greatest city but the proliferation of slums in Bombay makes it less of a city. Instead of suburbanisation we have the phenomenon of slumurbanisation. And all our cities are facing the same fate.

Here in New York, I find more migrants every time I visit this great city. My vision of New York as a city of sky-scrapers and marvels of high tech gets diluted by what I see in the subways and streets. Wall Street Journal (December 29) carried a perceptive article by Jum W Ferguson on California and the immigrant tremors there. He draws attention to Census Bureau's revised national projection which "bring home the message that immigration is materially affecting the size and makeup of the population. Californians might still be surprised; those close to the state's schools know they have gone from 75 per cent white 25 years ago, to under 45 per cent today. Hispanics are 37 per cent."

Ferguson comments: "The movement of millions of foreigners to the US is arousing efforts to stem the tide. To date, the American scene hasn't grown as ugly as in Europe, where violence against outsiders is more commonplace and political opposition to them more virulent. Partly, this is doubtless a function of a people's generosity. But the good-will is being stretched". We need not be reminded of the recent Los Angeles riots. According to the latest figures released by the Census Bureau (December 29), the largest number of immigrants to the US (over 30 per cent) came to the State of California. San Francisco and Los Angeles also grew faster than cities like New York. In fact, nine out of the ten fastest growing states in the US, are in the West.

To conclude, urbanisation in the 21st century will be far from smooth unless we tackle in a big way the problem of unemployment, infrastructure and ethnic violence arising out of migration. In this regard, American cities may fare no better than Indian cities. The big cities seem to share a common destiny all over the world.

SECTION VII

STATISTICAL APPENDIX:
BASIC DEMOGRAPHIC DATA FOR ESCAP ASIAN COUNTRIES, CHINA AND INDIA

I
Asian Countries
(ESCAP Region)

Table 1: Demographic Estimates for Asian Countries, 1992

Country or Area and Region	Mid-1992 Pop (thousands)	Average Annual Growth Rate (per cent)	Crude Birth Rate	Crude Death Rate
	1	2	3	4
ESCAP	3164792	1.72	25.6	8.4
EAST ASIA	1387055	1.28	19.3	6.5
China	1187997	1.38	20.3	6.5
Democratic People's				
Republic of Korea	22618	1.81	23.4	5.3
Hong Kong	5735	.68	12.2	5
Japan	124248	.31	9.9	6.8
Macau	484	2.26	17.3	7.1
Mongolia	2310	2.64	34.2	7.9
Republic of Korea	43663	.91	16.4	5.8
SOUTH - EAST ASIA	455607	1.87	27.2	8.4
Brunei Dasrussalam	270	2.29	24	4.4
Cambodia	9001	2.5	40	15
Indonesia	184350	1.64	25.2	8.8
Law People's				
Democratic Republic	4469	2.89	44.2	15.3

Malaysia	18597	2.27	27.4	4.7
Myanmar	43668	2.13	32.5	11.3
Philippines	65186	2.29	30.5	6.9
Singapore	2821	2.1	18.4	4.8
Thailand	57760	1.42	20.3	6.1
Viet Nam	69485	2.06	29.7	8.6
SOUTH ASIA	1234731	2.15	32	10.6
Afghanistan	19062	4.73	50.9	22
Bangladesh	111701	2.44	38.2	13.8
Bhutan	1612	2.29	39.6	16.7
India	879548	1.91	29.3	10.2
Iran (Islamic				
Republic of	59560	2.96	36.4	6.8
Maldives	232	3.52	43	7
Nepal	20577	2.49	38.1	13.3
Pakistan	124773	2.84	40.9	10.7
Sri Lanka	17666	1.26	20.9	5.9
CENTRAL ASIA	59933	2.3	29.8	6.9
Azerbaijan	7456	1.95	26	6.5
Kazakhstan	17091	1.54	23	7.6
Kyrgyzstan	4589	2.32	30.4	7.2
Tajikistan	5552	3.22	38.7	6.5
Turkmenistan	3859	2.72	34.9	7.7
Uzbekistan	21386	2.7	33.3	6.3

(Contd.)

Country or Area and Region	Total Fertility Rate	Infant Mortality Rate	Male Life Expectancy At Birth (Years)	Female Life Expectancy At Birth (years)
	5	6	7	8
ESCAP	3.1	62	64.2	66.7
EAST ASIA	2.1	26	69.6	73.3
China	2.2	28	69.1	72.4
Democratic People's Republic of Korea	2.4	25	67.5	73.8
Hong Kong	1.2	6	75.1	80.7
Japan	1.5	4	75.9	81.6
Macau	2.1	10	70.1	75.7
Mongolia	4.7	61	62	64.7
Republic of Korea	1.8	12	67.5	73.6
SOUTH-EAST ASIA	3.3	55	60.4	64.3
Brunei Darussalam	3.1	8	72.4	76.2
Cambodia	4.6	117	49.4	52.2
Indonesia	3	65	58.2	61.9
Lao People's Democratic Republic	6.6	99	49.3	52.3
Malaysia	3.5	15	68.6	72.8
Myanmar	4.2	83	55.8	59.1
Philippines	4	41	63	66.8
Singapore	1.8	7	71.7	77.2
Thailand	2.2	28	65.7	70.4
Viet Nam	3.9	38	61.7	66.1
SOUTH ASIA	4.3	90	59.2	59.6
Afghanistan	6.8	163	42.8	43.8
Bangladesh	4.8	109	52.9	52.4
Bhutan	5.8	130	47.8	49
India	3.9	88	59.9	60.4
Iran (Islamic Republic of)	5.8	38	66.4	67.5
Maldives	6.2	43	61.3	61.3
Nepal	5.5	100	53.8	52.7
Pakistan	6.2	99	58.7	58.8
Sri Lanka	2.5	25	69.4	73.6
CENTRAL ASIA	3.6	35	65.2	72.3
Azerbaijan	2.7	26	67	74
Kazakhstan	2.8	26	64	73
Kyrgyzstan	3.9	32	64	72
Tajikistan	5.1	43	67	72
Turkmenistan	4.5	55	62	68
Uzebekistan	4	38	66	72

(Contd.)

Country or Area and Region	Percentage aged 0-14	Percentage aged 60+	Dependency Ratio (percentage)
	9	10	11
ESCAP	32.3	8.1	68.4
EAST ASIA	26.4	9.9	56.9
China	27.4	9.1	57.3
Democratic People's Republic of Korea	28.8	6.6	54.9
Hongkong	20.3	13.3	50.6
Japan	17.4	18.5	56.1
Macau	24.3	7.3	46.1
Mongolia	40.8	5.1	85
Republic of Korea	24.7	8	48.7
SOUTH-EAST ASIA	36	6.2	73.4
Brunei Darussalam	33.3	7.4	68.6
Cambodia	41.2	4.4	83.9
Indonesia	34.8	6.1	69.4
Lao People's Democratic Republic	44	4.9	95.6
Malaysia	38	5.8	78.2
Myanmar	37.7	6.4	78.9
Philippines	39.1	5.1	79.3
Singapore	23.2	9.1	47.7
Thailand	31.3	6.5	60.8
Viet Nam	37.9	7.2	82.3
SOUTH ASIA	37.5	6.7	79.7
Afghanistan	41.2	4.6	84.6
Banglaldesh	41	4.8	84.5
Bhutan	38.7	6.2	81.5
India	35.5	7.3	75
Iran (Islamic Republic of)	45.9	5.7	106.8
Maldives	44.2	5.7	99.7
Nepal	43.3	5.1	93.6
Pakistan	43.8	4.6	94
Sri Lanka	31.7	8.3	66.6
CENTRAL ASIA	37.3	4.8	73.3
Azerbaijan	33	5	61.3
Kazakhstan	32	6	61.3
Kyrgyzstan	37	5.0	72.4
Tajikistan	43	4	88.7
Turkmenistan	41	4	81.8
Uzbekistan	41	4	81.8

(Contd.)

Country or Area and Region	Density (persons per sq. km.)	Percentage of Urban Population
	12	13
ESCAP	89	32.2
EAST ASIA	118	35.9
China	124	29.4
Democratic People's Republic of Korea	188	60.4
Hong Kong	5488	94.5
Japan	329	77.1
Macau	30.250	98.7
Mongolia	1	52.7
Republic of Korea	441	74.1
SOUTH-EAST ASIA	102	31.3
Brunei Darussalam	47	58
Cambodia	50	12.6
Indonesia	97	30.9
Lao People's Democratic Republic	19	19.9
Malaysia	56	44.7
Myanmar	65	25.3
Philippines	217	43.8
Singapore	4565	100
Thailand	113	29
Viet Nam	209	22.8
SOUTH ASIA	182	26.9
Afghanistan	29	18.9
Bangaldesh	776	17.7
Bhutan	34	5.8
India	268	25.7
Iran (Islamic Republic of)	36	58.9
Maldives	779	26.2
Nepal	146	10.5
Pakistan	157	33.1
Sri Lanka	269	21.8
CENTRAL ASIA	15	46.2
Azerbaijan	86	54
Kazakhstan	6	58
Kyrgyzstan	23	38
Tajikistan	39	31
Turkmenistan	8	45
Uzbekistan	48	40

(Contd.)

Country or Area and Region	Population	
	Projected to year 2010 (thousands)	Doubling time (years)
	14	15
ESCAP	4084288	40
EAST ASIA	1634128	54
China	1409946	50
Democratic People's Republic of Korea	29035	38
Hong Kong	6440	101
Japan	135090	223
Macau	588	31
Mongolia	3543	26
Republic of Korea	49486	76
SOUTH-EAST ASIA	577384	37
Brunei Darussalam	364	30
Cambodia	12959	28
Indonesia	208421	42
Lao People's Democratic Republic	7119	24
Malaysia	26138	30
Myanmar	61631	32
Philippines	89337	30
Singapore	3200	33
Thailand	71118	49
Viet Nam	97097	33
SOUTH ASIA	1748927	32
Afghanistan	33539	15
Bangladesh	177491	28
Bhutan	2465	30
India	1189396	36
Iran (Islamic Republic of)	95353	23
Maldives	372	20
Nepal	31047	28
Pakistan	197672	24
Sri Lanka	21592	55
CENTRAL ASIA	88545	30
Azerbaijan	10125	35
Kazakhstan	22550	45
Kyrgyzstan	6495	30
Tajikistan	8521	21
Turkmenistan	6085	25
Uzbekistan	34769	26

(Contd.)

Country or Area and Region	1990 GNP Per Capita ($US)	Contraceptive Prevalence Rate (%)
	16	17
ESCAP	1736	-
EAST ASIA	2865	-
China	370	72
Democratic People's Republic of Korea	-	-
Hong Kong	11490	81
Japan	25430	56
Macau	-	-
Mongolia	-	-
Republic of Korea	5400	77
SOUTH-EAST ASIA	931	-
Brunei Darussalam	-	-
Cambodia	-	-
Indonesia	570	48
Lao People's Democratic Republic	200	-
Malaysia	2320	-
Myanmar	-	17
Philippines	730	34
Singapore	11160	-
Thailand	1420	68
Viet Nam	-	53
SOUTH ASIA	444	-
Afghanistan	-	-
Bangladesh	210	31
Bhutan	190	-
India	350	45
Iran (Islamic Republic of)	2490	-
Maldives	450	-
Nepal	170	25
Pakistan	380	12
Sri Lanka	470	62
CENTRAL ASIA	-	-
Azerbaijan	-	7
Kazkhstan	-	22
Kyrgyzstan	-	25
Tajikistan	-	15
Turkmenistan	-	12
Uzbekistan	-	19

Notes :

   *   Refers to 1991

  **   Refers to 1990

  +   Refers to 1989

 ++ Refers to 1988

  x   Refers to 1987

 xx Refers to 1986

  #   Data for both sexes combined.

  @   Weighted averages, excluding Central Asian countries and some other countries reporting their elderly population as population aged 65+, instead of aged 60+, and the related dependency ratio.

  ~   Refers to modern methods only.

  ^   Percentage of Population aged 65+, and

$$\text{demendency ratio} = \frac{(\text{Population aged})\text{-}14 + \text{population aged } 65+}{\text{population aged } 15\text{-}64} \times 100$$

  \$ The total population for Pakistan has been cited from the United Nations World Population Prospects, 1992 Revision, in which it was assumed that about two thirds of Afghan refugees would return to their country in 1990-95. However, according to UNHCR via an electronic fact sheet, there were still about 2.3 million Afghans in Pakistan as of June 1992.

1. Exponential growth rate. The rate of increase takes into account international migration, and thus is not necessarily equal to the rate of natural increase.

$$2.\quad \text{Dependency ratio} = \frac{(\text{population aged } 0\text{-}14 + \text{population aged } 60+)}{\text{population aged } 15\text{-}59} \times 100$$

3. Surface area data used to compute density are from 1989 Demographic Yearbook (United Nations publication, Sales No. STESA/STAT/SER.R/19).

4. Where national data are not available, percentage of urban population for the country is cited from World Urbanization Prospects 1990, Estimates and Projections of Urban and Rural Population and of Urban Agglomeration (United Nations Publication, Sales No. E.91 XII.11).

5. Based on the assumption that the current rate of growth remains unchanged.

6. Data of GNP per capita are from World Bank, World Development Report 1992, Development and the Environment, 1992.

7. Contaceptive prevalence rate data are from (i) Demographic and Health Surveys World Conference, Proceedings, vol. I, 1991 and vol. II, 1991 (ii) Population Referecne Bureau, Inc., 1992 World Population Data Sheet, and (iii) Myanmar, Ministry of Home and Religious Affairs, Population Change and Fertility Survey, Preliminary Report, March 1991.

Source: ESCAP,1992 ESCAP POPULATION DATA SHEET, Population And Sustainable Development, Goals and Strategies into theTwenty-first Century, Fourth Asian and Pacific Population Conference, 19-27 August 1992, Bali, Indonesia.

ASIAN COUNTRIES
SELECTED SOCIAL INDICATORS 1992

	Adult Literacy M/F 1990	Secondary School Enrolment M/F 1986-89
	1	2
EASTERN ASIA		
China	84/62	50/37
Hong Kong	../..	71/76
Japan	../..	95/97
Korea, Democratic People's Republic of	../..	100/100
Korea, Republic of	99/94	91/83
Mangolia	../..	88/96
SOUTH-EASTERN ASIA		
Cambodia	48/22	45/20
Indonesia	84/62	53/43
Lao People's Democratic Republic	../..	23/22
Malaysia	87/70	59/57
Mynamar	89/72	25/23
Philippines	90/90	66/71
Singapore	../..	70/71
Thailand	96/90	32/28
Vietnam	92/84	44/41
SOUTHERN ASIA		
Afghanistan	44/14	10/7
Bangladesh	47/22	24/11
Bhutan	51/25	7/2
India	62/34	50/29
Iran (Islamic Republic of)	65/43	57/44
Nepal	38/13	35/17
Pakistan	47/21	26/11
Sri Lanka	93/84	63/74

(Contd.)

	Births Attended by Health Worker (%) 1983-90	Access to Health Services (%) 1985-90
	3	4
EASTERN ASIA		
China	94	90
Hong Kong	100	99
Japan	100	..
Korea, Democratic People's Republic of	100	..
Korea, Republic of	89	93
Mangolia	99	..
SOUTH-EASTERN ASIA		
Cambodia	47	53
Indonesia	49	80
Lao People's Democratic Republic	..	67
Malaysia	82	..
Myanmar	57	33
Philippines	57	..
Singapore	100	100
Thailand	71	70
Vietnam	95	80
SOUTHERN ASIA		
Afghanistan	9	29
Bangladesh	5	45
Bhutan	7	65
India	33	..
Iran (Islamic Republic of)	70	80
Nepal	6	..
Pakistan	40	55
Sri Lanka	94	93

(Contd.)

	Access to Safe Water 1985-88	Food Production per capita (1979-81=100) 1987-89
	5	6
EASTERN ASIA		
China	74	128
Hong Kong	100	61
Japan	..	97
Korea, Democratic People's Republic of	..	108
Korea, Republic of	79	96
Mangolia	65	91
SOUTH-EASTERN ASIA		
Cambodia	3	146
Indonesia	46	124
Lao People's Democratic Republic	29	116
Malaysia	79	142
Myanmar	33	120
Philippines	81	86
Singapore	100	86
Thailand	74	104
Vietnam	42	111
SOUTHERN ASIA		
Afghanistan	21	88
Bangladesh	81	93
Bhutan	32	121
India	75	113
Iran (Islamic Republic of)	89	87
Nepal	37	107
Pakistan	56	103
Sri Lanka	60	87

(Contd.)

	Agricultural Production per hectare arable land 1987	GNP per capita (US$) 1989	Health/ Education as % of GNP 1987
	7	8	9
EASTERN ASIA			
China	7.7	350	4.1
Hong Kong	10.0	10,350	..
Japan	1.9	23,810	10.0
Korea, Democratic People's Republic of	3.2	..	..
Korea, Republic of	5.0	4,400	4.3
Mangolia	.5	..	..
SOUTH-EASTERN ASIA			
Cambodia	1.8	..	..
Indonesia	3.8	500	3.9
Lao People's Democratic Republic	3.1	180	..
Malaysia	1.2	2,160	8.4
Myanmar	1.9	..	2.7
Philippines	3.5	710	2.7
Singapore	10.0	10,450	6.3
Thailand	1.7	1,220	4.7
Vietnam	6.1	..	..
SOUTHERN ASIA			
Afghanistan	1.0	..	..
Bangladesh	8.2	180	2.6
Bhutan	10.0	..	..
India	3.0	340	4.4
Iran (Islamic Republic of)	1.0	3,200	4.4
Nepal	7.0	180	3.6
Pakistan	2.9	370	2.4
Sri Lanka	4.6	430	5.4

Source : **The State of World Population 1992**, UNFPA, New York, 1992.

Asian Countries; Nuptiality - 1991

Country	Legal age of marriage		Percent age ever married of ages				Average age at first marriage	
			15-19		50			
	F	M	F	M	F	M	F	M
EASTERN ASIA								
China	20	22	4.2	1.4	99.8	95.4	22	23.9
Dem. People's Rep. of Korea	..	..	..	..	..	..	..	..
Japan	20	20	1.1	.6	95.6	96.1	25.8	29.5
Mangolia	18	18	..	..	..	..	..	..
Republic of Korea	20	20	.9	.1	99.7	99.5	24.7	27.8
SOUTH-EASTERN ASIA								
Brunei Darussalam	..	..	8.2	4.6	94.5	95.2	25	26.1
Cambodia	..	..	15.2	2.7	97.9	98.2	21.3	24.3
Indonesia	..	..	18.8	1.8	98.8	98.2	21.1	24.8
Lao People's Democratic Republic	..	..	..	..	..	..	..	..
Malaysia	b	b	10.3	1.3	97.4	96.3	23.5	26.6
Myanmar	..	..	16.8	6.7	94.1	96.5	22.4	24.6
Philippines	18	20	14.3	3.4	93.1	95.7	22.4	25.3
Singapore	21	21	2.3	.4	96.5	94.1	26.2	28.4
Thailand	17	17	17.5	7.1	96.2	97.6	22.7	24.7
Vietnam	18	20	10.9	4.3	97.1	98.7	23.2	24.5
SOUTHERN ASIA								
Afghanistan	..	..	53.6	9.2	99.1	96.3	17.8	25.3
Bangladesh	18	20	68.8	6.7	99.1	98.7	16.7	23.9
Bhutan	..	..	..	..	..	..	..	..
India	18	21	44.2	12.5	99.6	97.7	18.7	23.4
Iran (Islamic Republic of)	..	..	34.2	6.8	98.6	98.4	20.2	23.8
Maldvies	..	..	51.2	10.2	99.7	97.3	17.9	22.1
Nepal	18	21	50.8	25.9	96.8	92.9	17.9	21.5
Pakistan	..	..	31.1	7.5	97.9	95	19.8	24.9
Sri Lanka	21	21	10.4	.9	95.6	93.1	24.4	27.9

Source : United Nastions Nuptiality Chart 1991
Repared by the Population Division of the Department of International Economic and
Social Affairs of the United Nations Secretariat.

II
China: Basic Demographic Data, 1991

Table 2: China: Demographic Indicators

Region	Total Pop (0'000) 1990	National Income (in 100m yuan) 1990	Per Capita Gross National Product 1990
	(1)	(2)	(3)
CHINA	114333	14300	1522
Beijing	1032.2	361.8	4804
NORTH CHINA			
Tianjin	866.25	243	3463
Hebei	6158.88	704.6	1342
Shanxi	2898.9	301	1297
Neimenggu	2162.55	-	-
NORTH EAST CHINA			
Liaoning	3968	800	2445
Jilin	2483	327	1575
Heilongjiang	3543	566	1908
EAST CHINA			
Shanghai	1337	614	5512
Jiangsu	6766.9	1103	1945
Zhejiang	4238	726	1937
Anhui	5675	515	1036
Fujian	3037	380	1482
Jliangxi	3810.64	361.4	1117
Shandong			

(Contd.)

Region	Total Pop (0'000) 1990	National Income (in 100m yuan) 1990	Per Capita Gross National Product 1990
	(1)	(2)	(3)
CENTRAL SOUTH CHINA			
Henan	8649	736	1022
Hubei	5439.29	780	1224
Hunan	6127.79	590	1167
Guangdong	6346	1108.08	2222
Guangxi	4261	312.21	861
Hainan	662.8	78	1418
SOUTH WEST CHINA			
Sichuan	-	941.1	-
Guizhou	3267.53	211	783
Yunnan	3730.6	310	936
Xizang	-	-	-
NORTH WEST CHINA			
Shaanxi	3316	297	1125
Gansu	2254	194	1025
Qinghai	447.66	47	1385
Ningxia	470.2	48	1318.59
Xinjiang	1529.16	207.97	1655

(Contd.)

Region	Per Capita Gross Output Value of Industry and Agriculture 1990	Per Capita Annual Expenses of Urban Residents 1990
	(4)	(5)
CHINA	2732	1387
Beijing	8235	1787
NORTH CHINA		
Tianjin	8881	1522
Hebei	2382	1397.4
Shanxi	1525	1145.4
Neimenggu	1920	1050
NORTH EAST CHINA		
Liaoning	4616	1399
Jilin	2983	1127.53
Heilongjiang	3116	1090
EAST CHINA		
Shanghai	12723	-
Jiangsu	4944	1464
Zhejiang	4167	1769
Anhui	1138	1224
Fujian	2488	1567
Jiangxi	1777	1094.24
Shandong	3340	1408.08
CENTRAL SOUTH CHINA		
Henan	1779	1152.95
Hubei	2587	1294.56
Hunan	1809	1382.28
Guangdong	3925	2135
Guangxi	1345	1448
Hainan	887	1575
SOUTH WEST CHINA		
Sichuan	-	1354.45
Guizhou	1095	1217.4
Yunnan	1361	1367.37
Xizang	-	-
NORTH WEST CHINA		
Shaanxi	1847	1264.9
Gansu	1077	1245
Qinghai	1033	1199
Ningxia	1885.58	1270.55
Xinjiang	2384	1355.88

(Contd.)

Region	Per Capita Net Income of Peasants	Number of Staff & Workers (0'000)	Average Money Wages of Staff & workers
	1990	1990	1990
	(6)	(7)	(8)
CHINA	630	13989	2150
Beijing	1297	454.9	2614
NORTH CHINA			
Tianjin	1069	284.31	2438
Hebei	621.7	651.1	1997
Shanxi	603.5	437.8	2102
Neimenggu	*607	-	1846
	*906		
NORTH EAST CHINA			
Liaoning	776	1011.2	2150
Jilin	717.34	514.1	1888
Heilongjiang	670.8	855.3	1850
EAST CHINA			
Shanghai	1665	507.06	2885
Jiangsu	884	878.89	2125
Zhejiang	1099	-	2219
Anhui	539	483.6	1782
Fujian	764	310.8	2109
Jiangxi	579.61	384.08	1689
Shandong			
CENTRAL SOUTH CHINA			
Henan	482	692.61	1825
Hubei	602.08	692.68	2033
Hunan	545.69	548.88	2020
Guangdong	952	785.49	2929
Guangxi	499.76	311.8	1972
Hainan	652	105.64	1980
SOUTH WEST CHINA			
Sichuan	557.76	934.89	1980
Guizhou	452	220.39	1850
Yunnan	490	291.39	2112
Xizang	430	-	-
NORTH WEST CHINA			
Shaanxi	459.7	379.2	2042
Gansu	403	231.6	2439
Qinghai	559.78	66.19	2615
Ningxia	569.78	67.41	2252
Xinjiang	622.45	300.54	2272

(Contd.)

Region	Crude Birth Rate	Crude Death Rate	Rate of Natural Increase	Life Expectancy at Birth
	1990	1990	1990	1981
	(9)	(10)	(11)	(12)
CHINA	21.06	6.67	14.39	67.811
Beijing	13.01	5.81	7.2	72.034
NORTH CHINA				
Tianjin	15.61	5.78	9.83	71.069
Hebei	20.46	6.82	13.64	70.65
Shanxi	22.54	6.56	15.98	67.947
Neimenggu	21.19	7.21	13.98	67.042
NORTH EAST CHINA				
Liaoning	16.3	6.59	9.71	70.,804
Jilin	19.49	6.56	12.93	69.027
Heilongjiang	18.11	6.35	11.76	68.354
EAST CHINA				
Shanghai	10.31	6.64	3.67	73.011
Jiangsu	20.54	6.53	14.01	69.644
Zhejiang	15.33	6.31	9.02	69.705
Anhui	24.47	6.25	18.22	69.354
Fujian	24.44	6.71	17.73	68.606
Jiangxi	24.59	7.54	17.05	66.282
Shandong	18.21	6.96	11.25	70.235
CENTRAL SOUTH CHINA				
Henan	24.92	6.52	18.4	69.813
Hubei	21.6	7.3	14.3	65.849
Hunan	23.93	7.23	16.7	64.544
Guangdong	22.26	5.76	16.5	68.578
Guangxi	20.2	6.6	13.6	68.313
Hainan	24.86	6.26	18.6	-
SOUTH WEST CHINA				
Sichuan	19.11	7.66	11.45	64.311
Guizhou	23.09	7.9	15.19	61.94
Yunnan	23.6	7.92	15.68	61.453
Xizang	23.98	7.55	16.43	-
NORTH WEST CHINA				
Shaanxi	23.48	6.52	16.96	65.24
Gansu	2068	6.2	14.48	66.087
Qinghai	24.34	7.47	16.87	61.578
Ningxia	24.34	5.52	18.82	65.911
Xinjiang	26.44	7.82	18.62	61.289

(Contd.)

Region	Total Fertility Rate 1989	Planned Fertility Rate 1989	Unplanned Fertility Rate 1989	Birth Control Rate 1989
	(13)	(14)	(15)	(16)
CHINA	1.775	84.18	15.82	88.11
Beijing	1.3323	95.82	4.18	88.72
NORTH CHINA				
Tianjin	1.4116	97.06	2.94	91.56
Hebei	1.7997	88.6	11.4	86.13
Shanxi	-	83.51	16.49	89.82
Neimenggu	1.608	92.15	7.85	90.02
NORTH EAST CHINA				
Liaoning	1.3236	99.11	.89	89.01
Jilin		95.54	4.46	89.21
Heilongjiang	1.6081	82.04	17.96	89.26
EAST CHINA				
Shanghai	1.5081	99.39	.61	90.25
Jiangsu	-	87.09	12.91	89.9
Zhejiang	1.3144	94.85	5.15	92.06
Anhui	2.1286	77.71	22.29	88.06
Fujian	1.6049	62.95	37.05	90.08
Jiangxi	1.5837	75.95	24.05	88.61
Shandong	16479	89.25	10.75	90.69
CENTRAL SOUTH CHINA				
Henan	2.6069	84.61	15.39	90.1
Hubei	1.8119	82.91	17.09	87.94
Hunan	2.0762	69.93	30.07	88.06
Guangdong	1.7307	83.84	16.16	87.86
Guangxi	1.9294	82.58	17.42	83.68
Hainan	2.3709	78.2	21.8	84.56
SOUTH WEST CHINA				
Sichuan	1.5898	91.05	8.95	89.98
Guizhou	2.0908	76.27	23.73	82.9
Yunnan	2.2214	78.39	21.61	77.5
Xizang	-	-	-	-
NORTH WEST CHINA				
Shaanxi	2.0491	81.4	18.6	89.41
Gansu	1.839	85.3	14.7	87.3
Qinghai	1.9127	78.71	21.29	80.17
Ningxia	2.2425	75.05	24.95	82.92
Xinjiang	2.4535	80.16	19.84	62.18

(Contd.)

Region	One-child Certificate Rate 1989	Number of Hospital Beds (0'000) 1990	Number of Doctors (0'000) 1990	Attendance Rate of School-age Children 1990
	(17)	(18)	(19)	(20)
CHINA	18.1	262.4	176.3	97.9
Beijing	53.79	5.9	11.16	-
NORTH CHINA				
Tianjin	48.22	3.34	3.2	99.8
Hebei	12.61	14.6	8.7	99
Shanxi	12.67	9.8	6	98.9
Neimenggu	12.51	6.07	.9	97.09
NORTH EAST CHINA				
Liaoning	35.6	17.4	8.6	99.4
Jilin	26.45	8.3	5	98.89
Heilongjiang	25.33	11.01	7.2	99.02
EAST CHINA				
Shanghai	64.93	6.21	5.82	99.93
Jiangsu	35.52	14.54	9.94	99.9
Zhejiang	20.88	9.71	5.91	99.3
Anhui	9.51	9.58	5.9	-
Fujian	9.21	6.06	3.57	99.1
Jiangxi	6.05	8.26	5.2	98.2
Shandong	22.30	15.96	10.7	98.6
CENTRAL SOUTH CHINA				
Henan	10.08	18.21	9.94	98.78
Hubei	13.58	13.16	8.68	99.04
Hunan	8.84	14.68	6.5	98
Guangdong	8.84	11.41	8.11	99.25
Guangxi	5.65	6.9	5.12	96.97
Hainan	7.82	2.11	.714	98.9
SOUTH WEST CHINA				
Sichuan	27.18	21.55	15.17	96.4
Guizhou	5.29	5.31	3.7185	91.3
Yunnan	6.42	7.61	5.3	-
Xizang	-	-	-	54.5
NORTH WEST CHINA				
Shaanxi	12.73	7.8	5.9	98.05
Gansu	10.3	4.6	3.3	94.4
Qinghai	9.07	1.57	1.99	81.48
Ningxia	8.88	1.0045	.9185	93.9
Xinjiang	9.07	6.07	3.37	97.5

III
India: Basic Demographic Data, 1991

Table 3: India: Demographic Indicators

States	Pop in 1991 (in '000)	Density (Pop per sq. km.)	Annual exponential growth rate 1981-91 (per cent)
	(1)	(2)	(3)
INDIA	846303	274	2.14
1. ANDHRA PRADESH	66508	242	2.17
2. ARUNACHAL PRADESH	865	10	3.14
3. ASSAM	22414	286	2.17
4. BIHAR	86374	497	2.11
5. GOA	1170	316	1.49
6. GUJARAT	41310	211	1.92
7. HARYANA	16464	372	2.42
8. HIMACHAL PRADESH	5171	93	1.89
9. JAMMU & KASHMIR	7719	-	2.54
10. KARNATAKA	44977	235	1.92
11. KERALA	29098	749	1.34
12. MADHYA PRADESH	66181	149	2.38
13. MAHARASHTRA	78937	257	2.29
14. MANIPUR	1837	82	2.57
15. MEGHALAYA	1775	79	2.84
16. MIZORAM	690	33	3.34
17. NAGALAND	1209	73	4.45
18. ORISSA	31660	203	1.83
19. PUNJAB	20282	403	1.89
20. RAJASTHAN	44006	129	2.5
21. SIKKIM	406	57	2.51

(Contd.)

States	Pop in 1991 (in '000)	Density (Pop per sq. km.)	Annual exponential growth rate 1981-91 (per cent)
	(1)	(2)	(3)
22. TAMIL NADU	55859	429	1.43
23. TRIPURA	2757	263	2.95
24. UTTAR PRADESH	139112	473	2.27
25. WEST BENGAL	68078	767	2.21
UTs			
1. ANDAMAN & NICOBAR ISLANDS	281	34	3.97
2. CHANDIGARH	642	5632	3.52
3. DADRA & NAGAR HAVELI	138	282	2.89
4. DAMAN & DIU	102	907	2.52
5. DELHI	9421	6352	4.15
6. LAKSHADWEEP	52	1616	2.15
7. PONDI CHEERY	808	1642	2.9

(Contd.)

States	Sex Ratio (females per 1000 males)	Literacy Rate (per cent of 7 + Pop)		
		Persons	Males	Females
	(4)	(5)	(6)	(7)
INDIA	927	52.21	64.13	39.29
1. ANDHRA PRADESH	972	44.09	55.13	32.72
2. ARUNACHAL PRADESH	859	41.59	51.45	29.69
3. ASSAM	923	52.89	61.87	43.03
4. BIHAR	911	38.48	52.49	22.89
5. GOA	967	75.51	83.64	67.09
6. GUJARAT	934	61.29	73.13	48.64
7. HARYANA	865	55.85	69.1	40.47
8. HIMACHAL PRADESH	976	63.86	75.36	52.13
9. JAMMU & KASHMIR	-	-	-	-
10. KARNATAKA	960	56.04	67.26	44.34
11. KERALA	1036	89.79	93.62	86.13
12. MADHYA PRADESH	931	44.2	58.42	28.85
13. MAHARASHTRA	934	64.87	76.56	52.32
14. MANIPUR	958	59.89	71.63	47.6
15. MEGHALAYA	955	49.1	53.12	44.85
16. MIZORAM	921	82.27	85.61	78.6
17. NAGALAND	886	61.65	67.62	54.75
18. ORISSA	971	49.09	63.09	34.68
19. PUNJAB	882	58.51	65.66	50.41
20. RAJASTHAN	910	38.55	54.99	20.44
21. SIKKIM	878	56.94	65.74	46.69
22. TAMIL NADU	974	62.66	73.75	51.33
23. TRIPURA	945	60.44	70.58	49.65
24. UTTAR PRADESH	879	41.06	55.73	25.31
25. WEST BENGAL	917	57.7	67.81	46.56
UTs				
1. ANDAMAN & NICOBAR ISLANDS	818	73.02	78.99	65.46
2. CHANDIGARH	790	77.81	82.04	72.34
3. DADRA & NAGAR HAVELI	952	40.71	53.56	26.98
4. DAMAN & DIU	969	71.2	82.66	59.4
5. DELHI	827	75.29	82.01	66.99
6. LAKSHADWEEP	943	81.78	90.18	72.89
7. PONDI CHEERY	979	74.74	83.68	65.63

(Contd.)

States	Work Participation Rate (Workers as per cent of total Pop).			Pop 0-6 as percent of total pop
	Persons	Males	Females	
	(8)	(9)	(10)	(11)
INDIA	37.46	51.55	22.25	17.94
1. ANDHRA PRADESH	45.05	55.48	34.32	16.49
2. ARUNACHAL PRADESH	46.24	53.76	37.49	21.12
3. ASSAM	36.09	49.45	21.61	19.73
4. BIHAR	32.16	47.92	14.86	20.57
5. GOA	35.28	49.56	20.52	11.74
6. GUJARAT	40.23	53.57	25.96	16.53
7. HARYANA	31	48.51	10.76	18.98
8. HIMACHAL PRADESH	42.82	50.64	34.82	16.25
9. JAMMU & KASHMIR	-	-	-	-
10. KARNATAKA	41.99	54.09	29.39	16.63
11. KERALA	31.43	47.58	15.85	13.19
12. MADHYA PRADESH	42.82	52.26	32.68	19.78
13. MAHARASHTRA	42.96	52.16	33.11	17.11
14. MANIPUR	42.18	45.27	38.96	16.69
15. MEGHALAYA	42.67	50.07	34.93	22.18
16. MIZORAM	48.91	53.87	43.52	18.6
17. NAGALAND	42.68	46.86	37.96	17.15
18. ORISSA	37.53	53.79	20.79	16.89
19. PUNJAB	30.87	54.22	4.4	16.3
20. RAJASTHAN	38.87	49.3	27.4	20.13
21. SIKKIM	41.51	51.26	30.41	18.37
22. TAMIL NADU	43.31	56.39	29.89	13.33
23. TRIPURA	31.14	47.55	13.76	18.03
24. UTTAR PRADESH	32.2	49.68	12.32	20.27
25. WEST BENGAL	32.19	51.4	11.25	16.98
UTs				
1. ANDAMAN & NICOBAR ISLANDS	35.24	53.32	13.13	16.51
2. CHANDIGARH	34.94	54.33	10.33	14.92
3. DADRA & NAGAR HAVELI	53.25	57.5	48.79	20.46
4. DAMAN & DIU	37.63	51.63	23.17	15.53
5. DELHI	31.64	51.72	7.36	17.06
6. LAKSHADWEEP	26.43	44.17	7.6	18.3
7. PONDI CHEERY	33.08	50.55	15.24	13.67

(Contd.)

States	Scheduled Caste pop (per cent of total pop)	Scheduled Tribe pop (per cent of total pop)
	(12)	(13)
INDIA	16.48	8.08
1. ANDHRA PRADESH	15.93	6.31
2. ARUNACHAL PRADESH	.47	63.66
3. ASSAM	7.40	12.82
4. BIHAR	14.55	7.66
5. GOA	2.08	.03
6. GUJARAT	7.41	14.92
7. HARYANA	19.75	-
8. HIMACHAL PRADESH	25.34	4.22
9. JAMMU & KASHMIR	-	-
10. KARNATAKA	16.38	4.26
11. KERALA	9.92	1.1
12. MADHYA PRADESH	14.55	23.27
13. MAHARASHTRA	11.09	9.27
14. MANIPUR	2.02	34.41
15. MEGHALAYA	.51	85.53
16. MIZORAM	.1	94.75
17. NAGALAND	-	87.7
18. ORISSA	16.2	22.21
19. PUNJAB	28.31	-
20. RAJASTHAN	17.29	12.44
21. SIKKIM	5.93	22.36
22.. TAMIL NADU	19.18	1.03
23. TRIPURA	16.36	30.95
24. UTTAR PRADESH	21.05	.21
25. WEST BENGAL	23.62	5.59
UTs		
1. ANDAMAN & NICOBAR ISLANDS	-	9.54
2. CHANDIGARH	16.15	-
3. DADRA & NAGAR HAVELI	1.97	78.99
4. DAMAN & DIU	3.83	11.54
5. DELHI	19.05	-
6. LAKSHADWEEP	-	93.15
7. PONDI CHEERY	16.25	-

(Contd.)

States	Birth Rate (per 1000)	Death Rate (per 1000)	Natural increase rate (per 1000)
	(14)	(15)	(16)
INDIA	29.3	9.8	19.5
1. ANDHRA PRADESH	26	9.7	16.3
2. ARUNACHAL PRADESH	30.9	13.5	17.4
3. ASSAM	30.9	11.5	19.4
4. BIHAR	30.5	9.8	20.7
5. GOA	16.8	7.5	9.3
6. GUJARAT	27.5	8.5	19
7. HARYANA	33.1	8.2	24.9
8. HIMACHAL PRADESH	28.4	8.9	19.5
9. JAMMU & KASHMIR	-	-	-
10. KARNATAKA	26.8	9	17.8
11. KERALA	18.1	6	12.1
12. MADHYA PRADESH	35.8	13.8	22
13. MAHARASHTRA	26.2	8.2	18
14. MANIPUR	19.6	5.5	14.1
15. MEGHALAYA	32.4	8.8	23.6
16. MIZORAM	NA	NA	NA
17. NAGALAND	18.5	3.3	15.2
18. ORISSA	28.8	12.7	16.1
19. PUNJAB	28.6	8	20.6
20. RAJASTHAN	34.3	9.8	24.5
21. SIKKIM	26.5	8.8	17.7
22. TAMIL NADU	20.7	8.8	11.9
23. TRIPURA	24.4	7.6	16.8
24. UTTAR PRADESH	35.1	11.1	24
25. WEST BENGAL	26.7	8.1	18.6
UTs			
1. ANDAMAN & NICOBAR ISLANDS	19.9	5.7	14.2
2.. CHANDIGARH	14.1	4	10.1
3. DADRA & NAGAR HAVELI	30.4	11.4	19
4. DAMAN & DIU	27.8	9	18.8
5. DELHI	24.1	6	18.1
6. LAKSHADWEEP	27.1	4.7	24.4
7. PONDI CHEERY	18.9	6.4	12.5

(Contd.)

States	Infant Mortality rate (per 1000) live birth	Life Expectancy of birth (1981-88)	
		Male	Female
	(17)	(18)	(19)
INDIA	80	55.9	55.9
1. ANDHRA PRADESH	73	57.3	60.3
2. ARUNACHAL PRADESH	NA	NA	NA
3. ASSAM	81	52.4	52.5
4. BIHAR	69	54.9	52.3
5. GOA	NA	NA	NA
6. GUJARAT	69	55.9	57.9
7. HARYANA	68	61.5	59.5
8. HIMACHAL PRADESH	75	*58.5	*62.9
9. JAMMU & KASHMIR	-	*60.2	*60.7
10. KARNATAKA	77	59.8	62.4
11. KERALA	17	65.9	72.2
12. MADHYA PRADESH	122	50.6	51.8
13. MAHARASHTRA	60	60.1	62.8
14. MANIPUR	NA	NA	NA
15. MEGHALAYA	NA	NA	NA
16. MIZORAM	NA	NA	NA
17. NAGALAND	NA	NA	NA
18. ORISSA	126	53.6	53.1
19. PUNJAB	53	63	64.7
20. RAJASTHAN	77	53.5	54.3
21. SIKKIM	NA	NA	NA
22. TAMIL NADU	57	57.4	58.5
23. TRIPURA	NA	NA	NA
24. UTTAR PRADESH	93	52.3	49.6
25. WEST BENGAL	70	57.9	59.1
UTs			
1. ANDAMAN & NICOBAR ISLANDS	NA	NA	NA
2. CHANDIGARH	NA	NA	NA
3. DADRA & NAGAR HAVELI	NA	NA	NA
4. DAMAN & DIU	NA	NA	NA
5. DELHI	NA	NA	NA
6. LAKSHADWEEP	NA	NA	NA
7. PONDI CHEERY	NA	NA	NA

Notes: (1) Census was not held in Jammu & Kashmir (J & K) in 1991. The figures in col. (3) include projected population of J & K for the year 1991. However the rates in col. (2) + col. (4) - (19) exclude J & K.

(2) Figures of proporations in col. (2) to col. (13) are based on final population totals of 1991 Census while col. 14-16 are based on Sample Registration System (SRS) estimates of 1991.

(3) In col. 18+19 the life expectancy of birth is based on the age. Specific Death Rates averaged over 1981-88 as estimated by Sample Registration System (SRS).

(4) NA Stands for 'Not Available'.

* Relates to the period 1981-85.

Source : Registrar General, India, INDIA 1991: POPULATION DATA SHEET (MARCH 1993).

IV

Supplementary Tables
for India, 1991

Table S1: Inida 1991 Census final population Figures

INDIA

		Total	Male	Females
Area (in sq. km.)	:	3,065.027		
No. of States/UTs	:	32		
No. of Districts	:	452		
No. of Blocks	:	5,774		
No. of Villages (Inhabited)	:	580.702		
No. Villages (Uninbabited)	:	46,732		
No. of Union agglomuratinal	:	3699		
Total no. of Towns	:	4615		
No. of Occupied residential housed	:	147.011,586		
No. of Households	:	152,009.467		
TotalMale Females Populations**	:	846,302,688	:439,230,458	:407,072.230
Scheduled Caste 317	:	138,223,277	71,928,960	66,294
Scheduled Tribe	:	67,758,380	34,363,271	33,395,109
Population below age 7 years	:	150,421,175	77,322,151	73,099,024
Literates	:	359,284,417	229,536,935	129,747,482
Workers	:	285,932,493	221,658	64,273,909
I Cultivators	:	110,702,346	88,480,942	22,221,404
II Agricultural Labourers	:	74,597,744	46,164,447	28,432,997
III Livestock, Forestry, Fishing etc.	:	6,040,739	4,716,030	1,324,709
IV Mining and Quarrying	:	1,751,275	1,536,919	214,356

V (a) Manufacturing & Processing in Household industry	:	6,804,021	4,555,016	2,249,005
VI Construction	:	5,543,205	5,122,468	420,737
VII Trade & Commerce	:	21,296,337	19,862,725	1,433,612
VIII Transport, Storage and Communication	:	8,017,746	7,810,126	207,620
IX Others Services	:	29,311,622	23,995,194	5,316,428
Marginal Workers	:	26,198,877	2,705,223	25,493,654
Non Workers	:	524,436,566	210,844,351	313,592,215

**	Including projected population of Jammu & Kashmir.
All other figures exclude Jammu & Kashmir where 1991 Census was not conducted.

Source: National Informatics Centre, Planning commisoon and Office of Registrar General, India, NICNET CENSUS SERVICE, New Delhi, January 1993.

Table 2: Number of Main workers (In 000's) By Industrial Categories And sex India, 1981-1991

Industrial Category	Persons		Males		Females	
	1981	1991	1981	1991	1981	1991
1	2	3	4	5	6	7
Total Main Workers (1-IX)	220,698	278,940	175,892	216,018	44,806	62,922
I Cultivators	91,489	107,143	76,663	85,610	14,826	21,533
II Agricultural Labourers	55,436	73,752	34,672	45,482	20,764	28,270
III Livestock, Forestry, fishing, hunting, plantations, orchards and allied activities	4,962	5,306	4,298	822	1,008	
IV Mining and quarrying	1,275	1,717	1,118	1,504	157	213
V Manufacturing, processing, Servicing and repairs						
(a) In household industry	7,615	6,743	5,569	4,523	2,046	2,220
(b) other than household industry	17,328	21,649	15,715	19,210	1,613	2,439
VI Constructions	3,669	5,434	3,281	5,015	388	419
VII Trade and commerce	13,975	20,818	13,059	19,398	916	1,420
VIII Transport, Storage and Communications	6,070	7,843	5,906	7,639	164	204
IX Other services	18,879	28,535	15,769	23,339	3,110	5,196

*Excludes Assam and Jammu & Kashmir.

Source: Census of India 1991, Paper-2 of 1992: *Final Population Totals*. Tables 3 to 13 are also from *Census Paper No. 2 of 1992*.

Table 3: Decadal Change in the Main Workers and Each Industrial Category by sex During 1981-91, India

Industrial Category	Absolute increase/decrease (in, 000s)			Percentage increase/decrease			Percentage distribution		
	Persons	Males	Females	Persons	Males	Females	Persons	Males	Females
1	2	3	4	5	6	7	8	9	10
Total Main Workers	58,242,	40,126	18,116	26.39	22.81	40.43	100.00	100.00	100.00
I Cultivators	15,654	8,947	6,707	17.11	11.67	45.23	26.88	22.30	37.02
II Agricultural Labourers	18,316	10,810	7,506	33.04	31.18	36.15	31.45	26.94	41.43
III Livestock, forestry, fishing, hunting, plantations, orchards and allied activities	344	158	186	6.92	3.81	22.58	0.59	0.39	1.03
IV Mining and quarrying	442	386	56	34.68	34.50	35.94	0.76	0.96	0.31
V Manufacturing, processing, servicing and repairs									
(a) in household industry	-872	-1,046	174	-11.45	-18.78	8.48	-1.50	-2.61	0.96
(b) other than household industry	4,321	3,495	826	24.94	22.24	51.21	7.42	8.71	4.56
VI Constructions	1,765	1,734	31	48.09	52.83	7.98	3.03	4.32	0.17
VII Trade and commerce	6,843	6,339	504	48.97	48.55	55.02	11.75	15.80	2.78
VIII Transport, storage and communications	1,773	1,733	40	29.19	29.33	24.01	3.04	4.32	0.22
IX other services	9,656	7,570	2,086	51.15	48.01	67.10	16.58	18.87	11.52

*Excludes Assam and Jmmu & Kashmir.

Table 4: Sex Ratio (Females Per 1,000 Males) of Total Population and Population aged 0-6 years, 1961-1991

India/State or Union Territory	Year	Total population	Population 0-6 years
1	2	3	4
INDIA	1961	943	976
	1971	931	964
	1981	935	962
	1991	927	945
1 Andhra Pradesh	1961	981	1,002
	1971	977	990
	1981	975	992
	1991	972	974
2 Bihar	1961	994	988
	1971	954	964
	1981	946	981
	911	911	959
3 Gujarat	1961	940	955
	1971	934	946
	1981	942	947
	1991	934	928
4 Haryana	1961	868	910
	1971	867	898
	1981	870	902
	1991	865	879
5 Karnataka	1961	959	987
	1971	957	978
	1981	963	975
	1991	960	960
6 Kerala	1961	1,022	972
	1971	1,016	976
	1981	1,032	970
	1991	1,036	958
7 Madhya Pradesh	1961	953	982
	1971	941	976
	1981	941	978
	1991	931	952
8 Maharastra	1961	936	978
	1971	930	972
	1981	937	956
	1991	934	946

(Contd.)

India/State or Union Territory	Year	Total population	Population 0-6 years
1	2	3	4
9 Orissa	1961	1,001	1,035
	1971	988	1,168
	1981	981	995
	1991	971	967
10 Punjab	1961	854	894
	1971	865	899
	1981	879	908
	1991	882	875
11 Rajasthan	1961	908	951
	1971	911	933
	1981	919	954
	1991	910	916
12 Tamil Nadu	1961	992	985
	1971	978	974
	1981	977	967
	1991	974	948
13 Uttar Pradesh	1961	909	946
	1971	879	923
	1981	885	935
	1991	879	928
14 West Bangal	1961	878	1,008
	1971	891	1,010
	1981	911	981
	1991	917	967
15 Delhi	1961	785	923
	1971	801	909
	1981	808	926
	1991	827	915

Excludes Assam and Jammu and Kashmir.

Table 5: Sex Ratio (Females Per 1,000 Males) For Total, Scheduled cast, Scheduled Tribe and Non-Scheduled Caste/Scheduled Tribe population 1981-1991

	India/State or Union/Territory	1981				1991			
		Total Popn	Sch. Caste Popn	Sch. Tribe Popn	Mon-SC/ST Popn	Total Popn	Sch. Caste Popn	Sch. Tribe Popn	Non-SC/ST Popn
	1	2	3	4	5	6	7	8	9
	INDIA	935	932	983	930	927	922	972	923
	States								
1	Andhra Pradesh	975	971	962	977	972	969	960	974
2	Arunachal Pradesh	862	592	1,005	599	859	627	998	658
3	Bihar	946	966	993	937	911	914	971	905
4	Goa	975	956	845	976	967	967	889	967
5	Gujarat	942	942	976	936	934	925	967	929
6	Haryana	870	864	—	872	865	860	—	866
7	Himachal Pradesh	973	959	978	977	976	967	981	978
8	Karnataka	963	968	971	961	960	962	961	959
9	Kerala	1.032	1,022	992	1,033	1,036	1.029	996	1,038
10	Madhya Pradesh	941	932	997	923	931	915	985	916
11	Maharashtra	937	948	974	932	934	944	968	928
12	Manipur	971	956	975	969	958	973	959	957
13	Meghalaya	954	790	1,002	776	955	821	997	739
14	Mizoram	919	125	997	227	921	157	982	243
15	Nagaland	863	—	955	495	886	—	946	547
16	Oeissa	981	988	1,012	969	971	975	1,002	959
17	Punjab	879	868	—	883	882	873	—	885
18	Rajasthan	919	913	945	916	910	899	930	909
19	Sikkim	835	913	927	801	878	939	914	862
20	Tamil Nadu	977	980	968	976	974	978	960	973
21	Tripura	946	942	962	940	945	949	965	931
22	Uttar Pradesh	885	892	915	883	879	877	914	879
23	West Bengal	911	926	969	902	917	931	964	909
	Union Territories								
1	Andaman & Nicobar Islands	760	—	930	739	818	—	947	806
2	Chandigarh	769	—	770	790	810	—	786	
3	Dadra & Nagar Haveli	974	1,133	1,018	799	952	925	1,022	708
4	Daman & Diu	1,062	1,259	952	1,072	969	1,067	931	970
5	Delhi	808	813	—	807	827	834	—	826
6	Lakshadweep	975	—	1,002	646	943	—	994	442
7	Pondicherry	985	964	—	989	979	983	—	979

* Excludes Assam and Jammu & Kashmir.

Table 6: Total Population, Population Aged 7 and Above, Literates, Illiterates and Litteracy Rate by Sex and Rural-Urban Residence, India* 1981-1991

Population	Total Rural Urban	1981			1991		
		Persons	Males	Females	Persons	Males	Females
1	2	3	4	5	6	7	8
Total population	Total	659.30	340.76	318.54	816.17	423.56	392.61
	Rural	502.88	257.56	245.32	602.89	310.98	291.91
	Urban	156.42	83.20	73.22	213.28	112.58	100.70
Population aged	Total	536.21	278.04	258.17	670.17	348.47	321.70
7 years & above	Rural	406.19	208.31	197.88	490.13	253.07	237.06
	Urban	130.02	69.73	60.29	180.04	95.40	84.64
Illiterates aged	total	302.06	120.96	77.07	349.76	223.70	126.06
7 years & above	Rural	146.60	103.51	43.09	218.32	146.38	71.94
	Urban	42.47	16.16	26.31	48.60	18.08	30.52
Literacy rate	Total	43.67	56.50	29.85	52.19	64.20	39.19
among population aged	Rural	36.09	49.69	21.77	44.54	57.84	30.35
7 years & above	Urban	67.34	76.83	56.37	73.01	81.05	63.94

*Excludes Assam and Jammu & Kashmir.

Table 7: Literacy Rates for States and Union Territories, 1981 and 1991

India/State or Union Territory	Population in 1991 (million)	Literacy rate (per cent) 1981	1991
INDIA	816.17	43.67	52.19
States			
1 Andhra Pradesh	66.51	35.66	44.09
2 Aunachal Pradesh	0.86	25.55	41.59
3 Bihar	86.37	32.05	38.48
4 Goa	1.17	65.71	75.51
5 Gujarat	41.31	52.21	61.29
6 Haryana	16.46	43.88	55.85
7 Himachal Pradesh	5.17	51.18	63.86
8 Karnataka	44.98	46.21	56.04
9 Kerala	29.10	81.56	89.81
10 Madhya Pradesh	66.18	34.23	44.20
11 Maharashtra	78.94	55.83	64.87
12 Manipur	1.84	49.66	59.89
13 Meghalaya	1.77	42.05	49.10
14 Mizoram	0.69	74.26	82.27
15 Nagaland	1.21	50.28	61.65
16 Orissa	31.66	40.97	49.09
17 Punjab	20.28	48.17	58.51
18 Rajasthan	44.01	30.11	38.55
19 Sikkim	0.41	41.59	56.94
20 Tamil Nadu	55.86	54.39	62.66
21 Tripura	2.76	50.11	60.44
22 Uttar Pradesh	139.11	33.35	41.60
23 West Bengal	68.08	48.65	57.70
Union Territories			
1 Andaman & Nicobar Islands	0.28	63.19	73.02
2 Chandigarh	0.64	74.81	77.81
3 Dadra & Nagar Haveli	0.14	32.70	40.71
4 Daman & Diu	0.10	59.91	71.20
5 Delhi	9.42	71.94	75.29
6 Lakshadweep	0.05	68.42	81.78
7 Pondicherry	0.81	65.14	74.74

* Excludes Assam and Jammu & Kashmir.

Table 8: Literacy Rates By Sex Crencent 1981 and 1991

| India/State or Union Territory | 1981 | | 1991 | |
	Males	Females	Males	Females
1	2	3	4	5
INDIA	56.50	29.85	64.20	39.19
States				
1 Andhra Pradesh	46.83	24.16	55.13	32.72
2 Arunachal Pradesh	35.12	14.02	51.45	29.69
3 Bihar	46.60	16.52	52.49	22.89
4 Goa	76.01	55.17	83.64	67.09
5 Gujarat	65.14	38.46	73.13	48.64
6 Haryana	58.51	26.93	69.10	40.47
7 Himachal Pradesh	64.27	37.72	57.36	52.13
8 Karnataka	58.73	33.17	67.26	44.34
9 Kerala	87.73	75.65	93.62	86.17
10 Madhya Pradesh	48.42	19.00	58.42	28.85
11 Maharashtra	69.65	41.01	76.56	52.32
12 Manipur	64.15	34.67	71.63	47.60
13 Meghalaya	46.65	37.17	53.12	44.85
14 Mizoram	79.36	68.61	85.61	78.60
15 Nagaland	58.58	40.39	67.62	54.75
16 Orissa	56.45	25.14	63.09	34.68
17 Punjab	55.56	39.70	65.66	50.41
18 Rajasthan	44.77	14.00	54.99	20.44
19 Sikkim	53.00	27.38	65.74	46.69
20 Tamil Nadu	68.05	40.43	73.75	51.33
21 Tripura	61.49	38.01	70.58	49.65
22 Uttar Pradesh	47.45	17.19	55.73	25.31
23 West Bengal	59.93	36.07	67.81	46.56
Union Territories				
1 Andaman & Nicobar Islands	70.29	53.19	78.99	65.46
2 Chandigarh	78.89	69.31	82.04	72.34
3 Dadra & Nagar Haveli	44.64	20.37	53.56	26.98
4 Daman & Diu	74.47	46.50	82.66	59.40
5 Delhi	79.28	62.60	82.01	66.99
6 Lakshadweep	81.24	55.32	90.18	72.89
7 Pondicherry	77.09	53.03	83.68	65.63

* Excludes Assam and Jammu & Kashmir.

Table 9: Male-Female Differential in Literacy Rates for States and Union Territories, 1981-1991

India/State or Union Territory	Male-Female difference in Literacy rate (Percentpoints)		Sex Ratio (female) Literates per 1,000 male literates)	
	1981	1991	1981	1991
1	2	3	4	5
INDIA	26.65	25.01	491	564
States				
1 Andhra Pradesh	22.67	22.41	501	577
2 Arunachal Pradesh	21.10	21.76	331	478
3 Bihar	30.08	29.60	332	392
4 Goa	20.84	16.55	709	776
5 Gujarat	26.68	24.49	556	622
6 Haryana	31.58	28.63	397	505
7 Himachal Pradesh	26.55	23.23	571	678
8 Karnataka	25.56	22.92	542	633
9 Kerala	12.08	7.45	900	965
10 Madhya Pradesh	29.42	29.57	366	457
11 Maharashtra	28.64	24.24	549	636
12 Manipur	29.48	24.03	523	634
13 Meghalaya	9.48	8.27	752	799
14 Mizoram	10.75	7.01	781	836
15 Nagaland	18.19	12.87	578	701
16 Orissa	31.31	28.41	436	534
17 Punjab	15.86	15.25	623	678
18 Rajasthan	30.77	34.55	285	338
19 Sikkim	25.62	19.05	415	610
20 Tamil Nadu	27.62	22.42	581	681
21 Tripura	23.48	20.93	582	661
22 Uttar Pradesh	30.26	30.42	316	394
23 West Bengal	23.86	21.25	540	623
Union Territories				
1 Andaman & Nicobar Island	17.10	13.53	538	655
2 Chandigarh	9.58	9.70	653	681
3 Dadra & Nagar Haveli	24.27	26.58	442	472
4 Daman & Diu	27.97	23.26	678	698
5 Delhi	16.68	15.02	620	662
6 Lakshadweep	25.92	17.29	666	762
7 Pondicerry	24.06	18.05	679	770

* Excludes Assam and Jammu & Kashmir

Table 10: Literacy Rates by Rural Urban Redidence 1981-1991

India/State or Union Territory	1981		1991	
	Rural	Urban	Rural	Urban
1	2	3	4	5
INIDA*	36.09	67.34	44.54	73.01
States				
1 Andha Pradesh	27.85	61.00	35.74	66.35
2 Arunachal Pradesh	22.81	63.75	37.02	71.59
3 Bihar	27.70	61.77	33.83	67.89
4 Goa	61.63	74.33	72.31	80.10
5 Gujarat	43.57	71.00	53.09	76.54
6 Haryana	36.26	66.83	49.85	73.66
7 Himachal Pradesh	48.89	77.80	61.86	84.17
8 Karnataka	37.63	66.91	47.69	74.20
9 Kerala	80.31	86.91	88.92	92.25
10 Madhya Pradesh	26.30	64.55	35.87	70.81
11 Maharashtra	45.65	74.29	55.52	79.20
12 Manipur	45.03	62.61	55.79	70.53
13 Meghalya	34.39	75.09	41.05	81.74
14 Mizoram	69.17	89.46	72.47	93.45
15 Nagaland	45.62	76.13	57.23	83.10
16 Orissa	37.77	64.81	45.46	71.99
17 Punjab	41.73	64.96	52.77	72.08
18 Rajasthan	22.47	58.05	30.37	65.33
19 Sikkim	39.94	64.93	54.38	80.89
20 Tamil Nadu	45.00	73.25	54.59	77.99
21 Tripura	45.78	83.36	56.08	83.09
22 Uttar Pradesh	28.53	54.87	36.66	61.00
23 West Bengal	40.18	70.68	50.50	75.27
Union Territories				
1 A & N Islands	58.12	76.71	69.73	81.69
2 Chandigarh	53.27	76.24	59.12	79.87
3 Dadra & Nagar Haveli	30.29	65.70	37.00	78.44
4 Daman & Diu	50.42	75.29	61.55	81.61
5 Delhi	57.83	73.01	66.90	76.18
6 Lakshadweep	65.47	71.76	78.89	83.99
7 Pondicherry	56.17	73.25	65.36	79.88

* Excludes Assam and Jammu & Kashmir.

Table 11: Urban Rural Diferential in Literacy Rates For States And Union Territor:es, 1981-1991

India/State or Union Territory	Urban-rural difference in literacy rate (per cent points)		Rural/urban ratio of Literacy rate	
	1981	1991	1981	1991
1	2	3	4	5
INDIA	31.25	28.47	53.59	61.01
States				
1 Andhra Pradesh	33.15	30.61	45.66	53.87
2 Arunachal Pradesh	40.94	34.57	35.78	51.71
3 Bihar	34.07	34.06	44.84	49.83
4 Goa	12.70	7.70	82.91	90.27
5 Gujarat	27.43	23.45	61.37	69.36
6 Haryana	29.57	23.81	55.75	67.68
7 Himachal Pradesh	28.91	22.31	62.84	73.49
8 Karnataka	29.28	26.51	56.24	64.27
9 Kerala	6.60	3.33	92.41	96.39
10 Madhya Pradesh	38.25	34.94	40.74	50.66
11 Maharashtra	28.64	23.68	61.45	70.10
12 Manipur	17.58	14.74	71.92	79.10
13 Meghalaya	40.70	40.69	45.80	50.22
14 Mizoram	20.29	20.98	77.32	77.55
15 Nagaland	30.51	25.87	59.92	68.87
16 Orissa	27.04	26.53	58.28	63.15
17 Punjab	23.23	19.31	64.24	73.21
18 Rajasthan	33.58	34.96	38.71	46.49
19 Sikkim	27.99	26.51	56.89	67.23
20 Tamil Nadu	28.25	23.40	61.43	70.00
21 Tripura	37.58	27.01	54.92	67.49
22 Uttar Pradesh	26.34	24.34	52.00	60.10
23 west Bangal	30.50	24.77	56.85	67.09
Union Territories				
1 Andaman & Nicobr Islands	18.59	11.96	75.77	85.36
2 Chandigarh	22.97	20.75	69.87	74.02
3 Dadra & Nagar Haveli	35.41	41.44	46.10	47.17
4 Daman & Diu	24.87	20.06	66.97	75.42
5 Delhi	15.18	9.28	79.21	87.82
6 Lakshadweep	6.29	5.10	91.23	93.93
7 Pondicherry	17.08	14.52	76.68	81.82

* Excludes Assam and Jammu & Kashmir

Table 12: Per Cent Distribution of Total Population by Scheduled Castes, Scheduled Tribes and Now-Scheduled Castes/Scheduled Tribes 1981-1991

India/State or Union/Territory	Total Popn	1981 Sch. Caste Popn	1981 Sch. Tribe Popn	1981 Mon-SC/ST Popn	Total Popn	1991 Sch. Caste Popn	1991 Sch. Tribe Popn	1991 Non-SC/ST Popn
1	2	3	4	5	6	7	8	9
INDIA*	100.00	15.81	7.83	76.36	100.00	16.73	7.95	75.32
States								
1 Andhra Pradesh	100.00	14.87	5.93	79.20	100.00	15.93	6.31	77.76
2 Arunachal Pradesh	100.00	0.46	69.82	29.72	100.00	0.47	63.66	35.87
3 Bihar	100.00	14.51	8.31	77.18	100.00	14.56	7.66	77.78
4 Goa	100.00	2.05	0.07	97.88	100.00	2.08	0.03	97.89
5 Gujrat	100.00	7.15	14.23	78.62	100.00	7.41	14.92	77.67
6 Haryana	10.00	19.07	—	80.93	100.00	19.75	—	80.25
7 Himachal Pradesh	100.00	24.62	4.61	70.77	100.00	25.34	4.22	70.44
8 Karnataka	100.00	15.07	4.91	80.02	100.00	16.38	4.26	79.36
9 Kerala	100.00	10.01	1.03	88.96	100.00	9.92	1.10	88.98
10 Madhya Predesh	100.00	14.10	22.97	62.93	100.00	14.54	23.27	62.19
11 Maharashtra	100.00	7.14	9.19	83.67	100.00	11.10	9.27	79.63
12 Manipur	100.00	1.25	27.30	71.45	100.00	2.02	34.41	63.57
13 Meghalaya	100.00	0.41	80.58	19.01	100.00	0.51	85.53	13.96
14 Mizoram	100.00	0.03	93.55	6.42	100.00	0.10	94.75	5.15
15 Nagaland	100.00	—	83.99	16.01	100.00	—	87.70	12.30
16 Orissa	100.00	14.66	22.43	62.91	100.00	16.20	22.21	61.59
17 Punjab	100.00	26.87	—	73.13	100.00	28.31	—	71.69
18 Rajasthan	100.00	17.04	12.21	70.75	100.00	17.29	12.44	70.27
19 Sikkim	100.00	5.78	23.27	70.95	100.00	5.93	22.36	71.71
20 Tamil Nadu	100.00	18.35	1.07	80.58	100.00	19.18	1,03	79.79
21 Tripura	100.00	15.12	28.44	56.44	100.00	16.36	30.95	52.69
22 Uttar Pradesh	100.00	21.16	0.21	78.63	100.00	21.04	0.21	78.75
23 West Bangal	100.00	21.99	5.62	72.39	100.00	23.62	5.60	70.78
Union Territories								
1 A & N Islands	100.00	—	11.85	88.15	100.00	—	9.54	90.46
2 Chandigarh	100.00	14.09	—	85.91	100.00	16.51	—	83.49
3 Dadra & Nagar Keveli	100.00	1.97	78.82	19.21	100.00	1.97	78.99	19.04
4 Daman & Diu	100.00	3.56	12.70	83.74	100.00	3.83	11.54	84.63
5 Delhi	100.00	18.03	—	81.97	100.00	19.05	—	80.95
6 Lakshadweep	100.00	—	93.82	6.18	100.00	—	93.15	6.85
7 Pondicherry	100.00	15.99	—	84.01	100.00	16.25	—	83.75

* Excludes Assam and Jammu & Kashmir

Table 13: Decadal Growth Rate of Total, Scheduled Caste, Scheduled Tribe and Mon-Scheduled Caste/Scheduled Tribe Population 1981-1991

India/State or Union Territory	Total population	Scheduled Caste population	Scheduled Tribe population	Non-SC/ST population
1	2	3	4	5
INDIA*	23.79	30.99	25.67	22.11
States				
1 Andhra Pradesh	24.20	33.04	32.23	21.94
2 Arunachal Pradesh	36.83	38.81	24.75	65.19
3 Bihar	23.54	23.95	13.87	24.51
4 Goa	16.08	18.16	-45.51	16.08
5 Gujrat	21.19	25.51	27.08	19.73
6 Haryana	27.40	31.94	—	26.33
7 Himachal Pradesh	20.79	24.32	10.69	20.22
8 Karnataka	21.12	31.70	4.96	20.11
9 Kerala	14.32	13.22	22.75	14.35
10 Madhya Pradesh	26.84	30.82	28.46	25.35
11 Maharashtra	25.73	95.50	26.79	19.66
12 Manipur	29.29	109.01	62.94	15.04
13 Meghalaya	32.86	65.19	41.03	- 2.44
14 Mizoram	39.70	411.85	41.49	11.93
15 Nagaland	56.08	—	62.98	19.90
16 Orissa	20.06	32.69	18.89	17.53
17 Punjab	20.81	27.28	—	18.43
18 Rajasthan	28.44	30.30	30.88	27.57
19 Sikkim	28.47	31.74	23.47	29.84
20 Tamil Nadu	15.39	20.62	10.37	14.27
21 Tripura	34.30	45.34	46.14	25.37
22 Uttar Pradesh	25.48	24.83	23.72	25.66
23 West Bangal	24.73	34.00	24.04	21.90
Union Territories				
1 Andaman & Nicobar Islands	48.70	—	19.72	52.60
2 Chandigarh	42.16	66.58	—	38.16
3 Dadra & Nagar Haveli	33.57	33.76	33.86	32.36
4 Daman & Diu	28.62	38.32	16.88	29.99
5 Delhi	51.45	60.02	—	49.56
6 Lakshadweep	28.47	—	27.55	42.39
7 Pondicherry	33.64	35.85	—	33.21

* Excludes Assam and Jammu & Kashmir

Table 14: Population and Growth Rate of Million-plus cities In India, 1991

Sl.	City		State	1991	Growth Rate 1981-91 (Percent)
1	Greater Bombay	UA	Maharashtra	12,596,243	33.43
2	Calcutta	UA	West Bengal	11,021,918	18.73
3	Delhi	UA	Delhi	8,419,084	46.18
4	Maders	UA	Tamilnadu	5,421,985	24.99
5	Hyderabad	UA	Andhra Pradesh	4,421,985	24.99
6	Banglore	UA	Karnatka	4,130,288	39,87
7	Ahmadabad	UA	Gujrat	3,312,216	28.94
8	Pune	UA	Maharashtra	2,493,987	47.38
9	Kanpur	UA	Uttar Pradesh	2,029,889	28.94
10	Luchnow	UA	Uttar Pradesh	1,669,204	62.97
11	Nagpur	UA	Maharashtra	1,664,006	36.24
12	Surat	UA	Gujarat	1,518,950	64.21
13	Jaipur	UA	Rajasthan	1.518,235	64.21
14	Kochi	UA	Kerala	1.140,605	38.14
15	Vadodara	UA	Gujarat	1,126,824	42.54
16	Indore	UA	Madhya Pradesh	1,109,056	33.13
17	Coimbatore	UA	Tamilnadu	1,100,746	23.38
18	Patna	UA	Bihar	1,099,647	19.55
19	Madurai	UA	Tamilnadu	1,085,914	20.49
20	Bhopal	UA	Madhya Pradesh	1.062,771	58.51
21	Visakhapatnam	UA	Andhra Pradesh	1,057,118	74.27
22	Ludhiana	UA	Punjab	1,042,740	66.72
23	Varansi	UA	Uttar Pradesh	1,030,863	28.77

Worked out on the basis of provisional population totals, Census paper No. 2 of 1991. The 1991 figures are final figures as per Census Paper No. 2 of 1992. The growth rates have to be reworked after suitable adjustment for extension of city-boundaries.

SECTION VIII

GRAPHICS: INDIA 1951-91

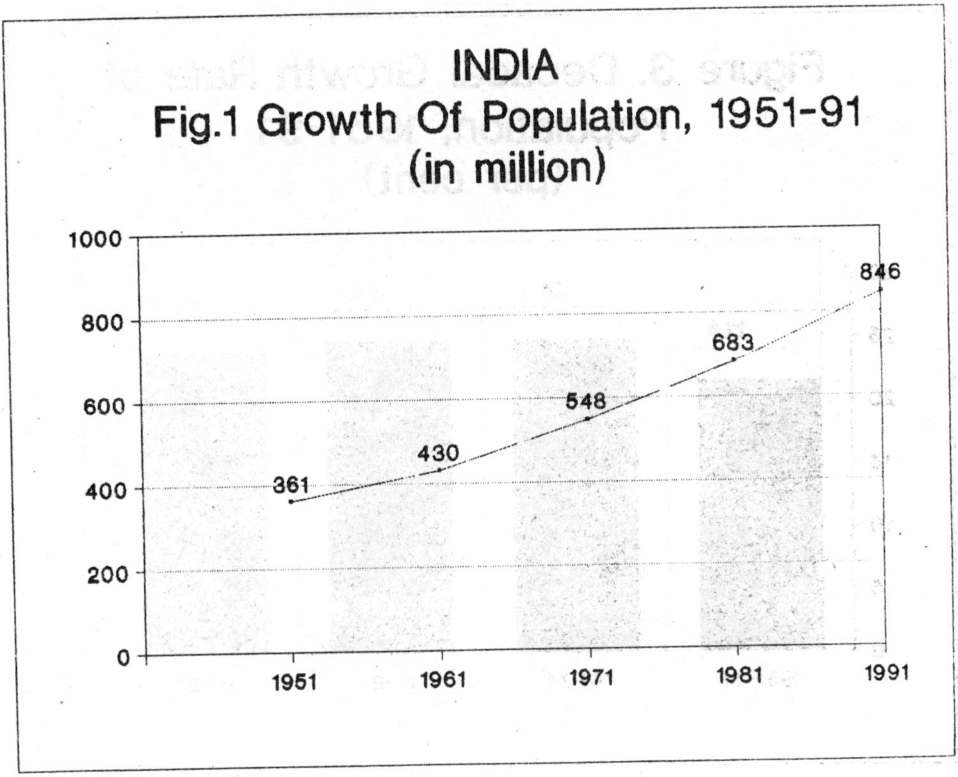

INDIA
Fig.1 Growth Of Population, 1951-91
(in million)
1000
800
600
400
200
0
846
683
548
430
361
1951
1961
1971
1981
1991

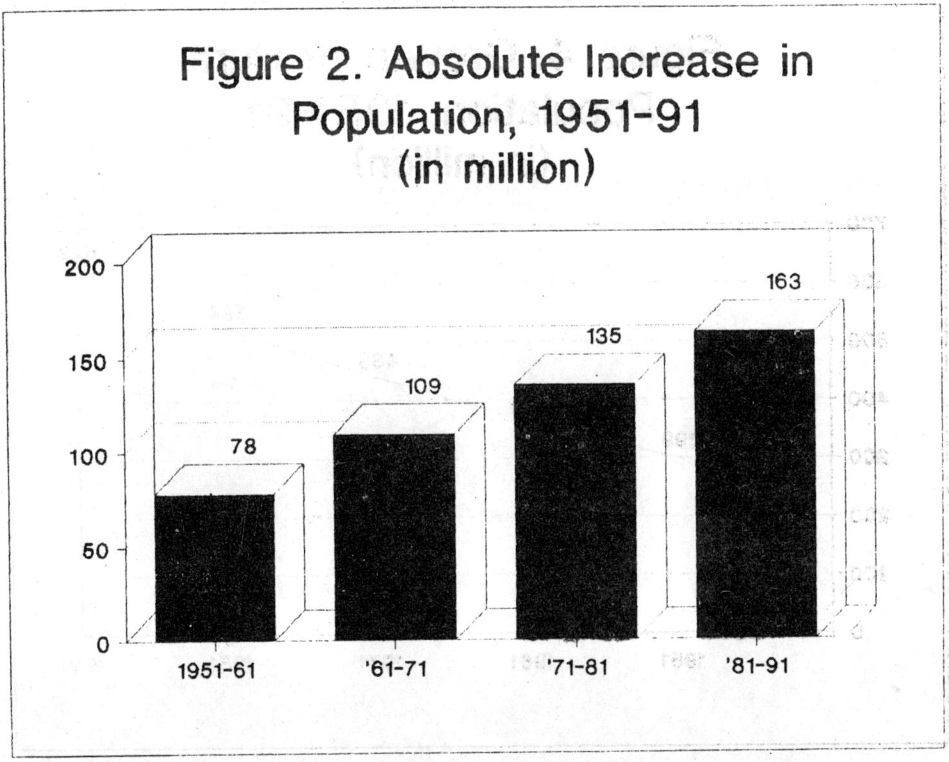

Figure 2. Absolute Increase in
Population, 1951-91
(in million)
200
150
100
50
0
163
135
109
78
1951-61
'61-71
'71-81
'81-91

Figure 3. Decadal Growth Rate of Population, 1951–91 (per cent)

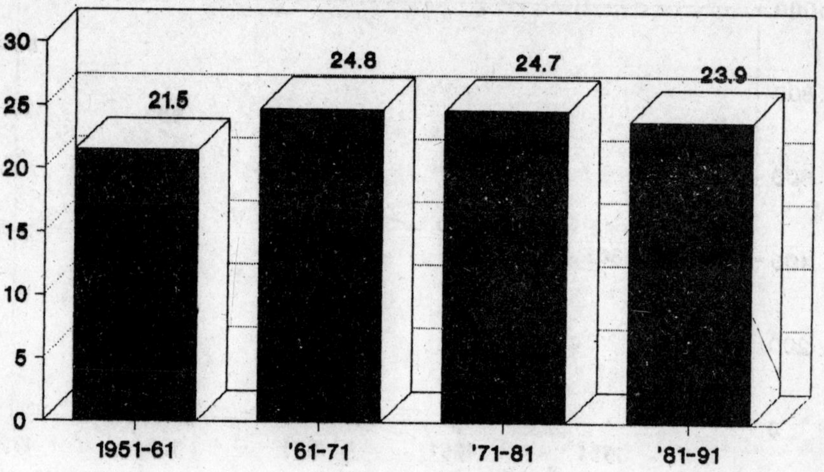

Figure 4. Growth of Rural Population, 1951–91 (in million)

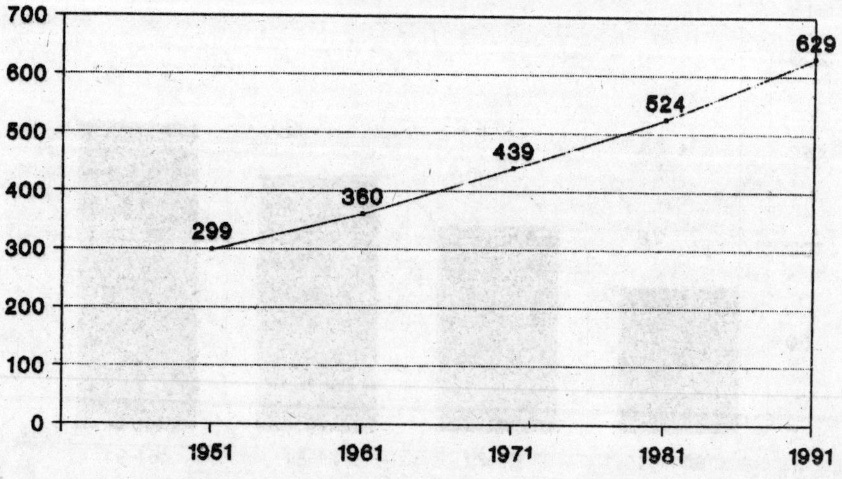

Figure 5. Absolute Increase
in Rural Population
(in million)

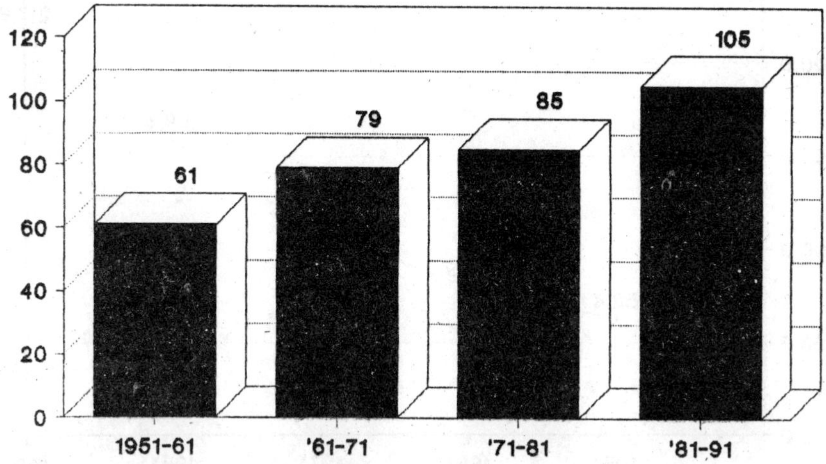

Figure 6. Decadal Growth Rate
of Rural Population
(per cent)

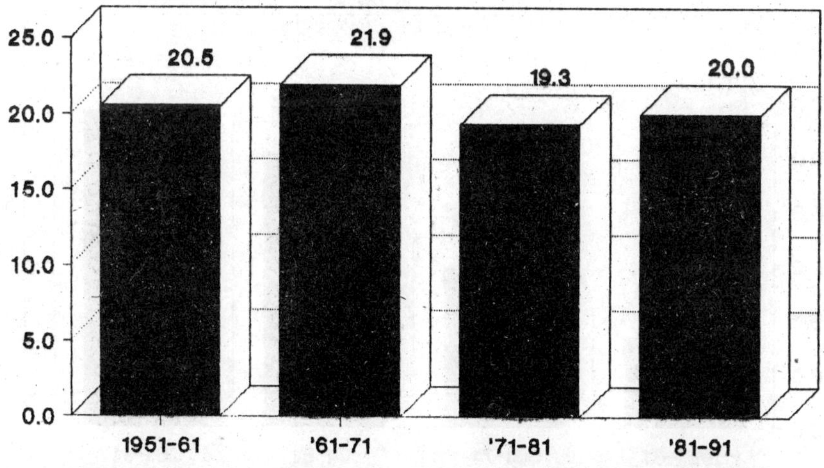

Figure 7. Growth of Urban Population
(in million)
250.0
200.0
150.0
100.0
50.0
0.0
62.4
79.9
109.1
159.5
217.6
1951
1961
1971
1981
1991

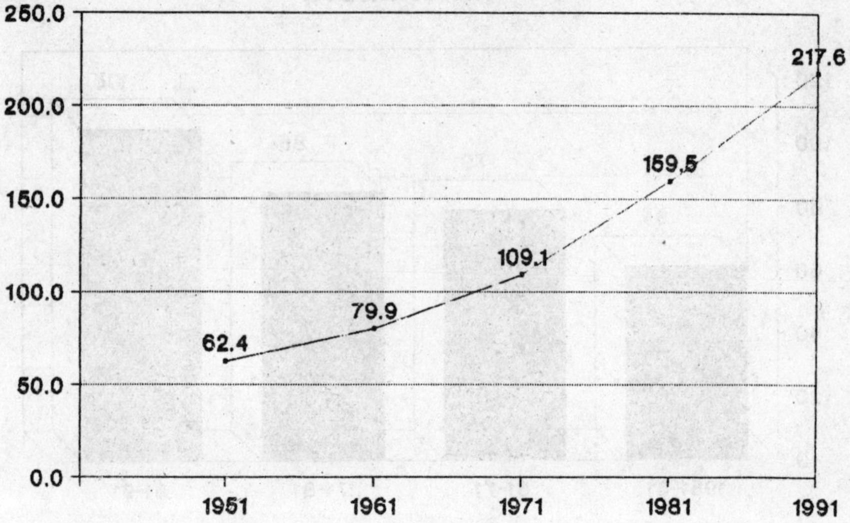

Figure 8. Absolute Increase in
Urban Population
(in million)
70.0
60.0
50.0
40.0
30.0
20.0
10.0
0.0
16.5
29.2
50.4
58.1
1951-61
'61-71
'71-81
'81-91

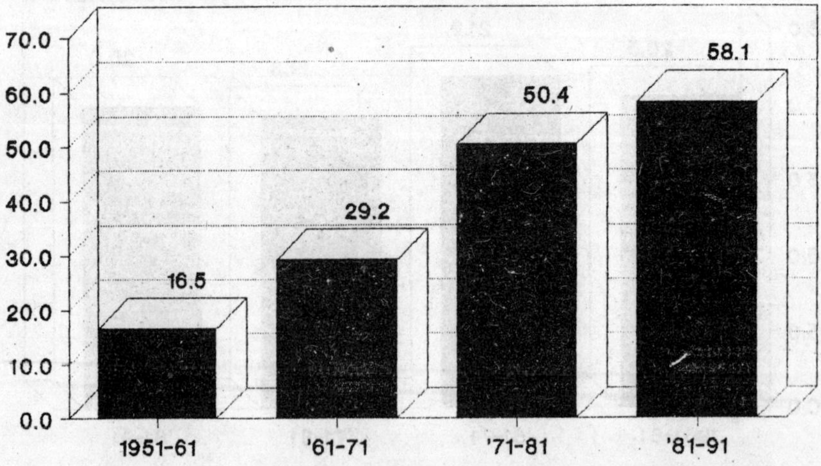

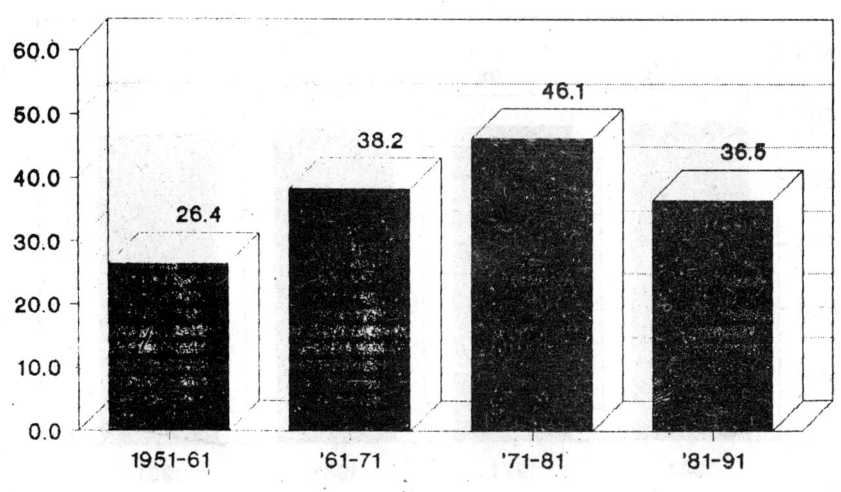

Figure 9. Growth Rate of Urban Population (per cent)

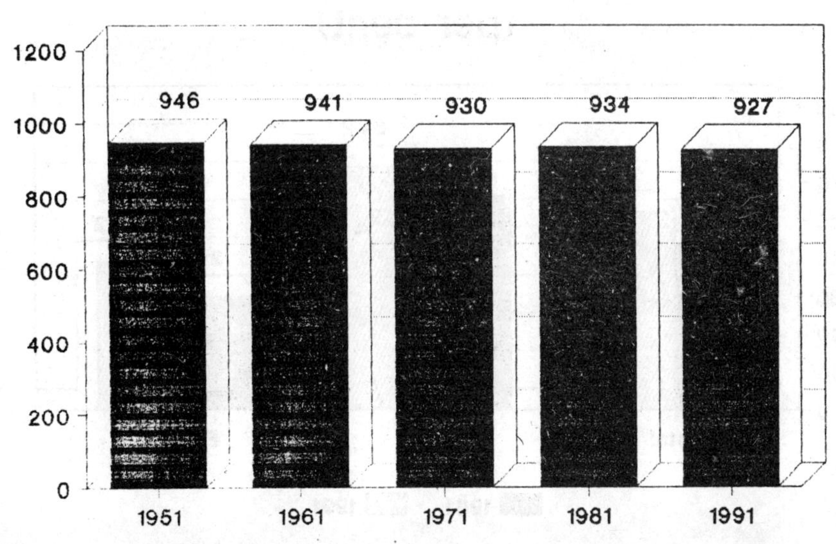

Figure 10. Sex Ratio (Females per 1000 Males)

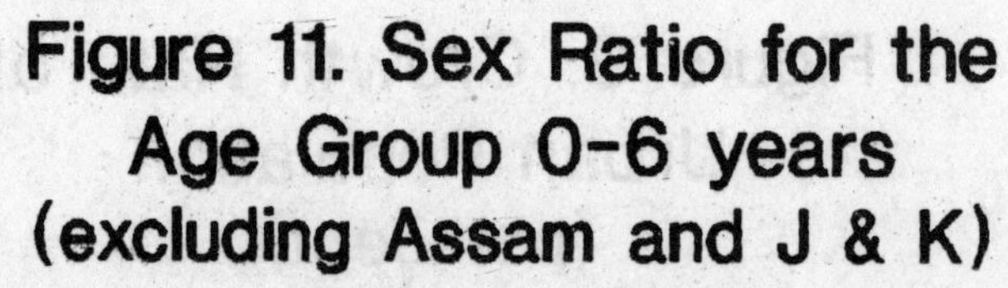

Figure 11. Sex Ratio for the Age Group 0-6 years (excluding Assam and J & K)

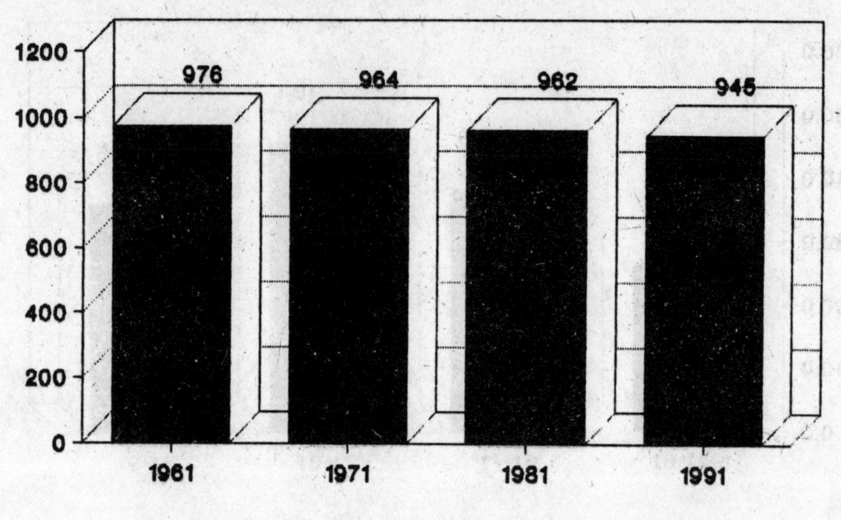

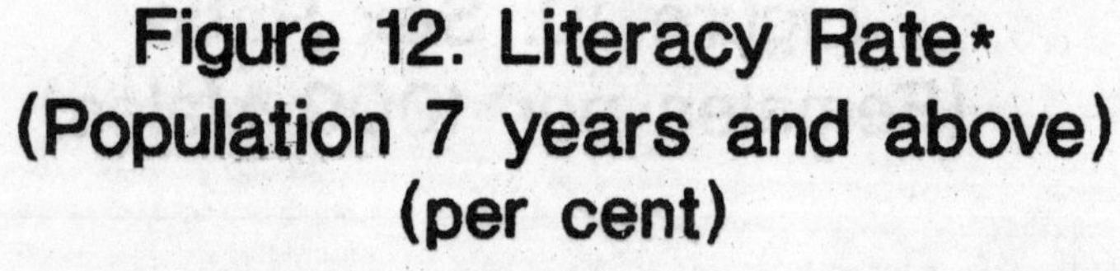

Figure 12. Literacy Rate* (Population 7 years and above) (per cent)

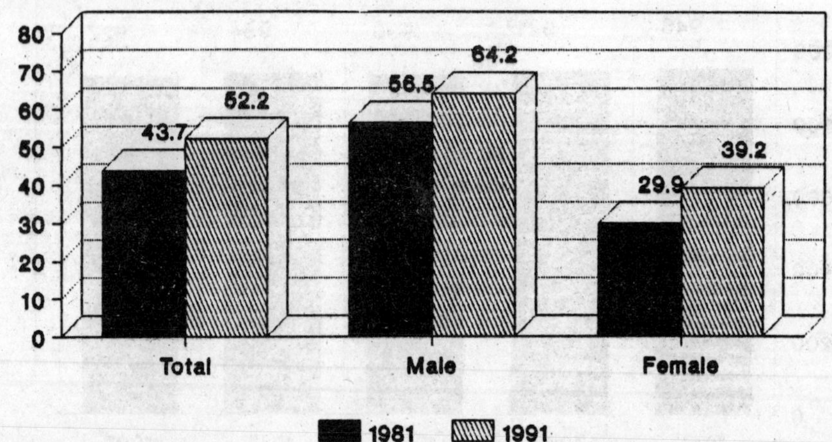

* excluding Assam and J & K

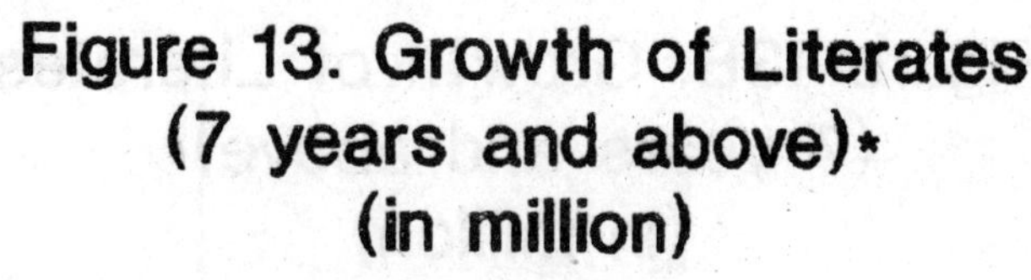

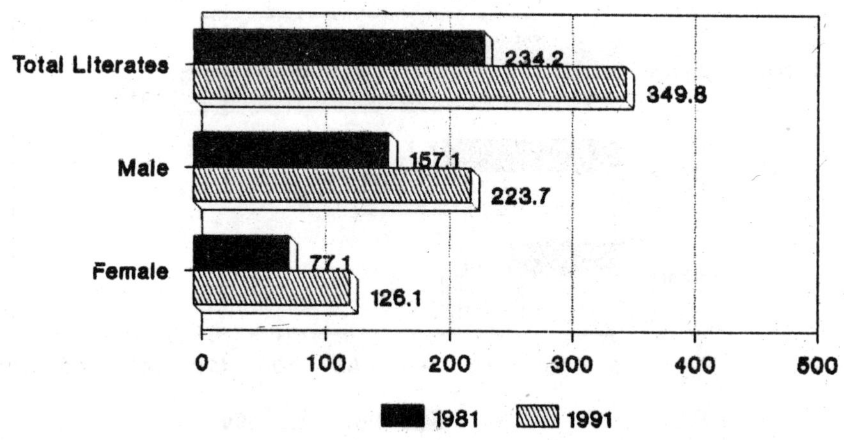

* Excluding Assam and J & K

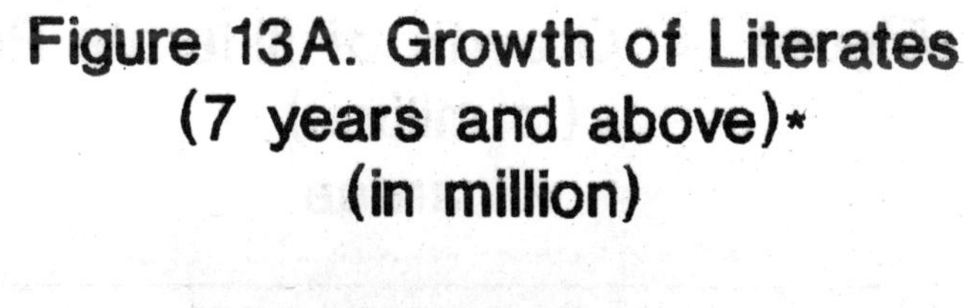

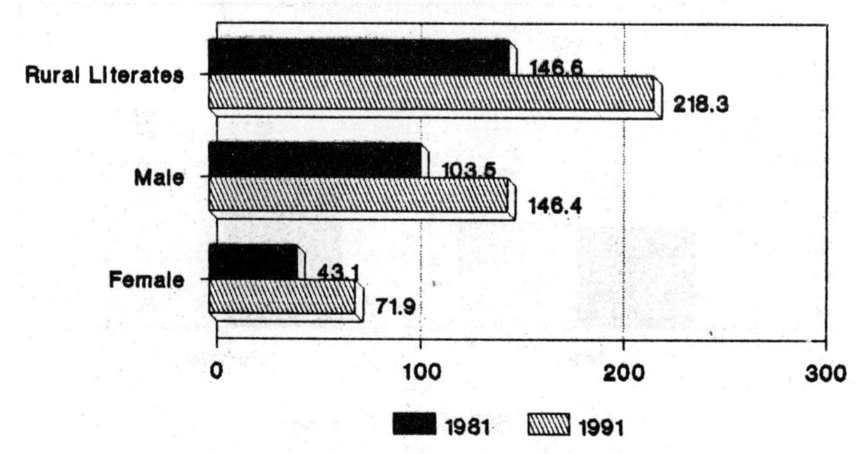

* Excluding Assam and J & K

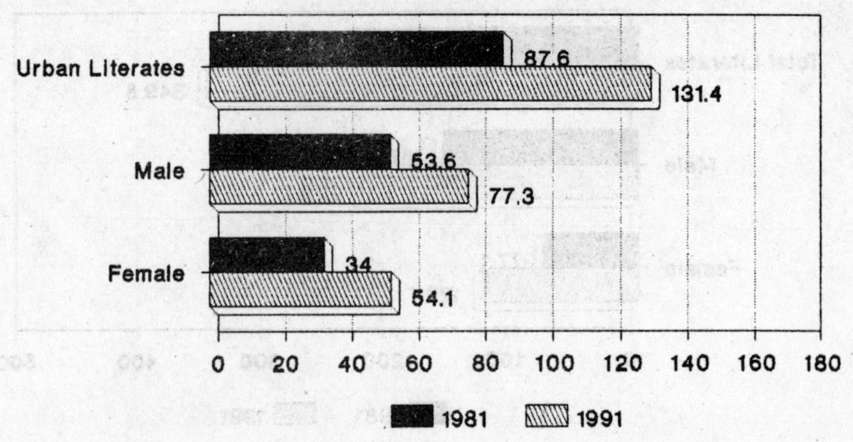

Figure 13B. Growth of Literates
(7 years and above)*
(in million)

* Excluding Assam and J & K

Figure 14. Growth of Illiterate Pop.
(in million)
All areas

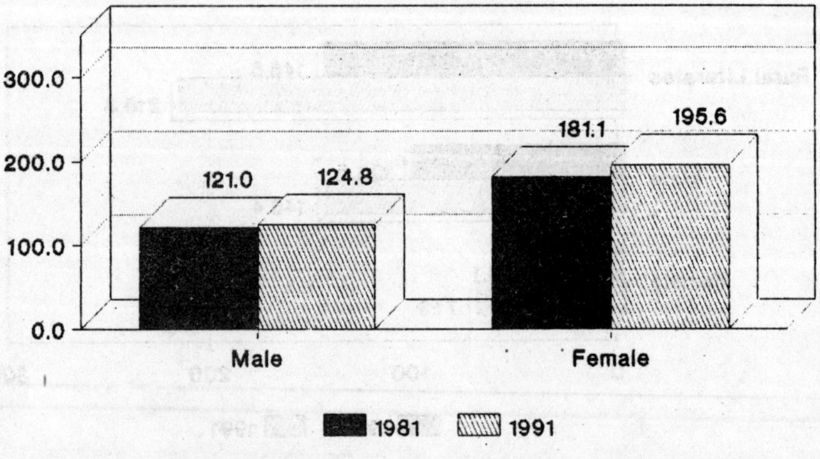

* Excluding Assam and J & K

Figure 14A. Growth of Illiterate Pop.
(in million)
Rural Areas 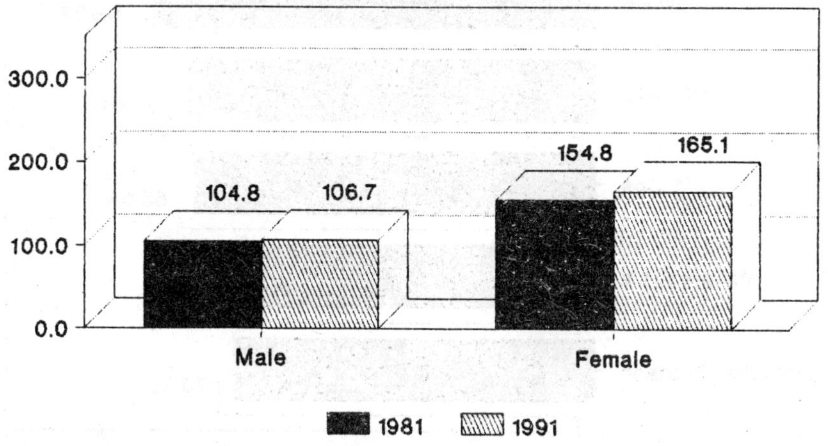
300.0
200.0
100.0
0.0
104.8
106.7
154.8
165.1
Male
Female
1981
1991
* Excluding Assam and J & K

Figure 14B. Growth of Illiterate Pop.
(in million)
Urban Areas 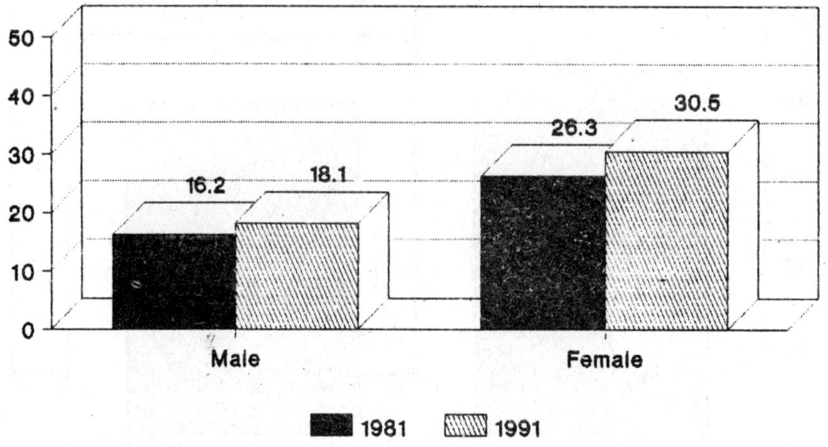
50
40
30
20
10
0
16.2
18.1
26.3
30.5
Male
Female
1981
1991
* Excluding Assam and J & K

Fig 15. States With The Male Literacy Rate Over 75 Per cent, 1991

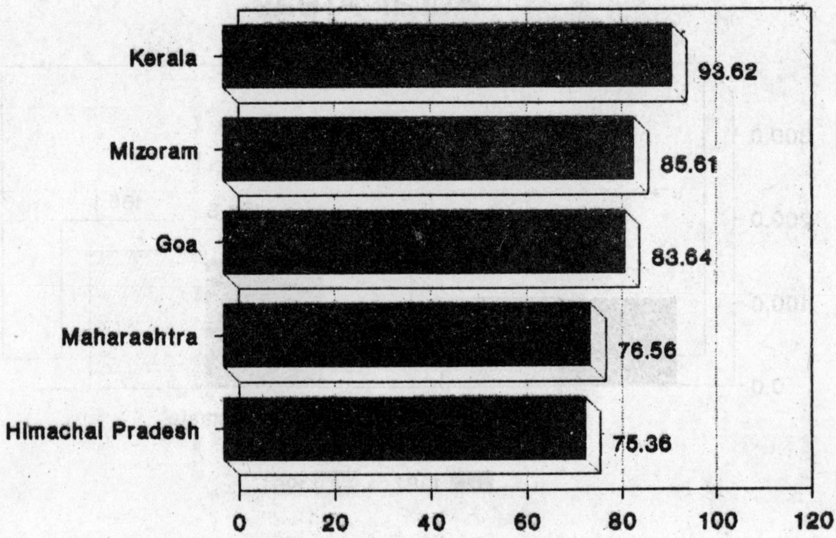

Fig 16. States With Female Literacy Rate Over 75 Per cent, 1991

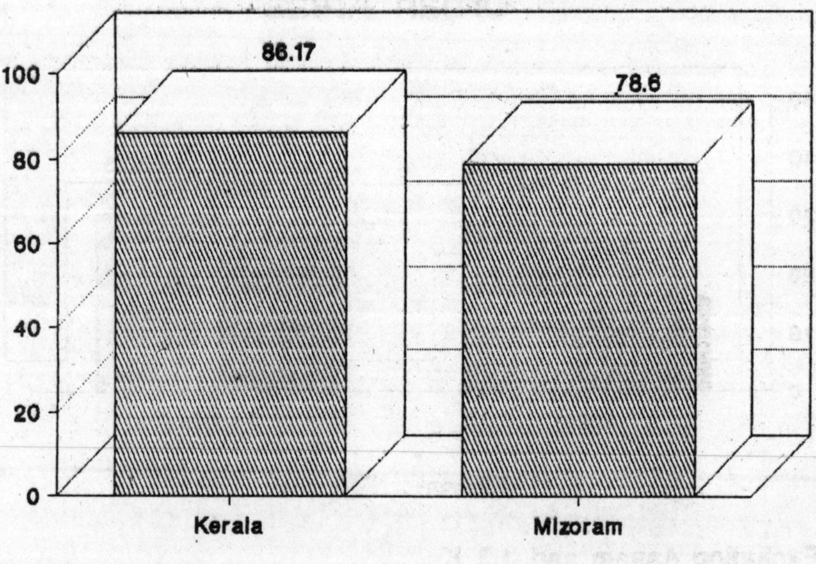

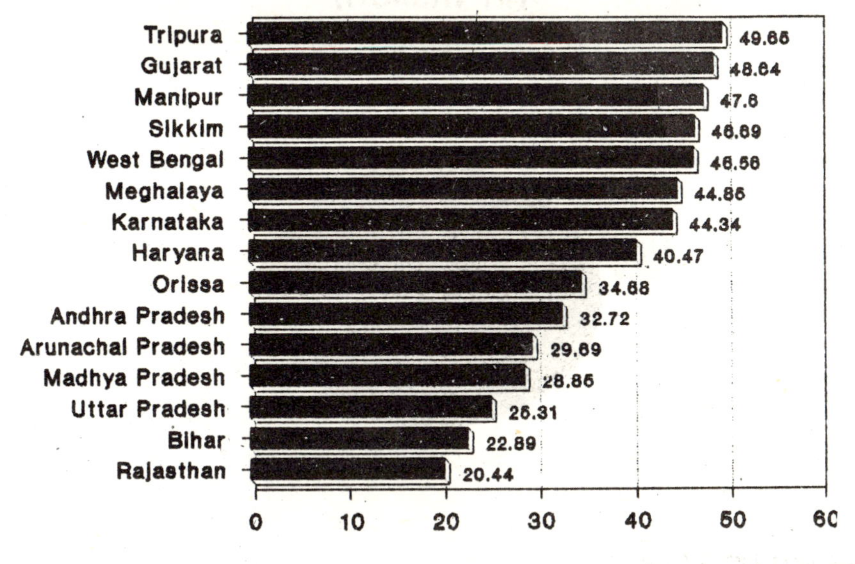

Fig 17. States With Female Literacy Rate Below 50 Per cent, 1991

Fig 18. Distribution of Main Workers: Primary, Secondary & Tertiary Sectors All Areas (R+U)

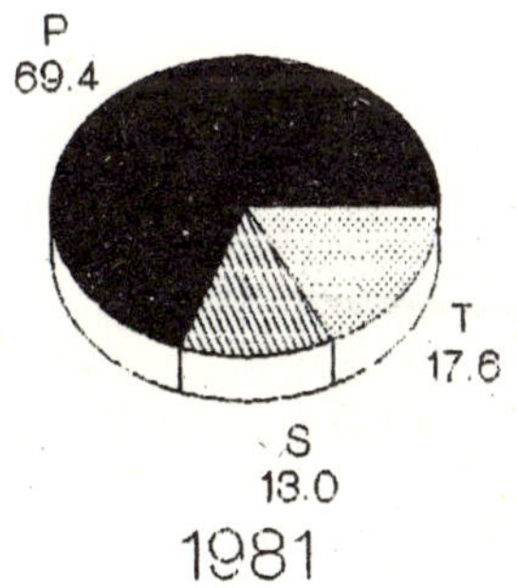

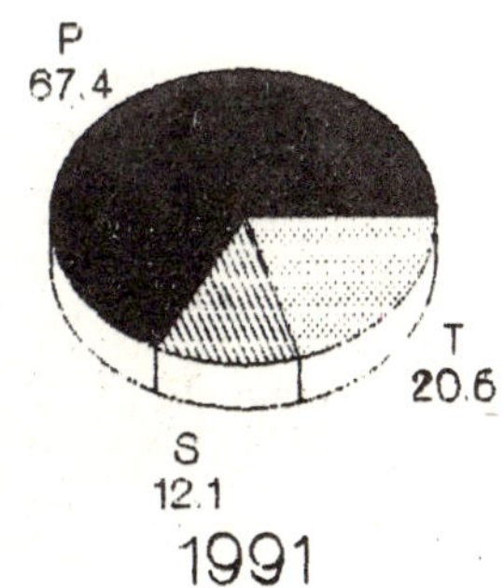

Excluding Assam, and J & K

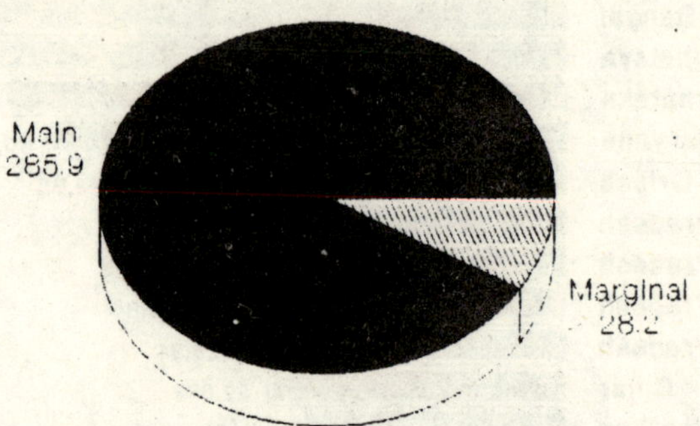

Fig 19. Main Workers & Marginal Workers*, 1991 (in million)

Total

* Excluding Jammu & Kashmir

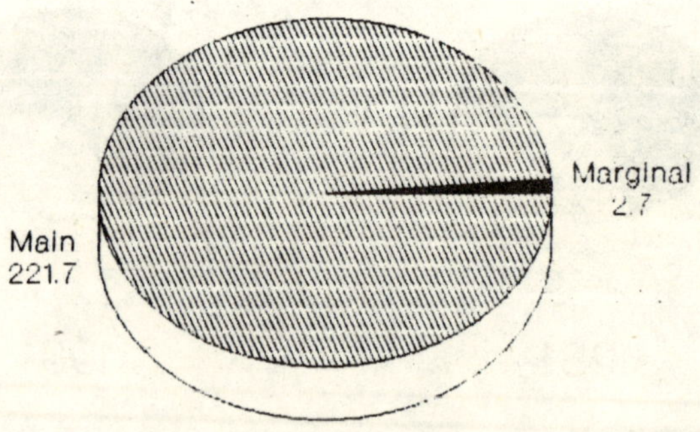

Fig 19A. Main Workers & Marginal Workers*, 1991 (in million)

Male

* Excluding Jammu & Kashmir

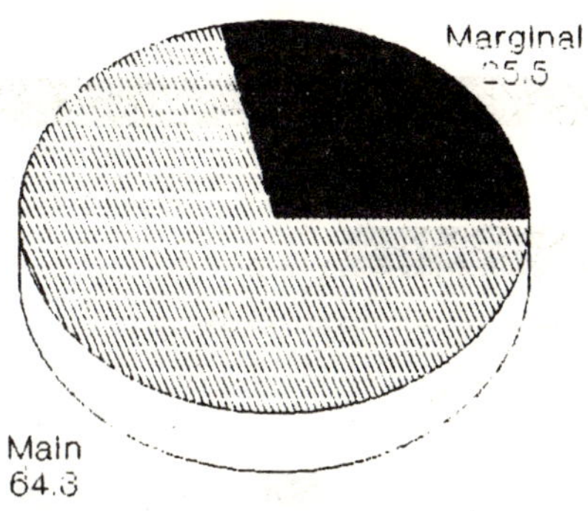

Fig 19B. Main Workers & Marginal
Workers*, 1991
(in million)
Female
Marginal
35.5
Main
64.3
* Excluding Jammu & Kashmir

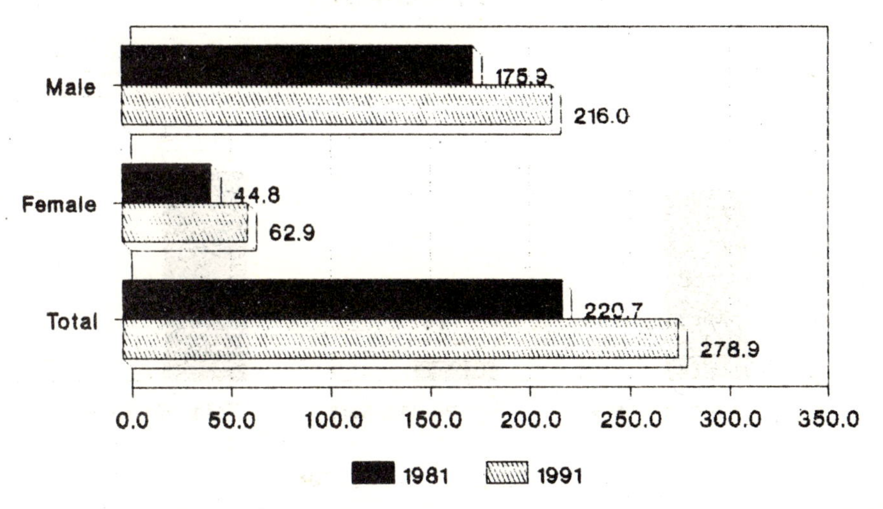

Figure 20. Main Workers*, 1981 and 1991
(in million)
Male
175.9
216.0
Female
44.8
62.9
Total
220.7
278.9
0.0   50.0   100.0   150.0   200.0   250.0   300.0   350.0
1981   1991
* Excluding Assam and J & K

Fig 21. Work Force Participation Rates, 1981 & 1991
(per cent of total population)

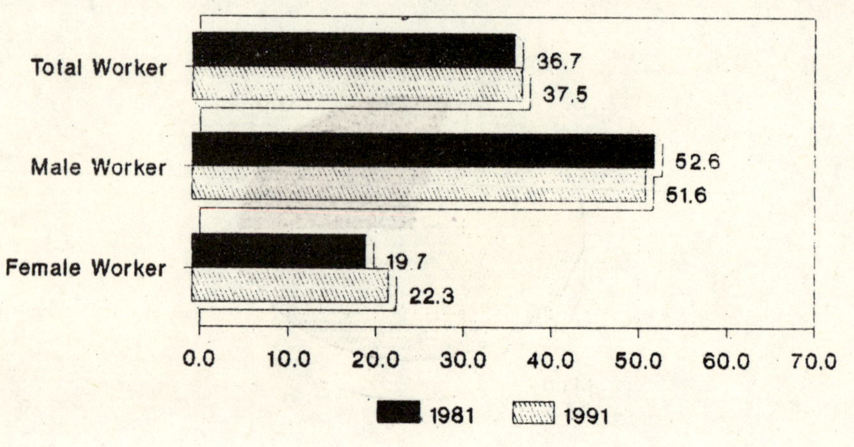

* Excluding Assam and J & K

Fig 22. Main Workers in Industrial Category V(b): Other Than Household Ind.
(in million)

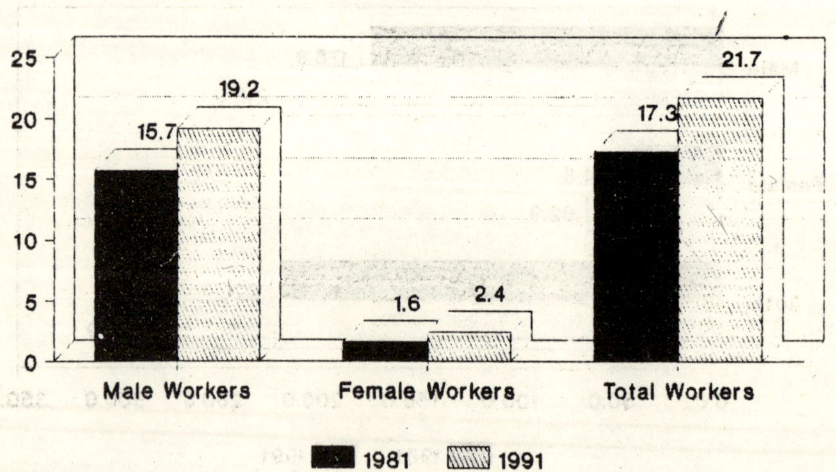

* Excluding Assam and J & K

Fig 23. Scheduled Caste & Scheduled Tribe Population*, 1991 (in million)

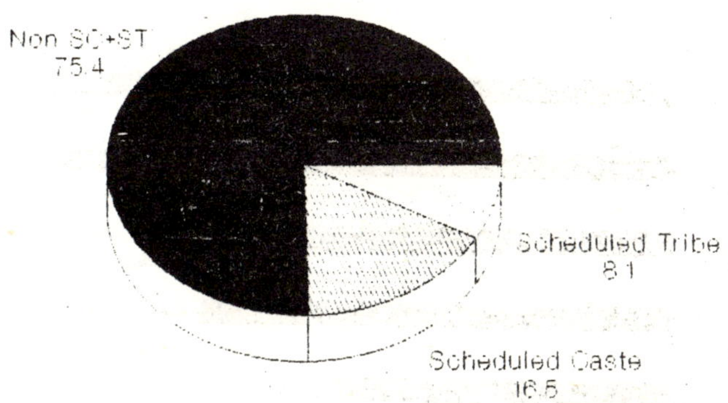

*** Excluding Jammu & Kashmir**

Fig 24. Outlay on Family Welfare Programme in Five-year Plans of India

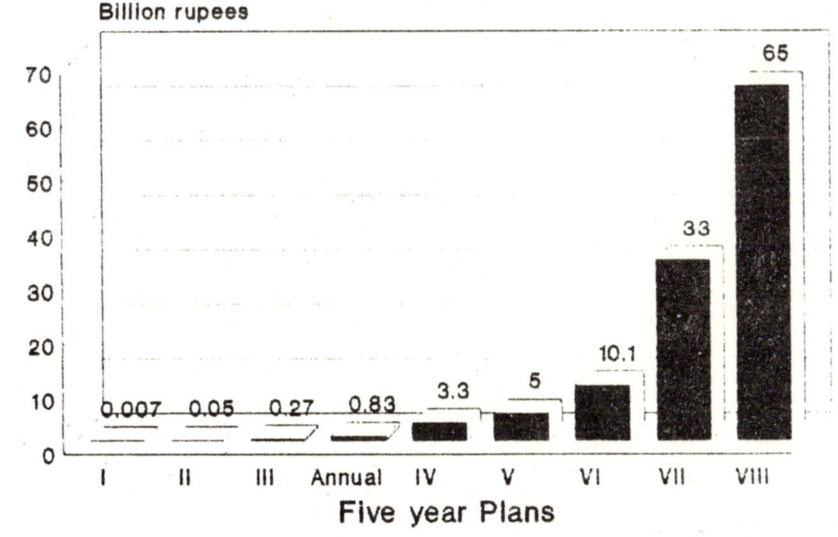

(one billion=100 crores)

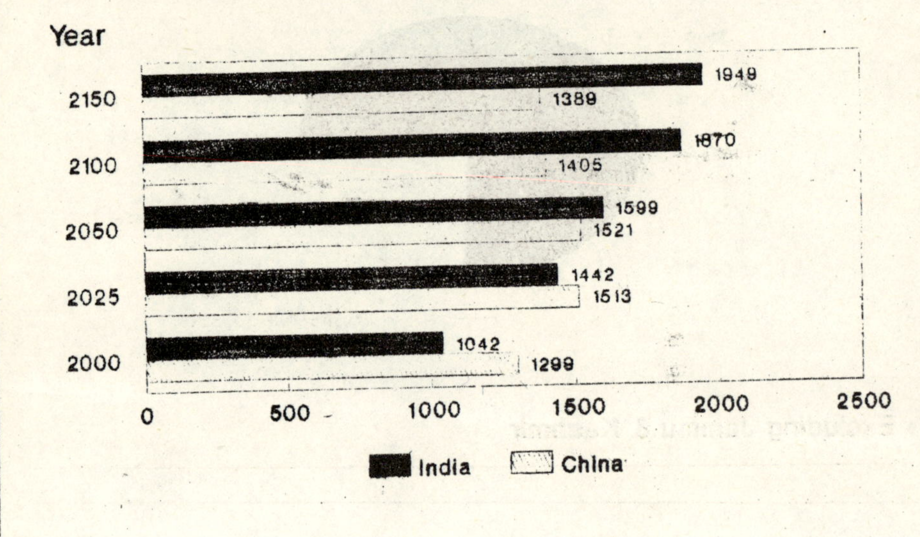

Fig 25. India and China: Long Term
Population Projections (United Nations)
(Millions)
Year
2150
2100
2050
2025
2000
1949
1389
1870
1405
1599
1521
1442
1513
1042
1299
0
500
1000
1500
2000
2500
India
China

Index